D0324098

7

GRAND
TO BE AN
ORPHAN

By the same author:

BOTH SIDES NOW
FAMILY QUARREL

GRAND
TO BE AN
ORPHAN

Reuben Slonim

CLARKE, IRWIN & COMPANY LIMITED
Toronto / Vancouver

Canadian Cataloguing in Publication Data

Slonim, Reuben, 1914-
  Grand to be an orphan

Includes index.
ISBN 0-7720-1389-6

1. Slonim, Reuben, 1914-   2. Authors, Canadian
(English) - Biography.*   3. Jewish orphans - Manitoba
- Winnipeg - Biography.   4. Jews - Manitoba -
Winnipeg - Education.   5. Rabbis - Ontario - Toronto
- Biography.   I. Title.

HV1010.W5S66   362.7'97924'0924   C83-098260-4

Printed in Canada

1 2 3 4 5 87 86 85 84 83

To the Alumni
of the Jewish Orphanage
and in memory
of my parents, Gisela and Meir,
my sister Rahel
and my brother Moshe.

Contents

Preface

The conversations of almost sixty years ago, as recorded in this memoir, are not verbatim, but their sound is true, their essence correct and their progression accurate. I have rendered them as they remain with me.

I do not use the accepted transliteration from Hebrew and Yiddish to English because Hebrew in the 1920s had a distinct Ashkenazic or Russian-Polish sound, as used by East European Jews, not today's Sephardic sound employed as the official accent in the state of Israel.

I am grateful to my fellow alumni of the Jewish Orphanage and Children's Aid of Western Canada and to our friends who have helped me remember: John Albert, Gertrude (Albert) Greenfield, Dorothy (Abrahamson) Segall, David Ackerman, George Ackerman, Boris Amromin, Morris Block, Morris Buim, Louis Buim, Reuben Buim, Mendell Blatt, Winnie (Barnett) Greenberg, Sadie (Butler) MacPherson, Daniel Butler, Frankie (Balbert) Stall, Harry Balbert, Esther (Balbert Fink) Colberg, Reuben Bider, Reuben Braunstein, Hershey Braunstein, Oscar Cantin, John Cooper, Bella (Nurenberg) Cooperman, Esther (Cooperman) Tuffs, Ted Chorach, Paul Chorach, Clara (Coblin) Segal, Morris Coblin, Serkie (Coblin) Skulko, Daniel Davis, Sam Dvorak, Harry Dvorak, Sidney Diamond, Louis East, David Favor, Morris Favor, Pearl (Finkelstein) Silver, Max Freedman, Babs (Faigen) Cohen, Abe Gold, Esther (Gold) Rubman, Mary (Gold) Landau, Sadie (Gelfand) Orenstein, Gaye (Gelfand) Selby, Mindel (Gelfand) Kagna, Ken Gutnick, Nelson Gutnick, Paul Gutnick, Gary Goodman, Maurice Gilman, Sam Gilman, Rae (Gold) Greenberg, Ms. Louis Greenberg, Kaushie (Gilman) Kassakoff, Ted Harris, Harry Harris, George Harrison, Babe (Tuberman) Hershfield, Sydney Koyle, Arthur Kushner, Bernard Kushner, Pearl (Lexier) Barnes, Frank Lexier, Perry Lexier, Helen (Leff) Goldberg, Adeline

(Litsky) Hoffer, Leon Leckie, Ruth (Leckie) Stein, Meyer Lecker, Bernice (Macklin) Marmel, Dr. Allan Macklin, Shirley (Mitchnik) Featley, Morrie Ostrow, Rose (Ostrow) Stitz, Mickey Ostrow, William Ostrow, Beckie (Ostrow) Verbitt, Miriam (Stein) Ostrow, Nathan Ostrow, Edward Posen, Sara (Rosenberg) Tregebov, Ernest Rosenblat, Saul Rothstein, Barney Ross, Ben Zion Steindel, Lillian (Slonim) Gordon, Ruth (Stein) Finkleman, Nettie (Stein) Shoub, Sidney Shoub, Eleanor (Shatsky) Burke, Sherry (Shatsky) Thompson, Irvin Simovitch, Rae (Simovitch) Gobuty, Ben Sturrey, Freda (Sturrey) Shieff, David Sturrey, Sheila (Sturrey) Berman, Clara (Shapiro) Krugel, Sam Stedman, Clara Stedman, Ruth (Stedman) Gerstein, Ann (Spenser) Hudson, Betty (Spenser) Delmonico, Jay Tobin, Ida (Schwartz) Winston, Sidney Winston.

Valuable aid in research was given by Dr. Arthur Frankel; my sister Lillian (Slonim) Gordon; Dr. Dorothy (Osovsky) Hollenberg; Barry Hyman, assistant archivist, Manitoba Provincial Archives; Esther Nisenholt, archivist, Jewish Historical Society of Western Canada; Miriam Ostrow; and Barney Yellen, executive director, Jewish Child and Family Service of Winnipeg.

I thank the Explorations Program of the Canada Council for its interest and support, and Professor William Berman, Jerelyn Craden, Ellen Eisenberg, Sol Kanee and Victor Sefton for their faith in the manuscript.

R. S.

Prologue

I was lucky; I lived in an orphanage. Most people think of an orphan home as Charles Dickens described it: a disreputable place where unwanted children were shunted to be reared haphazardly as an afterthought. My orphanage years were the most crucial and beneficial of my life. They taught me the pride of being a carrier of a 4000-year-old tradition, the glory of being human.

Some years ago in a fine review of my book *Both Sides Now*, in the *Canadian Author and Bookman*, Elsa Rosenberg wrote: "Reuben Slonim spent some of his formative years in the Jewish Orphanage in Winnipeg. I tell you this because it is easier to understand what makes Reuben run if one knows what made Reuben. It is difficult to grow up under those circumstances and not be bitter and aware of the shortcomings, hypocrisies and deceits of the establishment. Knowing this it is easier to understand Rabbi Slonim's writings and motivations, easier to understand why he is a maverick and why he has such a keen awareness and sensitivity to both sides of any question."

True enough, the Orphanage helped me to develop respect for an independent mind, but not for the reason Ms. Rosenberg suggests. If she, a friendly critic, concludes that the Home embittered me, what of the less sympathetic ones? That surely must be their impression and an easy explanation of my chariness of the establishment.

In the interest of accuracy, I must put the matter right; hence this book. My Orphanage was a congenial place, and the Jews who founded and supported it were kindly people. As an inmate I could observe the shortcomings of the community, but mostly I was aware of its generous heart.

The fact is that I did not bemoan my fate while in the Orphanage. I was much too busy with constructive activity ever to con-

trast my lot with that of other Winnipeg boys and girls. If anything, they envied me and the other residents of the Home.

Sholom Aleichem, the Yiddish raconteur, tells of a little boy
who was left an orphan in an East European _stetl_. He, like other
children, was addicted to mischief, tying a piece of paper on a cat's
tail in order to make her spin, or banging a stick on a priest's fence
to make all the dogs run out, or pulling the stopper out of Leibkeh
the water-carrier's barrel to make the water flow out.

"You're lucky you are an orphan," says Leibkeh to the boy,
"else I'd break your hand and foot. You may believe I'm not
lying."

The little boy believes. He knows no one will touch him because
of his orphanhood. "It's grand to be an orphan," he concludes.

That was my feeling in the Home. When I went to the movies on
Saturday afternoon to see Tom Mix and Hoot Gibson and there
was a long line at the box office, I was passed to the head of the
queue "because he's an Orphanage kid." Some of my peers at Luxton public school would say: "You're lucky to be in the Orphanage; you get to go on picnics, to the movies and the circus for free
and to parties with presents and lots of good things to eat."

The children of Winnipeg reflected the attitude of their parents.
The Orphanage was the jewel of the Jewish citizenry, the visible
proof of a compassionate community. It diminished the great tradition to have Jewish orphans sent to Protestant or Roman Catholic institutions. "It has always been our proud boast," said E. R.
Levinson in his first presidential report in 1917, "that we Jews attend to those of our own people in want or in need. Consequently
the fact that many Jewish children in Western Canada were housed
in Gentile orphanages aroused in our community considerable
alarm and a determination that such a condition should not continue."

Caring for orphans was one of the great good deeds, a _mitzvoh_.
When the building at 123 Matheson Avenue was erected in 1920,
the Jews of Winnipeg declared a holiday, as recorded by *The
Guardian*, a publication of the Israelite Press:

> That was a Jewish holiday. A holiday in which the Jew felt at his
> best, and showed himself up at his best. . . . A holiday in which
> for once heart and mind worked in perfect harmony, in wonder-
> ful unison, because the Jew beheld before his eyes that for which
> his whole soul yearns, that for which his whole being is fa-
> shioned, that which thousands of years of sublime teaching have

inculcated in him: the incarnate spirit of *tz'dokoh*, concern for others, keen appreciation of duty for fellow-beings. All these he saw in the magnificent edifice that stood before him, the Jewish Orphanage.

The throngs that kept continually revolving were an inspiring sight. Never did one see such real, genuine happiness. Smiles and jolly handshakes everywhere. Men and women and children, very old men and very young children, kept climbing up the white stone stairs. . . . And they climb down, peep into the dormitories with large, bright, airy windows and neat, comfy, immaculately clean beds, so many in a row, where the kiddies, the dear little fatherless souls, sleep, satisfied with today, unmindful of tomorrow, certain of the unfailing care of the Jewish community, happy in the tenderness of that collective maternity, the Jewish heart.

This embroidered statement may seem like hyperbole today, but it was not far from the communal attitude of the 1920s, 1930s and 1940s. "We can't restore to children their parents," I recall Board member David Spivak saying, "but we can give them what their parents would have wanted them to have: adequate shelter and clothing, nourishing food, a good education and a firm yet gentle hand." Spivak, his colleagues on the Board and the community that elected them were as good as their word. We had enough to eat and more. The undernourished were given supplemental provision. Oliver Twist, holding out his plate begging for a second helping, was for us a figment of an overactive imagination. It was quite a sight to see a long line of youngsters troop into Churchill's wholesale establishment on McDermot Street, enthusiastically trying on spanking new garments.

"Pick the colour you like," Mr. Churchill, who somehow acquired an Anglo-Saxon denomination on his way from Eastern Europe to Canada, would say. No regulation uniforms for us, as in Winnipeg's Protestant and Catholic orphanages of the time. We belonged to an institution but were treated as individuals.

Those charged with rearing us—the superintendent, matrons and teachers—were often more severe in their discipline than they needed to be, but this severity was balanced by their dedication and the affection of volunteers, who not only served on committees but befriended us and made us feel we were important to them.

Even as a nine-year-old I knew the officers and members of the

Board of Directors and greeted them by name: Allan Bronfman, of
distiller fame, the president, who established the Yechiel and
Mindel Bronfman scholarship fund for higher Hebrew education;
M. H. Levinson, the first vice-president, who·shook your hand
solemnly but warmly; second and third vice-presidents Mrs.
Goldin and bewigged Mrs. Saltzman, who could argue rings
around the men of the Board long before women were supposed to
know how to do such things; Charles Tadman, the Main Street
hardware merchant who usually invited you in for a chat when he
saw you looking at his show window; David Spivak, the cattle
dealer, who was an officer of the Home from the day of its incep-
tion to the day it closed in 1948; Dr. C. J. Bermack whose pince-
nez held by a black ribbon always shook and sparkled when he
greeted you; Riva Kanee, the Saskatchewan representative, who
seemed to regard her visits to the Home as pilgrimages; M. Aver-
bach, the pedagogue, who appeared to love the Orphanage Hebrew school as much as his own; Pansy E. Frankfurter, a south-
ender who spoke with impeccable preciseness, dressed in *haut
monde* and specialized in guiding the graduates of the Home into
the big, wide world; the aldermen, M. A. Gray and J. Blumberg,
who could always be relied on to negotiate with the municipal authorities for financial support; Dr. S. Rodin, who fished out
tongue depressors from his pocket at the least sign of a sore throat;
Max Heppner who vied with Allan Bronfman in setting up schol-
arships; A. Boroditsky, the soda-water king, and his brother M.,
who provided the drinks on holidays and at parties; J. Gershfeld,
who rarely missed a religious service; H. Feinstein, the peripatetic
propagandist, who insisted that "his" Orphanage was the best on
any planet; Leo Davis who habitually proffered a sweet from his
pocket; Mrs. I. Malcove, who called herself the "hoise" committee
because it was her job to look after repairs; Dr. I. Fried who pulled
my tooth instead of filling it because the pain of the drill was too
much for me; and the formidable ladies' brigade, the true experts
on child care—so I heard it repeatedly said by Spivak and Boroditsky, A.—Mrs. D. Spivak, Mrs. R. Schiller, Mrs. S. Coleman,
Mrs. M. Chess, Mrs. F. Bookhalter, Mrs. F. Mass, Mrs. L. Leipsic,
Mrs. M. Woladarsky, Mrs. Louis Phomin, Mrs. Galsky, Mrs. E.
Rafalsky, Mrs. A. Pesochin and Mrs. J. Guttman. I used to rattle
off their names with machine-gun rapidity to the huge amusement
of my mother, whose friends they were.

These volunteers had a collective personality. Some were very rich and others in modest circumstances, but they all gave from their hearts not from their wealth. So it seemed to one who was their beneficiary. They were genial to their charges but never condescending. They believed in educating the heart first and the head later. There was a calm about them all, a gentleness, an air of serenity, containment, wisdom perhaps. They walked and talked like people who knew where they were going and how they intended to get there. They had neither the thrusting impudence of the arrogant nor the practised humility of the fawning. They embraced us, literally and spiritually, and released our affection. There was competitiveness among them, weak and human as they were, but their ultimate goals were obvious even to children. They wanted acceptance, love, a promise of purpose and continuity.

There was not only a Board of Directors and a Ladies Society but a Girls Auxiliary, a group of young women headed by Pearl Finkelstein, who ferreted out our hobbies and provided activities for leisure hours. We had an ice-skating rink in winter, with the hockey equipment to go along, a baseball diamond, soccer field, a tennis court on the front lawn and volley ball net in the back yard. For those with less interest in sports like myself, the library, with its sets of encyclopedias, nineteenth-century English novels, magazines and newspapers, offered diversion.

Our physical and mental health were prime priorities. We were periodically examined by a committee of doctors. Their names have never left me: Hershman, Bermack, Kobrinsky, Granofsky, Rodin, Perlman, Rady and Peikoff. The dentists visited every six months—Gardner, Churchill, Fried, Zilz, Ben Ezra and Shragge. We were even measured psychologically. I recall Dr. May Bere administering tests in order to help sixteen-year-olds who were about to leave the Home choose a vocation.

We lived in attractive surroundings. Superintendent Osovsky described them to an Orphanage annual meeting in 1928:

Our extensive lawns like green carpets, bestrewn with multi-coloured flowers of all shapes and forms, guarded all around by hundreds of trees and shrubs of all kinds, present a picture which compels the attention of all passers-by. Our model vegetable gardens, where the stately rows of corn stalks stand out proudly . . . have aroused universal admiration. Many times people have commented that we own the most beautiful grounds in Winnipeg. We may gladly accept this compliment, because it is aimed not at one person, not at the administration only but at the whole Jewish community of Western Canada, which made possible such a beautiful national asset. However much it may cost, it deserves an even larger investment of time and energy in order that both friends and foes alike should be forced to admit that Jews know how to maintain and how to preserve a national treasure.

By a national asset he meant a Canadian one, not only a Jewish one.

Most of all we were given values, the ancient Jewish kind. We celebrated sabbaths and holidays joyfully and performed the meaningful rituals. We absorbed the message that a Jew must live up to a time-honoured code, that there was glory in carrying the identity of generations of sages, martyrs, scholars and saints, that they had passed a sacred heritage to us and that ours was the duty to bequeath it to those who would come after. If I was at variance with the establishment in later years, it was because I judged it, rightly or wrongly, in the light of this code. If I became what Elsa Rosenberg calls a maverick and insisted on independent judgment, it was not out of bitterness against a hypocritical and insensitive community, of which I had no awareness, but out of loyalty to the ancient tradition which Western Canadian Jews, through the Orphanage, handed me, as a runner hands a torch to his comrades and hopes it will be guarded faithfully.

The Jewish immigrants to Winnipeg and the West at the turn of the century lived for most of their lives in a confined community, alienated from the Gentile life around them. It never occurred to them to challenge their Judaism, its ritual, theology and morality. They did not feel, as a rule, that they had the right to question what the past told them was true and desirable, since God had ordained it. Living in an entirely Jewish milieu, their attitudes were confirmed rather than challenged by those with whom they came in contact. The pressure of the ghetto ensured a straitjacket conformity.

One need only observe the Jew today to realize how free he feels to pass judgment on the whole of Jewish tradition or any of its parts. He was born to political rights and economic opportunities, aspires to social acceptance and has access to the intellectual life of his country. The old theology has broken down. Supernatural sanction for Jewish living is no longer the norm. The modern Jew lives with and among Gentiles. He absorbs their ways of thinking and their modes of living. This contact shakes Jewish routines. As a citizen of the 1980s, the Jew properly feels he has the right to determine for himself his own attitude toward Judaism. He may reject it if he wishes.

But what a great many modern Jews fail to see is that such rejection carries with it a prior obligation—the obligation to understand. A Jew has the right to reject Judaism but not until he has first understood its psychological and spiritual values. He has the right to abandon traditional observances but not before he has made an effort to assess them in the light of Jewish striving. He has the right to choose a kind of life that will depart from Jewish loyalties and assimilate into the Gentile pattern. But he owes it to himself, to the Jewish group and to mankind first to evaluate the implications of his decision and the grounds on which it may be condemned by the protagonists of Jewish survival.

This obligation to understand before he rejects is real. No one who has any respect for his own intellect, no one who wishes to live as full and rich a life as he can, no one with any feeling of responsibility to the past of mankind and to its future can avoid that responsibility. If he comes to understand and still rejects, Judaism can have no quarrel with him. It must say to him: Go thy way in peace. But Judaism does have a quarrel with the person who accepts no responsibility and rejects before he understands.

This was not my problem. I had no hard choice to make as I was growing up and away from first-generation Jews. I was encouraged to question and challenge, as the following narrative will demonstrate. It almost seemed as if I was being dared to reject the values presented to me. In the Orphanage understanding of the Jew's striving arrived early and for the most part easily. There Jewish commitment came through joy as well as duty. There I was exposed to the flame from which I lit my own candle. In later years the candle often flickered under doubt and disillusionment, but it has burned steadily to this day.

I

A Pity for the Living

When a man reaches the vicinity of the biblical three-score-and-ten, he can look back to a specific period and say: these are the crucial years of my life. In my case, they were the years I spent as a ward of the Jewish Orphanage of Western Canada. In the Home I absorbed feelings, attitudes and convictions that entered into the fabric of my being and lasted for almost six decades.

The Orphanage came into existence just before World War I and ended its life shortly after World War II, a span of little more than three decades. For most Winnipeg Jews it is now beyond recall. They do not remember its pain and glamour, its tradition of severity, its lesson of compassion, its symbol as hope.

The first World War was a terrible time abroad, tearing at the fabric of loyalties. Jews fought on both sides of the conflict. As patriotic Germans, they were loyal to Kaiser and country. As patriotic Britons and Canadians, they were loyal to King and country. The devastations of war combined with the ravages of the influenza epidemic to make it a time of loneliness and suffering, a time of hunger and groping. War and pestilence produced orphans.

It was before the Holocaust and the annihilation of the six million. Jews were not so angry then, though their ancient sorrow still engulfed them. They were softer, gentler. The power generated by the state of Israel had not yet hardened them.

Winnipeg Jews, plunged in the common grief of the time, had strengths. Living at the gateway of the Canadian West, when communication was less developed than it is today, faith sheltered them. They believed that life was a deeply serious matter, demanding all the talent, shrewdness and competitiveness of which a human being is capable. Embedded in their faith was a prophetic element: every act brought consequences and therefore life was a concern which everyone had to account for.

Unsophisticated, parochial, they hoped with a passion. They could have written Tevye the dairyman's words: "As we say on Yom Kippur, the Lord decides who will ride on horseback and who will crawl on foot. The main thing is—hope! A Jew must always hope, must never lose hope. And in the meantime what if we waste away to a shadow?" Tevye was the folk hero of Winnipeg Jews. They took him to their hearts long before *Fiddler on the Roof* made him famous. They shared his unquenchable faith and produced the Orphanage.

To the Gentiles the Winnipeg Jewish community early in the century seemed like a monolith. Jews were non-Christians; that was a sufficient distinction. But a close look would have revealed them to be almost as divided as the generation of the tower of Babel. There were the "south-enders," the more modern who came before the turn of the century, and the "north-enders," the recently arrived. There was Shaarey Zedek, the synagogue that had a German-English fragrance, where Jews "worshipped," and then there was Rosh Pinah, where East European Jews *davened. Landsmanschaften*, fraternal organizations, sporting the names of old-country localities and attracting fellow-townsmen, proliferated: the Bessaraber Society, the Kiever Society, the Bobrover Hilfsfarein, the Propoisker Society, the Nikoleiever Farein, the Pavolicher Society and a dozen more.

But south-ender or north-ender, Propoisker or Nikoleiever, English or East European Jew, they joined hands in founding and promoting the Orphanage. It was a banner for bringing factions to submerge their differences and act together. First came the Canadian Jewish Orphans' Home on Selkirk Avenue, supported by the Hebrew Ladies Orphans' Home Association and B'nai B'rith, in 1912. A year later the Esther Robinson Orphans' Home appeared on Robinson Avenue. Rivalry for the privilege of caring for homeless children was strong, but the two institutions, under the leadership of attorney Max Steinkopf, manufacturer Lester Rice and real-estate broker A. H. Aronovitch, realizing that in unity was survival, merged soon after into the Jewish Orphanage and Children's Aid of Western Canada. The merger spawned confidence to build the stucco structure on Matheson Avenue. Funds came from Winnipeg and the West.

In a real sense the Orphanage belonged not only to city Jews but to those who were scattered across the three other western provinces. The first two decades of the century saw the Jewish population of the prairies grow from the hundreds into the thousands. Most of them, fleeing from the Russo-Japanese war and East-European persecution, stopped in Winnipeg on their way west. The city had become a bustling transportation and distribution centre. In it Jewish communal life had already taken on form and substance. There were Jewish educational institutions for their children and cultural opportunities for themselves. But a few adventurous ones pushed farther west and settled in the prairie towns that dotted the railway line at intervals or tried their hand at farming.

Jews of Propoisk, Yekaterinislav and Bratzlav settled in Snowflake, Othan and Whiskey Gap. These towns seemed to be fashioned from the same mould: a railway station and confectionery stand that served coffee and sandwiches, a grain elevator, post office, church, restaurant, invariably owned by a Chinese, and a general store usually presided over by a member of the covenant of Abraham.

These merchants prospered. They sold to farmers on credit—until harvest time—yard goods, overalls, shoes as well as staples like sugar, salt, hardware and kerosene, and bought butter, cheese and eggs. Their knowledge of the basic Slavic tongue gave them direct communication with Russian, Polish and Ukrainian tillers of the soil. During periods of drought they shared the suffering of the settlers, their customers, attending ecumenical church meetings, long before ecumenism became popular, to contribute their "silent money"—not the kind that jingled, as one Methodist minister expressed it—to drought relief.

On festivals and holidays, hungry for the presence of other Jews, they would travel to Winnipeg to attend services at the Orphanage synagogue, where they were enthusiastically welcomed as friends and supporters. Inmates of the Home, when ready to strike out on their own, often took jobs as helpers in prairie general stores and taught Hebrew to the children of the store owners on the side. Thus the Orphanage became part of the life-fabric of prairie Jews. They were also tied to the Home for the very best of practical reasons: almost half of the Orphanage children came from Saskatchewan, Alberta and British Columbia.

Jews from the West came to celebrate the opening of the Matheson Avenue building in 1920, when a gala was held to raise funds. A witness lyrically described the devotion of the guests to their "darling," the Orphanage: "(We) cannot drink in enough of that sacred atmosphere that pervades the building and cannot open wide enough our hands. As a young woman, happy and confident in her husband's arms, yields to all his entreaties, abandons herself completely, so the Jew has abandoned himself here in the arms of higher duty." He goes on embellishing this erotic image, then gets down to practical matters. "The building had to cost us only $75,000, says Levinson, the president, but the flu came and we had to make more room. Then the strike came and we had to pay more. And now it cost us $125,000. And we have collected, yes, only in one year, just $95,000. And the provincial government have found our institution so magnificent, so deserving, that even they could not resist its charm, and they gave us $10,000. Surely we don't want a mortgage on our Home!"

What a fund-raiser this unnamed enthusiast was. "No! is the emphatic, prompt echo of the Jewish heart. And there it goes—$1,000 for the key, says Silverman; $1,000 for the dining room, says Rosner. Warm up, people, the competition is keen—$500 here, $200 there. In another hour it is $15,000, and lo, it is $20,000. No more mortgage. The Home is our own and fully paid up. Here you are in your element, O Israel! You have paid for the orphans' Home. Oh, when shall you pay up the mortgage for your own home?"

In the Home we orphans escaped the vulgarity of the Jewish community, the working class trying to show the middle class they were capable of style and the middle class showing the working class their substance. We had no inkling of communal pretensions. The relationship of the Jews to the orphans was strong simply because we were innocents. If they were snobs, we did not feel it. Middle-class vulgarity draws on material surplus, and we worked on deficits.

However, we were infected by a disease the dwellers at the juncture of the Red and Assiniboine rivers themselves called "Winnipegitis." It is a malady known to every organized community. Its source is vanity and its symptom something best expressed by the Hebraized Yiddish word *b'rogez*. If your name is omitted from a publicity release, you become *b'rogez*. If you feel slighted at a committee meeting, you stamp out, *b'rogez*. Winnipegitis hit me the moment I entered the Orphanage on my first day. There on the vestibule wall, covering most of it, were large slabs of marble, emblazoned in gold lettering with the names of late presidents, ex-presidents and past presidents, chairmen and co-chairmen, committee members and alternates, Board members, Ladies Society executives, Girls Auxiliary officers. Woe betide superintendent Aaron Osovsky if in a speech crediting volunteers for a noble piece of work he mentioned only the chairman of the committee, the general, and forgot the foot-sloggers!

Nevertheless, humaneness and social decency proved stronger and broke through the miasma of Vanity Fair. The Jews showed their worst to their peers and their best to us in the Home. Their humaneness was part of their *yiddishkeit*, a better word than Jewishness, for it connotes moral standards and spiritual awareness. Jews were compassionate in those days between the wars. To be otherwise would have meant being un-Jewish, and was therefore immoral. In the Home we felt the full blast of this moral power.

It came from three cultures—Yiddish, Hebraic and Anglo-Saxon. The first was cosy and familiar, the second distant and sacred, the third real but not always hospitable. Its dominant instrument was, of course, the Yiddish tongue. Hardly a post-World War I Jew in Manitoba's capital was not touched by the pathos of Yitzhak Leib Peretz, the satire of Mendele Mocher Seforim (Mendele the Book Peddler) and the folksiness of Sholom Aleichem. These three had been transported in the baggage of the migrants from Russia and the Ukraine. They gave Winnipeg Jews a highly personal perception of the meaning of *rachmonis*, compassion or pity.

One fulfilled the requirements of *rachmonis* by contributing time, work and money to the Orphanage, but these were not enough. One had to become intimately involved with the children. Mrs. Rafalsky, a Ladies Society executive, whom we came to know as "party-maker" because she was always good for second helpings on festive occasions, showed the way. On visits to the Home she would scoop up a child in her massive arms, press him to her ample bosom and murmur tearfully: "My little *teibele* (pigeon), my poor little orphan, let your troubles be mine. *A rachmonis auf die lebedige*, a pity for the living." The last phrase was the war cry of the Ladies Society, and it didn't come to them accidentally. It was the invention of Sholom Aleichem, the title of one of his stories.

At every meeting of the Society, culture as well as charity was prominent on the agenda. The ladies believed deeply in self-development. And what better way for cultural escalation than to listen to a reading of one of the great Yiddish literary lights?

The favourite public reader was Harry Steinberg, a strong supporter though not a member of the Board and a cloak and suit manufacturer, who had the wit to see that Winnipeg, at the centre of an agricultural region, was ideal for the establishment of a factory that produced work-clothes for tillers of the soil. Steinberg rose quickly in the industrial world of his city. His rise was facilitated by a cheque-book in one hand—his largesse became proverbial—and a copy of Sholom Aleichem in the other. Few could dispense the flavour of Solomon Rabinovich, the name Sholom Aleichem was born with, as did the perpetually willing Harry. He spoke the Yiddish words not only with verve, style and enthusiasm but with obvious affection. It was even said that the overalls manufacturer clothed Sholom Aleichem in particularly unique raiment, which was almost like saying one could improve on the language of the holy Bible.

Harry's favourite Sholom Aleichem piece was "A Pity for the Living." He would customarily test his audience with the query: "What would you like me to read today?" Invariably the cry would go up, "A Pity for the Living." As often as the Ladies Society heard it, they would never tire of it and relished the tears that welled up in them at the telling of it, tears of joy and sadness, nourished by a hope more than two thousand years old: "They who sow in tears shall reap in joy."

Here is the tale, in condensed and abbreviated form:

On the eve of a holiday a distracted mother says to her little boy: "Here is some horseradish for you to grate. But close your eyes, you little fool, because if I catch you crying I'll smack you."

"Why does she have to call me a fool?" the child protests to himself as he sets about his task. "And why does she threaten to smack me before I've done anything? Is it fair? Is it kind?"

"Ho-ho," he says to himself, "if a person begins to think about things that are unfair and unkind. . ." And as he grates the horseradish, keeping his eyes closed, he begins to think.

—Of the time he visited the house of his closest friend and watched his friend's father, a *shohet* (a ritual slaughterer), slit the throat of a chicken casually, cold-bloodedly, without a tremor of compunction.

"Pinele," he had said to his friend, "your father is an *epikoros*, a heathen."

"And why is my father an *epikoros*?"

"Because he has no pity for the living. He killed that chicken and didn't even feel sorry for it." After which a quarrel had ensued, and now the little boy and Pinele are friends no more.

—Or of the time when the dog was scalded and the little boy had chased after it to comfort it and his father had come upon him running after the dog, had accused him of being a dog beater and had dragged him off to *heder* (Hebrew school) by the ear.

—Or of the time on a sabbath afternoon, when dressed in his *shabbos* best, he had wandered into the woods and come upon two peasant boys who had found a nest with fledgling birds and were beating them to death one after the other against a tree trunk. And he had not been able to stand it and had tried to stop them, only to get set upon for his pains, to return home to another beating at his father's hands for fighting and getting his sabbath clothes torn.

"I don't understand it," the child reasons to himself; "the *rebbe* (teacher) in *heder* says one must not harm a single living thing, not a fly nor an ant, not even a spider. For these too are God's creatures and suffer when they are hurt. If that's so, then why do people beat dogs, kill birds and slaughter chickens? And not birds and chickens only!"

What about Perele, the paralyzed baby girl from the house next door whom he used to carry about on pleasant days so that she might enjoy the sunlight, and who, whenever he lifted her, twined her thin arms tightly about his neck, for she loved him dearly as he loved her. And when the pogrom broke out, didn't men throw her out of the window so that her crippled body lay broken, bleeding, dead in the courtyard? And doesn't Perele's mother cry all the time? And doesn't his own mother say to her: "Sha, you mustn't cry. It was God's will. You mustn't sin."

Thinking of all this, the little boy begins to cry himself, the tears streaming down his face. "You little fool," his mother snaps at him, "I told you to remember to keep your eyes shut." And she slaps him for being stupid.

A touching story even in this mutilated form. But for the workers in the Orphanage vineyard it was more than just a story; it was a profound and wise scripture as well. For at one and the same time it spoke of two things: a hard, tragic fact of life and a moral inference from that fact.

The hard, tragic fact, seemingly so obvious but in their view requiring constant and deliberate emphasis, was that of the universality of suffering, the truth that to live is to suffer, that all life is a great fellowship of anguish. *Tsaar baale hayim*—there is an anguish in all that lives, an assertion I heard constantly from the Harry Steinbergs and the Rafalskys.

The moral inference they drew was simple: since all suffer, all merit pity. This was the foundation stone on which the Orphanage was built—that one must have mercy, for to be pitiless is the gravest sin of which a Jew or anyone else is capable.

Yet compassionate as they were and try as they might, Rafalsky, Steinberg and David Spivak, who sought to be living parents to the orphans and spent every spare hour with them, and their fellow-workers could not give the orphans a real family. There is a profound difference between an institution and a family. In the latter rules are often relaxed and suspended, a necessary procedure for the blending of souls. In the former rules prevailed without let-up. "Party-maker" tried to provide a mother's lap; she did not succeed. Even the orphans who had living mothers never knew maternal balm. When I visited my mother on Saturday afternoons, away from the Home, I felt like a guest. Our relationship had no chance to wear. I always had the feeling of putting on a suit of clothes for the first time or breaking in a new pair of shoes. There was no comfort in the visit and therefore no solace, although our attachment was strong and our affection demonstrative. Perhaps too demonstrative, to make up for the hours and days we did not share.

We were certainly a family of some kind at the Orphanage, bound by a fraternity we could not feel with boys and girls outside the institution. But it was a big family, too big, one that permitted no privacy, no warmth, no spontaneous love, no relaxed affection. There was no playfulness between adults and children. Our emotional weather was always extreme—harshness or compassion. Mild, moderate days were almost unknown. Such a radical environment was bound to affect our personalities. We suffered from physical and spiritual claustrophobia. There were fences all around us and fences in our minds.

The Home constituted a self-contained colony, and all its inmates, cooped up together day and night, were hourly exposed to public view and unable to choose what to reveal and what to hide. Lizzie Lecker, one of the prettier inmates, who had an artistic bent, once drew a picture of the Orphanage as a jail, with bars on the windows and locks and chains on the doors. It fell into the hands of Osovsky who punished her for biting the hands that fed her. How dare she interpret the loving ministrations of a caring community as oppression? But Lizzie expressed the instinctive feeling of all the orphans. We were sick of the rules binding us to unending routine and yearned for relaxation, for emancipation.

We were not a real family because of the distinctions an institution inevitably draws. In a family the recognized parental norm is to treat all children alike. Parents, whether they live up to the standard or not, become quickly aware that, whatever the differences, every child deserves an even break. In the Orphanage inequality was deliberately sharp and uncompromising. It was fostered by the system. If you were blessed with a good voice or a good mind and brought credit to the choir or distinguished yourself at school, you became a "favourite" and were treated with special consideration. The menial chores were not for you. But if you were just another plodding orphan, and a dullard to boot, you were ordered about with curt severity and assigned the dirty jobs. Favourites dry-mopped the linoleum floors and monitored the neat six-year-olds. All the others wet-mopped the bathroom floor, scoured the toilets or had to minister to the bed-wetters. The system inevitably produced jealousy and bitterness.

The favourites, of whom I came to be one, were protected, but they were also expected to contribute more to the "good name" of the Orphanage. Superintendent, matrons and teachers gave them extra time and attention, explaining to them the problems facing the Home, the Jewish community and the entire Jewish people. The favourites were expected to approach life in the Home as adults and were treated as such. They were encouraged to ask questions and usually received grown-up answers. Superintendent Osovsky and Miss Rose, the matron, would stimulate my curiosity about the Home's financial difficulties and how important it was to arouse Jewish adults to fulfil their "sacred obligations." My behaviour and achievements would help "sell the Home," they said. They expected me to be bright and breezy all day and every day. But I didn't feel like that. I felt bleak and very young and ineffective. I did not know how to develop a chameleon talent for conformity and contradiction. I endured favouritism like a hairshirt, a secret penance for getting married to life's realities too soon. I worried about the burdens I had to carry and was doubtless abrupt, irritable and withdrawn.

The institutional environment was further accentuated by an exaggerated stress on physical cleanliness. The superintendent considered himself an expert on intellectual, culinary, educational and
musical subjects, but on matters hygienic he was without peer—
overseer, police chief and supreme court. The floors, walls and
windows had to be not only clean but antiseptic. There was always a disinfectant in the air. Cleanliness was not just next to god-
liness; it was worshipped as the deity. Dirt was Satan, evil incarnate, a wickedness to be fought against and eradicated. None of
the favourites was ever dirty. Familiarity with soap and water was
the first requisite for being "chosen" from among the helots and
elevated.

All things considered, we were perhaps best described as an institutional family. We were branded with the mark of separateness
as Orphanage kids and as Jews. The two merged into each other,
taking some of the edge off both. We were left with the feeling
that, orphans or not, Jewishness was an integral part of our being.
Like the mark of circumcision we would never get rid of it.

Since the Home was supported by Jews and the orphans were
wards of the Jews, we had to be symbols of what was authentically
Jewish. Trouble was nobody could agree on the definition. In the
1920s and 1930s denominationalism had not yet arrived in Winnipeg. The city's isolation saved the Jewish community from the
inroads of Reform and Conservative Judaism. All Jews were either
orthodox or secular, bound by a common language, Yiddish.
Logic should have governed in the Home and Yiddish should have
been the language of discourse, as it was with my parents and me.
Strangely, however, the language of Sholom Aleichem, beloved
by the sixteen thousand Jews of the city en masse, was a foreign
tongue among the inmates. It was neither taught nor spoken,
though it was the mother tongue of Osovsky, the nurses and the
Hebrew teachers and the language of the dramas superintendent
Osovsky wrote and directed, with the orphans as players.

English was the necessary communicating instrument in the
Home because of the varied backgrounds of the inmates. There
were children from the Maritimes and the prairies, from assimilated origins where only an echo of Jewish identity was heard.
Still, logically, Yiddish should have been taught by the Hebrew
teachers. One of them, Mr. Rachlis, did make feeble attempts at
bringing *mameh-loshen* (the mother tongue) into the classroom,

but without official encouragement they were doomed to failure.
My mother could not understand the neglect of Yiddish. It seemed
to her as if *dos pintele yid*, the essential Jewish core, had been
abandoned.

Clearly the Orphanage reflected the *kultur-kampf* (culture conflict) of the community. Secularists and religious Jews had initiated
separate educational streams. The former had built Y. L. Peretz
school, where Yiddish reigned supreme; the latter promoted the
Talmud Torah, where modern Hebrew was the language of instruction and the ancient Hebraic texts the subjects of the curriculum. While the protagonists of both schools used Yiddish for
everyday speech, the Hebraists were reinforced by the orthodox
and the Zionists who loved the vernacular Yiddish but were convinced that classical Hebrew, the language of the Jewish past, had
to be the cultural mine for the Jewish future. The Orphanage,
bound to accept the disposition of the majority, mirrored the content of the Talmud Torah.

Hebrew-Yiddish dissension was the lesser of the two headaches
that plagued the Orphanage administration. All agreed that religion, whatever the language, had to be the important ingredient in
training the orphans. Even the Yiddish secularists, priding themselves on tolerance, conceded a significant place to religion. The
question was: how much and what kind? That orthodoxy must
prevail, no one had any doubt, but of orthodoxy there was no
limit. Dietary laws, sabbath and holiday observance, separation
of the sexes, daily prayers—these were the orthodox demands.
The ultra-orthodox insisted on substance to the last detail. The
liberal orthodox wanted style as well as substance.

The result was compromise, acceptable to the so-called liberals
but anathema to the ultras who never ceased complaining that the
Home was being led by a pack of revisionists who were shaping it
into a den of assimilationism. On at least one occasion the complaint produced a scandal.

One Saturday morning Rabbi Israel Isaac Kahanovitch appeared at the sabbath service to deliver a sermon commemorating
an Orphanage anniversary. Orthodox law required that he walk
all the way from Flora Avenue, where he lived, to the Home on
Matheson, a distance of several miles. The exertion must have left
him tired and irritable. He was an impressive man, though small of
stature, with a full black beard, wearing a Prince Albert coat and a
black, wide-brimmed hat, which emphasized his dark complexion.

He spoke in measured cadences like rhythmic waves beating against a shore. Even a boy of nine was mesmerized. But the cadences fell out of line that morning.

Before the sermon the boys and girls of the choir had sung their hearts out. They had put on display the best in their repertoire. Everybody knew about the girl choristers, but no one brought them up as an issue. When publicity pictures were released, only the boys were shown, in skull-caps and prayer shawls, surrounding their cantor-director. That there were females in the choir was an open secret, a fact if not approved universally, still to be tolerated. Somehow that morning the rabbi was not prepared to overlook the forbidden feminine presence.

As the female voices soared, his dark face turned white. When his turn to speak came, he did not change his big hat for a skull cap, as was his custom, but mounted to the altar rapidly. Instead of beginning softly, a great piercing cry issued from him: "A *hillul hashem*, a desecration, has occurred here today!" There followed a thunderous and highly charged polemic on the evil of women's voices in the synagogue. He cited the Bible, the Talmud, the authoritative responsa and the medieval commentaries. Finally, in a voice that dropped a few decibels, heavy with emotion, he warned that such violation of the sacred tradition could only result in further sin and ultimate apostasy.

The homily shook the Orphanage to its foundations. Actually the controversy that followed had nothing to do with the issue, just with the suitability of the rabbi's verbal onslaught at such a time and on such an occasion. Even some of his ultra supporters felt that the issue could have waited to be discussed in a less sanctified atmosphere.

Kahanovitch's sermon had an ironic effect. It galvanized communal support for the girls in the choir. It pointed up the war between "the forces of light and the forces of darkness," between the modernists and medievalists. It set the stage for a revision of all the religious ritual performed in the Home.

The orthodox clamoured for three daily services—morning, afternoon and evening. Only the morning service was agreed upon and limited to boys of bar-mitzvah age, to train them how to put on *tephillin* (phylacteries). Dietary laws were observed in the kitchen, but the ultras complained that they were more symbolic than actual, since the non-Jewish waitresses, ignorant of the basic requirements of *kashrus*, often cut corners and there was no *mash-*

giah (ritual supervisor) to control them. However, the kosher status quo remained. A short grace preceded every meal and a somewhat longer blessing followed, but not the extensive post-prandial service orthodoxy demanded. Sabbath eve services were abbreviated and held in the dining-room rather than in the synagogue on the third floor. Sabbath was a sacred day but not a "blue" one. It was not so severe as to forbid riding to the theatre on Friday evenings to see a film, as the ultras wanted. Saturday morning and holiday services remained untouched, perhaps as a concession to the ultras. They were long, arduous and cathartic exercises.

The struggle over ritual and prayers impelled liberal supporters of the Home to call for a more meaningful approach to religion. As a result of their clamouring, an innovative morning prayer was instituted just before the daily breakfast. Superintendent Osovsky was in the forefront of the liberal forces. He trained the boys to cover their heads during prayers at mealtime but to uncover them when they ate, an innovation the orthodox mightily condemned. He caught the imagination of Orphanage supporters of every label in a public address in which he cited the fifth verse of the new morning prayer, a quotation from Proverbs: "Hearken, my child, to the instruction of thy father, and despise not the teaching of thy mother." For orphans, who have no mother or father, he said, the community plays the parental role. His audience loved the thought the little ones were praying for their benefactors daily. Indeed, it was Osovsky's wit that won the day for revisionist ritual in the Home.

Liberals were also enchanted with the last verse of the new morning prayer, an expression of gratitude to the Creator of the universe for having made the orphans Israelites. In the orthodox prayer book this blessing is negative: "Praised art thou, O Lord, for not having made me a Gentile." Making the gratitude positive was a constructive change, in the liberal view, helping to give the orphans a strong confidence in themselves and their origins. In later years the Conservative movement in the U.S. also changed this blessing from the negative to the positive.

The progressive victory should have alienated the ultras and divided the community, but the fission did not occur. In American communities of the 1920s orthodoxy and Reform met head on over the issue of religious training in orphanages and one or the other eventually withdrew support. A special factor prevented such a schism in Winnipeg. No one challenged the supremacy and validity of orthodoxy as such but rather how far it could go without becoming fanaticism. For the rabbinic forces Jewish law was clear and unchangeable. For the liberals Jewish law was to be respected but applied with leniency in regard to orphans. Always, always, *rachmonis*, a pity for the living.

Ironically, a decade after he had been supplanted as superintendent by H. E. Wilder, Osovsky sided with the anti-revisionists. He opposed Wilder's deletion of the word orphanage from the official name and the substitution of the title Children's Home. Orphans, in the Anglo-Saxon tradition of Dickens, connoted a special breed. The word was pejorative. In Hebraized Yiddish the word *yesoimim*, orphans, connoted all the pathos and tenderness of the ancient concept of compassion. *Yesoimim* was the battle cry of Osovsky against those Orphanage workers of the late 1930s who reduced the size of the Board of Directors and opted for the foster home system, thus leading to the dissolution of the Home as an institution. These innovations meant less involvement by members of the community, which in Osovsky's eyes implied anti-orthodoxy and assimilation, the gradual loss of Jewish identity.

What happened in the Home in the 1920s over religious training was really a battle between mind and heart. Heinrich Heine once said that the Greeks of the Periclean Age, for all their dazzling attainments, were only striplings, whereas the Hebrews were mature men. The Greeks revered great intellect. The Jews did, too, but they revered a great heart more, for a Jew, if he be truly a Jew, is compassionate, and compassion consists in an awakened and mature heart.

Max J. Finkelstein, a barrister, a director of the Orphanage Board and eventually its president, echoed Heine's words in a talk on radio station CKY in 1932 and applied them to the Home. He took his listeners back to the ancient days when the Greeks were masters of the world in matters of culture and government.

It was the custom in the world-famous city of Sparta, second only to Athens among the cities of Greece, to expose upon Mount Taygetus any child born into the world which the authorities thought would likely become a public charge. The unfortunate child was left there upon the mountain top until the ravages of the elements and the beaks of the vultures destroyed the body, and the gods took back the soul of the little one which, had it been left to live, might have become a burden upon a community too busy with the making of war and the chiseling of statues to pay attention to the frail little human thing.

Ah, not so in ancient Israel. No unfortunate child was exposed on the sacred Mount Zion. The laws of the land protected the weak against the strong. The widow and the orphan were given special rights and privileges. No unfortunate individual was to suffer in order that the state might be rid of a probable burden. Thus you have the essential differences between the Greek culture of art and beauty and the Jewish culture of justice and mercy.

Perhaps that is why Mount Olympus, home of the ancient Greek gods, is silent and deserted while practically the whole civilized world today takes its law from Mount Zion and the word of God from Jerusalem. Winnipeg is in the best traditions of ancient Israel with its fine philanthropic institutions of the Jewish community. Among the noblest of such institutions and one that is, perhaps, the most outstanding is the Jewish Orphanage whose field of endeavour extends from the Great Lakes to the Pacific Ocean.

A noble speech, calculated to appeal to pride of origin and the tradition of the heart. It was this kind of heart that responded to the needs of the orphans on Matheson Avenue. This personal attachment to the Home, identifying it with an ancient heritage, persisted well past World War II. And when the building was finally razed, staunch supporters like David Spivak and Aaron Osovsky mourned it with the sorrow of the mourners over the destruction of Jerusalem's ancient Temple.

The supporters of the Home performed two poetic acts. First they engaged in a flight of imagination. They got out of the prison of themselves and identified with the orphans, sharing their bruised bewilderment. In this respect their act of pity was closely akin to artistic insight, to the glimpse into others of the novelist or portrait painter.

Imagination and identification made them believe that mercy was a sign, not of weakness, as Nietzsche argued, and the Nazis after him, but of strength. A stupid person cannot pity. He lacks the required imagination. The immature person, the narcissist who has never outgrown his infantile self-centredness, cannot pity, because he is unable to concern himself with anyone else. The morbid soul, the person who hates himself, cannot pity, because in identifying with others he comes to hate them also. Only a healthy soul is capable of pity, and a strong mind of mercy. So Winnipeg Jews reasoned sixty years ago.

I go back to my days in the Home not just for nostalgic self-indulgence, but because they tell me that the incapacity for pity is a terrible, loathsome disease, and that there is something even more terrible—wilful pitilessness. We are all human, with the power of compassion. We are all human, with the tendency to suppress this power, deliberately, cold-bloodedly, and say: "Do not tell us, we do not wish to hear. Do not show us, we do not wish to see." And if by chance we should see and hear against our will we harden our hearts.

This is not a new response, but I doubt whether ever before in history has there been so much of it in the world. A thousand evidences around us, on every continent, testify how widespread, how deep-seated in us these days is wilful pitilessness. Wars starve the bodies, blast the minds, twist the characters and wreck the prospects of millions of children. They cause mass starvation and the bombing of civilian populations, bringing the stress and tragedy of violence on those all of us—American, Canadian, British, Russian, Israeli, Arab—care most about, our children. Pitilessness must be checked or it will destroy us. It will grow in us, making us capable of ever greater brutalities until we become dehumanized and our world perishes. For without mercy, as without justice, humankind cannot endure.

It is for this reason I remember the Home and seek to acquaint others with it. In those days, in a little colony called the Jewish Orphanage, people not only mourned the dead; they pitied the living.

II

"Orphan"

Walking up the tree-lined street on that summer morning, I looked about wonderingly, not as one seeing it all for the first time—for the Orphanage was familiar—but rather as one who sought something he had never imagined he would be seeking here. From now on this was no longer a place where I went on a visit, but a home for years on end—five as it turned out. I walked slowly, even pausing occasionally. I was going to become an orphan that day and had my bundle of belongings with me. I was on the threshold of my ninth year.

I imprinted on my keen memory the wide expanse of five acres fenced in all around, the potato patches, the substance of the black soil—I with my unfenced spirit, my soil-seeking roots and as yet unformed personality. That was prairie land to the west, where I was to discover that circuses made their seasonal pilgrimages. The flat land—I had never seen rolling country in my life—stretched all the way to Main Street where lumbering street-cars, with their quaint cow-catchers, could be faintly heard.

To the south a row of neat middle-class houses—no less than palaces to me for I had never lived in anything but a cottage—girded the dirt road, unrelieved by such apparitions as shops. Matheson Avenue was an incipient Jewish suburb where "the rich" had moved, those who had surmounted their immigrant generation and achieved the status of factory owners, manufacturers of ladies' coats and dresses and men's suits.

To the east more potato patches and vegetable gardens, leading to some nondescript habitations to which I paid no attention. They belonged to the original Matheson Avenue Gentile dwellers who had preceded the *nouveau riche*.

And to the north prairie again, stretching interminably and ending somewhere at Kildonan Park, a half-hour's street-car ride away.

These, then, formed the boundaries for my next five years. At their centre reared the Home, a three-storied stucco structure, with a peaked-tile green roof, dormer windows, a well-manicured lawn in front and a gravel-covered driveway beginning and ending at Matheson, forming an arc that enclosed several flower beds. How strange it all was for I was now an orphan, thus created by the decision of an official and the stroke of a pen. Actually my mother and father were alive. The contradiction was annoying if comprehensible.

The Home was not only for orphans, although they made up the bulk of its population. Its official name was Jewish Orphanage and Children's Aid of Western Canada. I was in the category of children's aid. My father, a *shohet*, had been felled by a stroke, and my mother undertook the support of her two little daughters and son, ten, eight and nine respectively, and her husband. She was finding the undertaking physically hard and spiritually forlorn until, happily, the Home advertised for a cook. The Orphanage's need and my mother's want made a perfect match. She would become the tetrarch of the kitchen, working on its spacious wooden blocks that served as tables and sweating over the huge stoves, living in one of the rooms reserved for staff, and her three children would become part of the orphan populace. As consideration for the care and education of her children, her salary was reduced to twenty dollars per month. Though the increment was low, it was a most convenient arrangement. She was near her children, though contact with them was restricted, and her husband, because his crippled condition required special care, was confined first to a hospital in Selkirk, about thirty miles north of Winnipeg, then to the Jewish Old Folks Home in the city's north end.

My father was a pitiful sight, shuffling his left leg, the left arm hanging aimlessly, the fingernails long, large and encrusted. His beard was overgrown, a sort of ginger colour with streaks of grey. His speech was a jumble of sounds, although he could still recite well-remembered prayers. Illness deprived him of the facility to read. He was just past fifty but the ravages of apoplexy added twenty years to his figure and face.

There were six children in our family, born in two shifts. A decade separated two older brothers and a sister from the three who were in the Home. The older ones had left years before, Lily, Rosie and I remaining as "jewels" in the depleted case.

My father was a warm and affectionate man, with an occasional flash of temper but with a special fondness for little ones and a tendency to indulge them. Years before, he had given me my first introduction to the Five Books of Moses. During my first lesson, with Mother present, he let drops of honey fall on the page and let me bend to lick them so that study of Torah should be sweet to me. I still have the book with the sticky page.

Father's illness dulled his senses and reduced his understanding, but the demonstrative affection for his three little ones never slackened. His kisses were moist and strong, and as he tried to say the words "my jewels," tears of frustration would stream down his cheeks.

The incident that led Mother to put him in an institution centered on a wallet with twenty-five dollars in it, money she had earned as a cook at several catered affairs. The batch of one-dollar bills represented a month of meals for the family of five. Father had picked up the wallet, still believing himself to be head of the household, but could not remember what he had done with it. First he said it was in the wood-pile stacked against the house. I helped to remove every stick of wood, hunting for the coveted cash, then restacked the pile as it was. Subsequently he stoutly maintained, as far as we could make out, that he had dropped the wallet ten blocks away, an unlikely story, since he could not have walked a single block by himself. But I traipsed after Mother to verify his contention. We returned crushed with disappointment. Her words still ring in my ears: "What did you do with the money that is life for us? Who will now feed our helpless children?" For answer my father wept, and his wife and children wept. The tears were bitter yet comforting. We cried for each other.

That decided the issue of what to do with Father. No hospital would accept him. In those days medicine knew little about strokes. Their crippling effects were accepted as inevitable, to be endured by the patient and his family. But Father's illness was destroying his family as well as himself. The Selkirk institution for the mentally disabled was the only one that would admit him. Mother paid for his upkeep, visiting him twice a week, bundling us up to take along on Saturday afternoons so that he might catch a glimpse of his three children, the only balm to his helplessness.

For Father, Selkirk hospital was an abomination. The meals were not kosher, and nothing could persuade him that in sickness violation of dietary observance was permissible. His body, his very soul, kept wasting away. He would plead with Mother in the broken sounds that passed for speech to take him away from the residential horror, but she was adamant. She showed no mercy to him, then sobbed all the way home, blaming herself for an impossible predicament.

Father would often appeal to me, his eyes tearful and pleading. I could make out the words, "Away, away." He would open the little volume of Psalms, always at his bedside, and make me read aloud: "I lift up mine eyes unto the hills; whence cometh my help?" pointing to the word "ezri" (my help) and then to me. I sensed that he expected me to be the instrument of his salvation, for he was turning to me when all else failed, but I was bewildered and mystified. His sadness pierced me and left me confounded.

Mother was a strong spirit. An unlettered woman, she would complain about her weakness and inadequacy. Like Job she would curse the day she was born. But seeing us look at her with wondering eyes, she would regret her words and assure us that it was simply her sorrow speaking. She underestimated her powers. In later years—she died at eighty-six—the ailments of old age crept upon her. But until then she handled her problems with strength and boldness. Despite her near illiteracy, she was a natural public speaker. In 1938, on my return to Winnipeg to address the twenty-fifth anniversary dinner of the Ladies Society, she was called upon for "a few words." Her speech electrified the audience and stole the show. It was a comfort for her to know that, given the opportunity, she could have achieved intellectually more than she did.

As a cook she had few peers. Her K-rations—knishes, kreplach, kasha soup—were the pride of the family when she was young and the celebration of the community when she turned professional in order to feed her children and support her husband. It was when Father was at Selkirk that the Orphanage's offer arrived. Mother must have been relieved to see that the next years of her life, though hard and humbling, were neatly set out and clearly delineated.

But for me, mounting the few steps of the Home and entering the high-ceilinged room which was the superintendent's office, life was a great jumble. I set down my bundle and seated myself on a wooden bench, worn smooth by many waitings, set against the wall. One of its legs emitted a slight thump under the sitter's weight. I had been told to wait, and wait I would, but that did not mean I would accept whatever fate was handed to me.

I began to be irked by a surging sense of loneliness, acute and clear at one moment, dull and vague at another, a sensation that was not going to leave me during my five years at the Home. From now on I was in other people's hands, at their beck and call.

The Home had now become my starting point. I was homesick, although I could not focus on any particular residence to which I was attached. For the first eight years of my life the family had moved at least five times—from a dwelling at Aberdeen and Sinclair, a kind of farmhouse out on the prairie where I was born; to Charles and Flora where Father worked as a caretaker in the Talmud Torah (Hebrew school) while preparing to receive his *kabbalah*, the traditional licence to practise the craft of *shohet*; to 218 Avenue G South in Saskatoon, where he was a jack-of-all-synagogue-trades (*shohet*, teacher, cantor and preacher) and where illness cut him down; and back to Winnipeg where we moved from one house to another in search of some measure of security. My homesickness was not so much for a particular place as for a desired relationship, in which Mother cooked only for the family, Father earned a living as most fathers seemed to do, and I could bring friends to a proper residence. The Home did not provide such a relationship, but now I would always be starting out from there.

As I sat waiting for the superintendent, Aaron Osovsky, I felt hatred—for the secretary, pretty as she was, who smiled and found time to make jokes and kept answering the telephone with a cheerfulness that served to include the whole world but excluded me, and for my fate. I felt contempt. Call this an office, with a long table in the centre, a desk for the secretary in one corner and the superintendent's desk in another, all jammed together as in a warehouse for second-hand furniture? I felt mutiny. If they don't call me soon, I'll show them. I'll tell them nothing, not about my school certificate or my Hebrew training. I'll just let them think I'm ignorant. Do what you want with me. Treat me like an orphan; you're going to anyway.

Osovsky finally arrived. Having prepared my defiance, I looked him straight in the eye. The Old Man smiled. It was a rare reaction for him. He may have smiled at other times during my years at the Home, but I was not aware of it. Behind his smile he may have been thinking: This little snit may show bravado now, but wait till he learns who is boss.

He motioned to me to follow him and led me up the stairs on "the boys' side" to a dormitory with some thirty-odd beds, pointed to a bed in the middle row, said, "That's yours," and disappeared. I resented being so utterly ignored and left to my own devices. Nobody had so much as said a decent word to me since I had entered the building as an orphan. Was the whole thing perhaps a mistake? I smarted at my own foolishness. I should have asked more questions when being led off to the dormitory: Where's the light? Where do you go for meals? Where and how do you get washed? Or don't you wash? But I was shy and questions did not come easily to me.

On a previous visit I had seen some grubby little characters around the place who looked as if they had never been introduced to soap and water. What particularly stung me was that the other inmates were probably out there somewhere, listening to things, doing things that needed to be done, while here was I alone.

Suddenly a tall, severe woman appeared. "You're the new boy," she said, as if there were no question of the fact, in a clipped English accent, and ordered me into the washroom which contained a row of toilet stalls and urinals, two rows of wash basins, two bath tubs and a shower with two water outlets designed for group cleansing.

"Take your clothes off," said the English accent. I hesitated. Miss Hoey, owner of the clipped voice, tolerated no nonsense. In two shakes she had stripped me naked and there I stood in the shivering embarrassment of a nine-year-old.

"Get under the shower," came the clipped voice again. This time I hopped to it. Down came the cold spray, squeezing a horrible squeal out of me. Miss Hoey, a traditionalist out of John Bull country, believed in the salutary influence cold water produced by freezing a child into subservience. She soaped me down from head to foot and rinsed me as if I were no more than an insensitive utensil. She threw a towel at me. "Rub down." Miss Hoey did not open her mouth when she talked; only her lips moved.

"Sit down." She pointed to a small, narrow bench. With a feline spring she was behind me applying a clipper to my hair. I was so astonished I forgot to cry. She made short shrift of my locks, then doused my head with coal oil, a fluid she believed in with the passion of a pilgrim kneeling at a shrine. "Coal oil destroys lice," she intoned with perfervid fanaticism, failing to add that its vile odour depressed the spirit and demolished the soul.

Then and there Miss Hoey would have instilled in me a permanent bias against the English and the Scots, for she was a descendant of both strains. Fortunately when I registered at Luxton public school later in the week, I came under the influence of the exquisite English-Scottish Miss McLelland, who was as charming and attractive as Miss Hoey was severe and forbidding; her lilting voice uplifted me just as Miss Hoey's disheartened me.

Each day that followed brought something new. Not only did I have to get acquainted with the other boys, some fifty of them, but I had to fall into the routine and learn to abide by the house rules until they became second nature. Each boy, as did each member of "the girls' side," had a morning task—to wet-mop the terrazzo hallways or dry-mop the linoleum dormitory floor, clean the wash basins or monitor a younger child. In addition to the large dormitory there were two rooms for boys under school age who needed help in dressing and hygiene. One was occupied by youngsters whose kidneys operated normally and the other was for the bed-wetters, known as the pisties or pishers. The fragrance that issued from the latter room of a morning was acrid and foul. Anyone assigned to monitor one of the pishers considered himself born under an unlucky star.

All things were performed in response to a bell. We were awakened at seven by an electric bell operated by the superintendent from his suite. A cow-bell summoned us to line up in the basement playroom for breakfast. The same cow-bell signalled the recitation of the *motzi* (blessing before the meal). A bell interrupted the meal when announcements were to be made. A bell invited us to say the blessings in unison after the meal. A bell commanded us to line up for lunch, for an afterschool snack of peanut butter and honey sandwiches or apples in season, for the start of the Hebrew classes and again for supper. We lined up in groups, according to the table to which each was assigned. A monitor supervised each table, ladling out the soup and distributing the portions. A table monitor thus possessed power, and used it with a cruelty and tyranny only children know how to apply. If you were out of favour, you received the dregs of the popular dishes and large helpings of detested ones. The monitor usually reserved choice morsels for himself, naturally. On bean soup and stew days he was liberal to his charges. On cinnamon-rice-and-raisin days he was as autocratic as a Roman consul.

The orphans were not like neighbourhood boys you knew, with whom you larked about for a few hours. These were boys who had come together from all possible extremes, and you were thrown among them at all possible hours of the day or night, even when you slept and washed. The institution, cruel and humane at the same time, was a large chest into which everyone was flung haphazardly and jumbled together. Individual privacy was unknown, intruded upon by others who were not merely a source of entertainment but determined whether your existence would be life or hell.

They were different from one another, these orphans, yet similar and eager to be alike. Stretch out your hand and take your pick —say, the seven or eight boys from a common mother and two fathers, whose broken family was repaired by the Home; or the three boys whose parents died in the influenza epidemic of the first World War and for whom the Home was refuge and healer; or the boy and girl of a mother without visible means of support and a father whom they never knew; or the boy who was left abandoned during the Petlura pogrom in the Ukraine and was shipped to the east coast, thence to the Winnipeg Orphanage which made a specialty of caring for the exiled.

The Orphanage population, collected from Winnipeg, the Canadian West and European upheavals, comprised a hydra-headed tribe, each head alternately laughing, howling and snapping at the other in a cacophony of words. Each of us was divided and subdivided—one part trapped by reason and specious logic, another lost and wandering and yearning to be found, a third clinging childlike to a legendary past, still another armed and watchful against the encroachment of authority.

While the orphan population was not a family in the accepted sense, it was composed of a series of family cells whose identities were fiercely maintained. Ties of blood were overemphasized just because the institution tended to minimize them. My sister Lily was so overprotective of her little sister Rosie and me that other inmates knew they would have to answer to her if they tangled with one of us. She was the mother hen and we her chicks. She was bold enough to stand up to the superintendent, arms akimbo, if she felt an injustice had been done to one of her "brood." She was one of the few who could force the Old Man into retreat. "Who do you think you are," he would fling at her as he walked away, "the Empress of China?" Though uttered in derision, it was a prized title to Lily, an indication of how to perform one's duty to family.

So it was with the Eis brothers, Abie, Louis, Morris and Roy.

They were powerful youngsters, each able to take care of himself in a one-on-one confrontation. As a combination, they were physically unbeatable. When their tempers flared, I would give them a wide berth. Their parents were both dead, and I do not recall that they were ever visited by other relatives. This aloneness sharpened their loyalty to each other.

Yet all four brothers could be warm and devoted friends to members of other family cells. Abie, who later became Al, slept in the bed next to mine in the dormitory, and after lights out we would engage in whispered conversations, he wanting to know all about my parents and relatives. He was a good listener and an even better talker. In his later years he became a redoubtable salesman and travelled in the U.S. and Canada inaugurating programs to boost morale among industrial workers. Abie and the Old Man often clashed, the boy taking physical punishment without flinching.

His brother Louis was in constant trouble and no stranger to beatings or the ultimate retribution, overnight imprisonment in the shoe-room, an enclosure for the storage of our sabbath footwear, shoe polish and brushes. Light in this room was controlled from the outside. It was windowless and without artificial ventilation. We were warned never to put on the light for the miscreant inside, but the warning was unenforceable and ignored. This black hole of Calcutta was the bane of Louis' young life; he invariably emerged from it weak and groggy. My mother would protest this severe discipline to the Old Man who would remind her that her duties were to feed the children not to train them. "A *rachmonis*, a pity for the living," she would murmur as she slipped Louis something to eat. The unusual form of punishment did not seem to affect him. He became a fine citizen and businessman in London, Ontario.

His brother Morris was known as a "bad kid," constantly castigated and penalized. The youngest of the four brothers, Roy, also succeeded in regularly arousing the ire of the Old Man, often without cause. Roy fought overseas, married an English girl and brought her to Toronto where they had several children before he died at an untimely age.

The Ackermans, whose parents succumbed to the flu epidemic, constituted another family cell—Ben, a handsome youth, Dave, the quiet one and a talented saxophonist, and Georgie, the boy with the golden voice who delighted the holiday congregation with his solos. The only one Osovsky laid a hand on was Dave, who lives in Toronto now and remembers the beatings feelingly, though in perspective. Ben was sent to a Saskatchewan town as a helper in a general store, gradually took over the enterprise and became a prosperous merchant. Dave remained faithful to his first love, music. Georgie was sent to the *yeshivah* in Chicago. He dropped out of the rabbinical course and became a cantor in Charlotte, North Carolina.

The Gilmans, Maurice, David, Sam and Kaushie, were also bereft of mother and father. In habits and dress they were neat as pins and methodical as clockwork. Their refinement elicited the deference of peers and staff alike. They did not seem to need any kind of discipline. After homework sessions they always left the library table as clean as they found it. Maurice and Sam entered the business world and became affluent. Kaushie left for the U.S., where she married. David, a gifted student, accompanied me to the Chicago *yeshivah*, which he left after a couple of years, moving to the university where he specialized in accountancy.

Romances between Orphanage alumni were few and marriages even fewer, perhaps because the Home's disciplined atmosphere discouraged affairs or because familiarity took away the required mystery. Yet Miriam Stein and Nathan Ostrow, who came into the Home as infants, saw each other almost every day of their young lives, took the male and female leads in plays, walked together to and from school, studied together in Hebrew class and sang together in the choir; they now live together in Toronto, having been married for almost four decades.

My own contact with girls in the Home was considerable. There were girls and girls. A great many were silly little schemers and screamers, snivelling or warbling. I always dreamed of a girl who was the sort to confide in, possessed of hidden charm, a girl worth spending a lot of breath on, with a lot of calm and studied indifference.

The girls in the Home were mostly odd creatures to me. My sister Lily, for example, had a friend, a pimply-faced girl whom I so detested that we frequently came to blows. She was "the terror" of the girls' side and of the nurses. The worst of the boys—and I can recall some magnificent ruffians—were not a patch on her. She was a screeching little slut, with eyes and nose constantly dripping, probably the offspring of a family which had not had a smooth time of it.

Then there were the bigger girls, four or five years ahead of me, who grew tall and started sprouting breasts. They would plague me as I sat reading in the library. What they really wanted was to get up close. At eleven, I couldn't stand this offensive nearness and momentary clinging. I would report such behaviour to the other boys who heaped up a mass of contradictions and imponderables with their whispered yarns. The stories and tales were far removed from anything I saw in real life. The inference for me was this—the beauty that is in love, the nobility in a boy-girl relationship do not exist in real life; they are figments of imagination in books like the Biblical Ruth or the novels of Sir Walter Scott—until Rita, the girl I married, came along and I started believing that reality, Scott and the Bible all belonged to the same world.

Like all teenagers, in the year of my bar-mitzvah I became interested in girls and began to look at the Orphanage females with a fresh eye. There was one girl, Sarah, tall, fair and clear-eyed, about three years older than I, who would vie with me in reading every book that came into the library. During the winter she was in charge of the books. Sundays and most evenings when she was around I would spend in the library. People began to say that my inordinate liking for literature was astonishing.

My dreams about girls included Miss Rose, the nurse who supplanted Miss Hoey, that redoubtable English nanny who believed in cold showers and coal oils. Miss Rose took me through the first year of my life in the Home. She had the knack of imparting some of the fascination of the good hours to the dull ones. She was invariably neatly dressed in a remarkably white uniform that had both a tinge of festivity and a hint of mourning about it. You never found her with such things as stains or other objects of ridicule usually attached to teachers or other adults. The near perfection with which she kept her routine in hand came to her naturally by virtue of her dignified demeanour. She was not a person to remonstrate with. Her word had the force of truth and her merest suggestion the power of law. She was not above conspiring with her favourites against Osovsky. Often she called me to account gently, in a soft voice, making me feel like somebody who had taken a beautiful vase and deliberately smashed it and was now thoroughly ashamed for having done so. She did not make undue use of her authority to reprimand when it came to me, knowing how sensitive I was in regard to her. It was she, with her loving care, who helped me make the years bearable.

I was drawn to a few of the orphans and neutral to most. I took immediately to Robert Rodos who was always fired up about something, the spittle punctuating his enthusiasm; to Roy Schloss who was called Porky, but never to his face, whose thick lips turned white when he ate herring in vinegar; to Melvin Bobrin who was constantly driven by the Russian pogrom he had witnessed and felt that he understood life more deeply than I. They became my good friends mostly because they flattered me and contributed more to the friendship than I knew how. In those early days I harboured a dislike for Ben Ackerman, a youth the girls admired, because as "a big kid" he could ridicule me with impunity: "You sing loud, don't you? You think loud is good, don't you?" He was right, of course. I did sing up at choir practice and religious services because I wanted to be noticed. It took me a long time to forgive Bennie for understanding the subtleties of voice modulation and for wounding my vanity with his sophistication.

Nicknames abounded. Some for obvious reasons were known as Red, Fats, Pisher, Lefty. Others bore the soubriquets Scotty (because his family name was Barnett, reminiscent of the Hebrides) and Lobey, the origin of which was never adequately explained. This engrafting of nicknames was foam cast up by the seething waves of our social adjustment, effervescing into something new with each day. There were rarely calm days. If the routine pursued an even course, along came a wild youngster who brought off something and stirred up a furore. And if the orphans happened temporarily to conform, along came authority and instituted all sorts of new rules, restrictions, requirements and other nuisances which again put the place in an uproar. Life at the Home usually simmered and rose to a boil.

I cannot remember a single week when the name of a miscreant did not appear on "the board." Actually there were two blackboards on either side of the dining-room, one for the boys and the other for girls, as if misbehaving required sexual separation. Your name went up if you broke a rule or invented your own misdemeanour. Nothing seemed to give the Old Man more relish than to chalk up a name. He would write it with such vigour that the chalk often broke. We would laugh, causing him to turn livid. Name-on-the-board meant withdrawal of privileges for a week or two or three, depending on the severity of the crime. It meant staying home when others went to the picture show Friday nights and confinement Saturday afternoons when permission was given to visit friends and relatives on the outside. Anyone who received a beating for a violation automatically got his name on the board. It was a kind of double jeopardy, a sort of fine and imprisonment.

Among the orphans themselves there raged a secret struggle, invisible on the surface, until our political hierarchies had become permanently shaped, titles conferred and positions on the social scale alloted. We became aware repeatedly that without a certain measure of mutual agreement life would remain well-nigh impossible until such time as we acquiesced, one by one, in the sacrosanct, unwritten laws of the "yard" and dormitory. One incident from the initial period of the struggle coincided with my first days in the Home.

When the Old Man pointed out my bed to me in the middle row, I had no inkling that the site of a bed was a symbol of position in the orphan hierarchy. Bennie Ackerman, the recognized leader of the big kids, slept in the bed in the southwest corner of the dormitory where cross-ventilation made sleep most comfortable. One of the Bell brothers, also conceded big kid priority, occupied the bed in the south-east corner, another advantageous spot. Other big kids slept in beds along the west wall where a row of windows provided air and lower but still coveted prestige. The little kids were assigned the middle row, and those who were lowest on the totem pole slept in beds along the windowless east wall. Ah, the vanity of social distinctions. In the East European synagogue a position at the east wall was the most prestigious of all vantage points.

One evening, shortly after the bell had rung for nine o'clock bed-time, Roy Eis, one of four brothers who had a reputation for skill with their fists, was outraged on coming into the dormitory to see that some of the older boys had parked themselves on his bed. He went over and protested, claiming that they were making his bed filthy with their shoes, scraping them against the bedding. Ignoring his remonstrances, they remained engrossed in lively chatter, whereupon Roy gave the nearest boy a shove and tried to heave him off the bed. He had tangled with Sammy Lennis, another gladiator with a record of triumphal fisticuffs, who yelled at his assailant. Roy in turn cursed Sammy roundly and concluded:

"You're not gonna park your feet . . . not gonna walk all over my bed any more. D'you hear? Not on your life!"

"Quite sure of that? Who's gonna stop me?"

"Let's see you. Just try."

Without another word Sammy jumped on the bed and to everyone's horror proceeded to trample all over it with his muddy
shoes. Nobody said a word. As "a new kid" I was dumbfounded.
Roy, his eyes wide and staring, gasped and rushed out of the dormitory.

Several days later, Friday evening, boys and girls over eight
were taken to the Metropolitan Theatre downtown to see a picture
show, as was the custom. Roy's name was on the board for some
misdemeanour, a not infrequent occurrence for him, and his privileges were suspended. When the gang came back late at night, he
was nowhere to be seen. It was only when the lights were turned
on in the dormitory that his antagonist saw what had been done to
his own bed. All the bedding was smeared with human excrement
which exuded an atrocious stench.

We wanted to laugh, all of us. The very thought of Roy squat-
ting there, straining to befoul the bedclothes was enough to make
anyone go into spasms. But we didn't dare. We guessed what the
consequences of such vindictiveness would be.

The following morning, the sabbath, before the three-hour
prayer session, Sammy and Roy were out in the yard squaring off
for what proved to be the bloodiest fist-fight I had ever seen.
Sammy was big-boned with large shoulders and a muscular chest.
Roy was younger, frailer, fully a head shorter but with the speed
and venom of a serpent, darting in and out and getting his licks in
with sharp jabs to the nose and mouth. After a while the most fun-
and-spectacle-loving of the onlookers lost their appetite for the
cruel and unimaginative combat and stepped in to put an end to it.

Both combatants remained crimson faced for some time after.
Roy seemed becalmed after his act of revenge. Sammy ran off to
the Old Man and waited outside his door until he was given an audience. But no decision came from the court on high. No one was
punished. We learnt from this that the Old Man did not like people
to run to him weeping and complaining. He had his hands full with
a thousand other matters. So long as internal disputes did not get
to the outside, thereby affecting the reputation of the Home, orphans were expected to shift for themselves, settling their differences "inside the family."

The incident was but one of many. Their repeated occurrence,
and the fact that they almost invariably ended up in a bloody
fight, set the boys pondering the ways of the world. If all should be
at the mercy of the worst bully in the Home, no one would be able

to depend on having so much as a pillow under his head, to say nothing of pilfering, damage to clothes and personal belongings or breaking into lockers which were as sacrosanct, but certainly not as secure, as a bank's safety deposit vault. Hence the orphans, following the sociological law of any civilized society seeking peace and order, began to cast about for some self-imposed, tacitly accepted *modus vivendi*. A minimal degree of group restraint was called for. To maintain such self-government, we naturally had to accept and tolerate the authority of a selected few older, level-headed ones who would be able to represent the populace as a whole.

Thus was developed the social strata of big kids and little kids, the latter submitting to decisions of the former. The big kids had full awareness of their own importance. With a mixture of surprise and contempt they would sometimes notice some miserable little shrimps roaming about the yard. They were, to the big kids, so ridiculously pathetic that it was inconceivable they would ever amount to anything. When the yard had to be cleared of paper and other rubbish, and orders went out from the Old Man that he expected everybody to pitch into the hated task, it was the fate of the little kids to be corralled for the major duty.

The Old Man was aware of the system. Strong and powerful as he was, he used it to establish his absolute authority and broke through it at will whenever expediency demanded. For example, little kids passed out of their pejorative category when they were considered old enough to attend the Friday evening picture show, but despite this, they still had to fulfil the behavioural requirements in order to earn a ticket of admission to the theatre. The power of reward and punishment was retained by the Old Man at all times. In the middle 1930s, after my time, when Osovsky was replaced by H. E. Wilder, a man of considerably less fire and assertiveness though with progressive ideas, the big kids ruled the little ones and controlled the rites of passage even in defiance of the ultimate authority. Wilder sought to break the system without success.

From the first, I resisted the little-kid, big-kid stratification. Something in me protested at having to take sides just because I belonged to a particular class. The Roy-Sammy confrontation gave me my first insight into partisanship and left me with little enthusiasm for it. Little kids were on Roy's side, big ones on Sammy's. But wasn't it possible both were wrong? Wasn't it just as bad for Roy to befoul Sammy's bed as for Sammy to muddy up Roy's? Ah, said the little kids, but Sammy did it first. Always the argument: Who did it to whom first? That was also the question of Osovsky, the nurses and the Hebrew teachers. Who started it? No one ever taught the orphans the more crucial question: How do you stop it? What is the right thing to do now that the contretemps is in full force? As a nine-year-old I had not yet the sense to ask these questions. Being a new kid I escaped the pressure to choose between the Roy and Sammy camps. In later disputes I attempted to seek the issues rather than the sides at considerable cost in suspicion and unpopularity. To be moderate among the orphans, I discovered, was to take up an exposed position, and I was often condemned and belaboured from both sides. It has been no different in the years following. In my five years at the Home I was never a big kid or a little kid, just a non-conformist kid. I have been a non-conformist kid ever since.

III

"Old Man"

The Orphanage made up my everyday life to a degree no parental home could have done. It took over that delicate substance, time, which is ordinarily at one's own disposal and did what it pleased with it, cutting and clipping, adapting and sticking, reforming and moulding me into shape. More accurately, it was not the institution that shaped me, but the superintendent, Aaron Osovsky.

The superintendent, the overlord of the Orphanage, the absolute ruler of the entire staff, had his hand in everything. All lived by his grace. Much of the time he just hovered about, keeping an eye on the general order. If a Hebrew teacher wanted to put you out of class and have it brought home to you that this was a punishment rather than a reward, he sent you to Osovsky's office. And as you waited there until he arrived, you could already hear along your spine and at the base of your skull the things that would be said to you and what the future would be made to hold in store for you.

Osovsky had not been formally trained for his job; his schooling was minimal. One of seven children, he was born to poor parents in the Crimean village of Yazir, where there was hardly enough for material sustenance, let alone higher education. But like most Jewish children, rich or poor, in Czarist Russia, he was sent to a *heder*, where he studied Scripture and commentaries. Before bar-mitzvah age he was apprenticed to a confectioner. After immigration to Canada with his wife in 1904, in flight from persecution and war, still in his twenties he laid railroad ties for the CPR, then tried his hand at his trade with Paulin Chambers bakeries in Winnipeg. Later a venture as an independent candymaker failed. I used to hear Orphanage Board members say that Osovsky was not a businessman. But there was no question of his prodigious thirst for learning and his natural literary bent which expressed itself in writing and public speaking. He transmitted respect for knowledge to his own six children—who became proficient in pedagogy, pharmacy and medicine, three of them becoming physicians—and to the Orphanage wards. Torah, knowledge, he would say, paraphrasing a Yiddish proverb, is the best of all merchandise. It was doubtless his idealism and grasp of traditional values that inspired the Board of Directors to engage him as superintendent in 1920, a post he held for thirteen years.

He was a rather good-looking man, not too tall, with grey in his hair. Though his voice was somewhat hoarse, he raised it unsparingly. Sometimes he gave you an impatient swipe with his fingers if you were within reach. Once he grabbed me by the scruff of the neck and threw me across the terrazzo floor simply because I had opened the office door and he was on his way in and I in his path.

The most awesome thing of all was his silence. All of a sudden he came upon you slinking along a corridor during a lesson period. You freeze into immobility before he can bat an eyelid, but all he says is "Nu?" and bars your way. There he stands and there you stand. "Nu?" He seems to look at you not with his eyes but with that Nu of his, and you look at him speculatively. After a long silence he again comes out with one Nu, which could mean anything and everything: Nu, what's happened this time? Nu, what are we going to do about you? Nu, admit it yourself! Nu, are you going to ask for another chance this time?

If truth be told, the Old Man was like some avenging fury, casting his dread over the whole Orphanage throughout the years. No detail escaped his observation, his knowledge and his vindictive memory. He knew the names of all the inmates, their lineage and ancestry as far back, it seemed, as ten generations. The near desperate war he waged against the wild horde of ravenous, insidious little beasts under his care wasted away his strength and told on his nerves.

Yet he did not allow his driving ambition for the Home and its welfare to diminish, ever seeking to improve its system. Once he decided that the vegetable gardens could provide produce winter as well as summer. He had a root cellar built where the yield was stored. In a statement to the annual meeting of the Home in 1928 he reported that the cellar contained "everything a capable and efficient housewife needs to make the tastiest meals: 310 bushels of potatoes, 40 bushels beets, 40 bushels carrots, 25 bushels parsnip, 500 heads cabbage, twelve barrels of pickled cucumbers, 200 quarts of home-made pickles, 200 squashes. All these in addition to lettuce, radishes, cauliflower and parsley will satisfy our requirements for a whole year."

The storeroom in the basement of the Orphanage building was the repository for all other foods. It contained two large refrigerators, one for *milchige* or dairy products and the other for *fleischige* or meat comestibles, the separation arranged in accordance with orthodox religious requirements. On numerous shelves were white enamelled cans of sundry other foodstuffs, the containers tightly sealed and plainly labelled. "I take great care," said the Old Man to the 1928 Board, "that everything that goes to the children's table from this room shall be kept sweet and fresh." He planned the menus two weeks in advance, and a special dumbwaiter which led up into the kitchen received the provisions in the exact quantities specified by the menu card. Efficiency and care were the man's middle names.

What didn't he fight for! Tables and chairs and the other furniture had to be kept undamaged and the floors spotless. There were such matters as clothes to be bought and stored, the care of plants and flowers in the gardens, the bushes and trees on the front lawn, the general property and tools; damage inflicted on plumbing by careless scalliwags; unruly behaviour at meals or in formal classes, as well as a host of special matters: obstreperous inmates, bothersome parents who would insist on visiting outside the regular visiting hours, thefts, fights, three cases of injury daily, outlawed games (gambling, cards), keeping members of the Board of Directors at bay and Ladies Society interlopers from lifting the lids of boiling pots on the huge kitchen stoves, prowling about like foxes in the vineyard; not to speak of the pack of troubles he had with members of the staff—the rivalry among the nurses and Hebrew teachers. I didn't know much about these, of course, but the adult quarrels sometimes exploded into the open to the astonishment of the orphans. Hoarse, worn out, dedicated to his cause, devoted to his charges, intent on keeping the spark of pedagogic vision from dimming, he went grubbing about the corridors, the yards and the precincts of the Home, preserving the vitality and industry of what he was proud to call a house of learning and doing.

Though he was regarded as some wrathful deity, the test of his mentorship was in this: No sooner had his charges left the Home than their feelings for him turned to fond admiration. They may have felt the pain of his beatings for years after and remembered his frothing rages and thunderous indignation, yet they later rendered him the unswerving devotion of a child to his father.

Perhaps they sensed, even through the beatings he administered, that he was capable of entering into the world of a child. In his annual report of 1926 he told of a boy standing at the auditorium entrance after a morning service in which two of the orphans observed *yohrzeit*, the anniversary of their parents' death, and recited *kaddish*, the memorial prayer. The boy was in tears.

"What's the trouble, child?" Osovsky asked.

"Nothing," he answered angrily.

"Come now, what is it?" the Old Man insisted. "Did somebody hurt you? Are you sick?"

"No."

"What then?"

"Gee," he burst out, "some children have no parents, but they are happy. They can at least say *kaddish*—and I—"

The boy was not an orphan, technically. He had been abandoned by his parents. "One must understand the nature of children to realize the tragic meaning of such a condition," said Osovsky. "The world of childhood is one of self-centred relativeness, a world of imagery rather than reality. He sees those who, like him, are fatherless and motherless. Yes, but they at least have their *yohrzeit*, and they can say *kaddish*. What has he got? Where does he belong? An orphan? Then why doesn't he observe *yohrzeit*? Not an orphan? Then where are his home and his parents?"

The Old Man understood that the realization that one is abandoned is keener and more hurtful because it generates a sense of shame. His sensitivity to a child's needs was doubtless profound but it did not always come through in his handling of the inmates.

There he was at the doorway of the dormitory, two minutes after the awakening bell had rung, shaved and shiny, in a finely pressed suit, four fingers of one hand in his jacket pocket, the thumb sticking out, scrutinizing the boys as they turned out. The lay-a-beds had their blankets pulled off them unceremoniously. "The day is short, the work is great and the workers lazy," he would roar. It was one of his favourite quotations from the Ethics of the Fathers in the Talmud. I wondered if the ancient rabbis who wrote that aphorism realized how obnoxious it would become to a band of fifty-odd striplings who longed to dawdle a bit in order to get the sleep out of their eyes and limbs.

But no dilly-dallying with the Old Man. Quickly into your B.V.D.s; then your long, black stockings held up by broad elastic bands; pants next, buckled just below the knees, knicker fashion; after which you made your bed, the spread tucked under the mattress in just the right angles at the corners. If any lumps showed, the Old Man would unfeelingly grasp the bedclothes and jumble them up, and you started again. Then swiftly into the washroom where the containers of liquid soap had to be tipped again and again. His omnipotence was always there, urging you on as if this were a steeplechase. "The ears, the neck, the neck, the ears," he would cry, and if you missed a spot his thumb would jab your cheek or your chin. You prayed he would not be standing by as you brushed your teeth, for he was an expert on dental hygiene and if he found your method incorrect, he would grasp your hand and "assist" you and your gums would ache the rest of the day.

He usually disappeared for about half an hour while we did our chores, sweeping, dusting, mopping and helping the six-and-seven-year-olds to wash and dress. As we trooped into the dining-room after line-up, there he was standing near a table at the entrance, inspecting us for any lapses in dress or antisepsis.

Breakfast began with the *modeh ani*, the morning prayer, followed by the *motzi*, the thank-you for bread. The meal consisted of oatmeal—we called it porridge—or farina and milk, great chunks of bread and peanut butter, jam and postum. Fruit juice and whole milk were given only to the "underweight" table, the skinny ones. The cow-bell, which signalled the prayers preceding the meal, was rung again by the Old Man for the grace after eating. We were permitted to talk as we ate, but if the hum of conversation became shrill, he would ring the bell in anger, quiet would descend and it would take some minutes before the drone of voices rose once more. So it went at dinner (the noon-meal) and supper, usually a meat menu for the former and dairy food for the latter. The separation of meat from milk was adhered to according to traditional requirements, although orthodox Rabbi Kahanovitch thought the system lax.

Always the Old Man was there, supervising, overseeing, pinching, pushing someone down, raising another up. Mornings he would stand in his usual place sipping a cup of hot water and lemon. Evenings he was prone to make announcements, deliver a little speech on the significance of events in the world, such as the accomplishments of the Jews in Palestine, or utter a little homily on food and behaviour.

He considered himself a specialist on nutrition and carried on a running feud with the Ladies Society on the issue. The ladies viewed nourishment as their natural province and insisted on participating both in its procurement and preparation. Osovsky argued that feeding the orphans was his responsibility. The detailed negotiations of buying the provisions and designing the menus were to be conducted under *his* auspices. If my mother as cook offered a suggestion, he would fix her with a condescending eye and inquire: "Since when did you become an expert on nutrition?" Sometimes Mother would circumvent his orders with a culinary embellishment of her own. If it worked he ignored the disobedience. If it did not, he would indignantly proclaim his supremacy. But during her several years as cook in the Home, my mother sided with the Old Man against the ladies, many of whom were her friends and co-workers in the Society. As between his summary orders and the ladies bursting into the kitchen to sniff what was cooking and offer unasked-for advice, she infinitely preferred the former. She would occasionally concede—for her a remarkable admission—that the Old Man was an expert cook and baker himself and could be relied upon for balanced meals. Besides, she would argue, he was scrupulously honest in his dealings with suppliers, driving hard bargains to the profit of the Home.

Generally the ladies were content to lose the battle concerning food, but they retaliated on the issue of his sexual excursions. The buzzing at their sewing sessions was never more concentrated than when the talk centered around the superintendent's exploits with the nurses—there were three, for the boys, the girls and the infants. We were innocent, as the Yiddish saying goes, yet knowing. We heard the gossip and had no compunction about disseminating it, yet the rumour-mongering was not all thin air.

Shortly after I entered the Home I underwent a tonsilectomy in what we called the hospital room, where minor ailments were treated. The day after surgery I was in one of the beds, with the nurse examining my throat. The Old Man strolled in. Oblivious to my presence, he engaged the nurse in rapid Russian conversation. Except for Miss Hoey, who left shortly after my arrival in the Home, all the nurses spoke Russian, Yiddish and English in that order of preference. They were East European and had received their training in their countries of origin. Russian was doubtless used by them as a way of circumventing "the little pitchers with big ears." There I lay with the language of Lenin and Stalin bearing down on me like a machine-gun. Suddenly the nurse and the Old Man were locked in an ecstatic embrace. As they searched each other with their lips and hands, it became evident even to a nine-year-old that this was not conduct appropriate to a hospital room.

A door banged somewhere, and they parted as explosively as they had come together. The incident was baffling, and when next I saw my mother I asked for an explanation. *"Narishe sachen* (foolish things),*"* was her comment, obviously embarrassed. I did not understand at the time that by foolish she meant: If they had to surrender to their libidos, they should have been more circumspect. It was not unusual for the orphans, girls as well as boys, to swap such eye-witness accounts, and to embellish them in the telling.

Though the Old Man may have succumbed to unauthorized sexual behaviour, where he detected it in the orphans he was uncompromising, treating it as an evil to be rooted out with Biblical severity. In those days school children did not receive formal family education. Our curiosity was insatiable, and it was fed by the Old Man's dalliance which, in the intimacy of the Home, was difficult to hide. Frequently after lights out he would enter our nurse's room, and the small window that looked out into the dormitory was lit up far into the night. We could hear the murmuring and speculated on what was going on. In this respect his example was far more impressive than his precept.

Even as children we wondered how the Old Man's wife took his dallying. She was a diminutive woman with a humped back, soft-spoken, wearing a pince-nez that gave her the appearance of a pussy-cat poking her paws into everything. We loved her. We called her *Meemeh*, the Yiddish for aunty, but it came out Meemee, an appelation that served to exaggerate her feline appearance. The contrast between herself and her virile-looking husband impelled some in the Ladies Society to find grounds for the Old Man's amorous excursions, but they were never excused or justified. In the end they constituted one factor that forced his resignation as superintendent.

Meemee was not as submissive as she looked. Sometimes she took a stand against her husband and insisted on compassion when he was harsh. One of his obsessions was correcting the behaviour of the boys in the washroom. Off the playroom in the basement was a washroom with several toilet stalls, a urinal in a cubicle and a shower section that was never used. Instead of relieving themselves close to the urinal the youngsters would stand at the entrance of the cubicle and perform. As a result the floor was always messy and foul-smelling.

One day the Old Man caught a little kid contributing to the messy floor. In his rage he gave the youngster a violent shove. The boy slid along the cubicle floor and landed in the urinal. There he lay, unable to move, soaked in urine and moaning over his hurt. Meemee happened by. She hesitated to enter the boys' washroom, but she was moved by the sobbing that came to her. Seeing the little fellow's predicament, she lifted him with all her strength, washed him, found him a change of clothing and calmed his sobs with a glass of milk and a sweet. "How did you get into such a mess?" she asked. "Mr. Osovsky did it to me," came the reply. "*Sha, shtill,*" said Meemee, "it will all pass."

The Old Man's precepts, more often than not, were accompanied by beatings. He did not spank; he beat. If a stick was handy, so much the better. The beatings varied according to sex, open-handed slaps for girls, fists for boys. He was not less sparing in blows to his own son than to us. He knew nothing about the kind of progressive training that insists there is no bad child. He declared himself to be theologically orthodox, believing in reward and punishment, individual responsibility and individual merit. There was no condescension, no allowance made, no concession to childish weakness. According to his lights, good and evil obtained in children as in adults. The one had to be fostered, the other excised. Orthodoxy loves neatness, and in all things the Old Man was neat.

Since life was such a serious business, there was no room for humour. I cannot recall Osovsky ever telling us a funny story. Sam Ostrow, the choir director, bubbled with them. Shimon Frankel, the Hebrew teacher, used wit to make his lessons palatable. But for the Old Man life was essentially drama, tension, sadness and sorrow, a struggle to survive against hostile forces, as the Jew had struggled throughout the ages. He had wit for his audiences in the community, but not for us.

For this reason he seemed less interested in the emotional and intellectual growth of a child than in education and culture per se. He was devoted to Yiddish as a living culture and to Hebrew as an ancient bond essential to Jewish survival. English was a necessary ingredient of everyday reality, but suspect. It was a potential vehicle for assimilation as were Persian and Greek in the past.

His favourite theme, in sermons and lectures delivered in the synagogue, was the necessity of resistance to assimilation and the retention of Jewish identity. The Yiddish word *assimilazia* became part of the vocabulary of the orphans. At public school we would shun the Christmas ceremonials—the tree, the class party and the gifts—as manifestations of *assimilazia*. When the Lord's Prayer was recited, we kept our lips compressed lest the words enter into us, contaminate us and create in us *assimilazia*.

On holidays and festivals he hammered at the theme. Purim, which commemorates the near-annihilation of the Jews of Persia in the early fifth century before the Common Era, would not have occurred had the Jews not succumbed to the lure of the culture around them. Why did Esther, the heroine, who intervened on behalf of her people, change her name from Hadassah, a good Hebrew denomination, to a version of Astarte, a pagan goddess? Why was Mordecai called by the name of the Babylonian god Marduk? They tended toward assimilation, said the Old Man, and that placed them in great danger.

Similarly the generation of the Maccabees fell victim to the culture of the Greeks and their pagan obscenities. The festival of Hanukkah was a warning lest we do likewise. On Tisha b'Av, the ninth day of the fifth Hebrew month, the day of fasting and mourning for the ancient Temple destroyed by the Romans, we were told of Titus, who tempted the Jews with the attractions of the civilization emanating from the banks of the Tiber. "Beware, beware!" the Old Man intoned. It could happen in the peaceful and integrated atmosphere of North America where, now that ghetto barriers had been broken down and new freedoms granted, the seduction was more subtle and therefore more perilous.

Osovsky believed that anti-Semitism and assimilation went hand in hand. The more the Jew aped the Gentile the greater the latter's contempt for him. I heard in the Old Man's words more emphasis on the menace of external pressures than on the need for internal imperatives. One had to be a Jew in spite of the Gentiles and in defiance of them. The Old Man spoke of "the heritage of our people" and appealed for loyalty to it, but he never quite succeeded in explaining what it was. The ritualistic observances? We breached as many as we honoured. We spent hours in the synagogue on the sabbath, but violated the orthodox prescription by riding the street-car on the holy day. *Davening* (praying)? We did a good deal of it, but still fell short of orthodox requirements. Yiddish vernacular and culture? While the Old Man used it as the language of his sermons—occasionally he would treat us to an English address but never seemed comfortable with it—most of the orphans did not speak it well or even hope to.

Heritage, as it came across to us, meant that we were different. We were different within a difference, a minority twice persecuted, once by the cruel Gentiles and then by a cruel fate, once for having been born Jews and then for having been made orphans. Our protectors were determined to make up our lack of *mazel* (good fortune). They could not do much about the disadvantages of being Jewish, but they would provide us with a destiny that would dispel our orphanhood.

The Old Man believed in his work with a passion. He was convinced that he was not only salvaging human wreckage but redeeming it, making it a valuable component of the Jewish people, who had a special purpose in the world. He was forever sharing his triumphs of transformation with the public, in reports to the Board of Directors and at annual meetings, in speeches and whenever he could con a newspaper editor into publishing them. In 1931 he wrote a "Fragment From My Diary" for the local Anglo-Jewish weekly about three of his charges who were saved by the Home. The circumstances were patently embellished and the language somewhat overblown, but the piece revealed a man to whom the highest good was working with children. It told of how the Home saved three children from a drunken, wife-beating father and a slovenly irresponsible mother.

"Three souls saved for society. Three lives moulded into useful and beneficial members of a community, who otherwise might have been a menace and a danger." Osovsky wrote: "I turned back to my desk with a lighter heart, for 'tis a job worth doing." Could a private home have done for those children what the Orphanage did? By no stretch of the imagination, claimed Osovsky. A children's institution is essential to a community. It alone by expert care and training can stop up communal gaps, repair parental neglect and bring a child through to a new life. For this reason Osovsky fought the foster home system which was first proposed in the 1930s and was eventually adopted more than a decade later, rendering the Orphanage superfluous.

In 1934 the Old Man was forced to leave his beloved institution for a variety of reasons. A major factor was his wrangling with some of the traditional veterans of the Home, such as David

Spivak. These were his natural allies against the advocates of more modern ways. The Old Man lost them, perhaps because he ceased to cultivate them. When the suggestion arose of a new superintendent in the person of H. E. Wilder, whose brother was on the board, a stampede occurred in this direction. The 1934 report of the president says that Osovsky "was asked to reconsider his decision but stated definitely that he was determined to leave." Evidently he had become sated with the disloyalty of old friends, unfounded criticism of his conservative ways and a constituency that was aware of how other orphanages were being dismantled. Perhaps the Old Man saw the certain dissolution of the institution to which he had given thirteen rich and enterprising years and did not wish to preside over its demise. A new generation of volunteers was taking over, younger people who were demanding the application of new sociological rules, the streamlining of administration, the abolition of corporal punishment. Once Osovsky was out of office, a consultant was brought from Chicago to appraise the Home. His report recommended the substitution of foster homes for institutional care.

No longer bound by the caution of a public servant, the Old Man thundered his opposition. He jeered at the advocates of foster homes, calling them provincials, late bloomers in the field of social work. They were simply aping the Americans. It was President Taft, decades before, he said, who had called a conference of social workers and produced the method of placing children in private homes rather than institutions, a method that had had only modest success.

"What is the meaning of 'foster mother'?" asked Osovsky, who always liked to get down to origins. "The word 'foster,' " he wrote in 1939, "means to nurture, to train. Happy the child, deprived of a natural mother, who could find a foster mother that understands the demands of child-training, knows the demands of loving a child not her own and has the ability to make her mere wish a command that elicits obedience! But in heaven's name, where are these ideal foster mothers? Were they to be found in every Jewish home, we would have no concern for the younger generation and the problem children who populate the courts and the jails."

The Old Man was taking the argument far afield, but his passion could not be contained. He saw the institution he had built and nourished falling away, and while his reason grasped the fact his heart could not accept it.

He contended that the Jewish Orphanage of Western Canada was unique in its sponsors and character. In the U.S. and eastern Canada orphanages had been founded by German Reform Jews. He called them *deutsche yahudim*, a derisive term for liberal American Jews who had discarded the ancient observances and eliminated all references in the prayer book to the Jews' national identity. The migration of these central European *yahudim* had occurred decades before the great immigration waves from Eastern Europe, where most Jews still clung to the ways of their fathers. The German Jews founded the Jewish welfare organizations and orphanages and impressed upon them their assimilationist concepts and customs. When orthodox Jews appeared upon the scene, their orphans had no alternative but to turn to the Reform organizations for help.

Thus, Osovsky concluded, orthodox children were reared in institutions bereft of all that was sacred to the traditional Jew. In Montreal, which harboured the oldest Canadian Jewish community, such a development also occurred, but the orthodox would not accept the jurisdiction of the *yahudim*. They founded their own institution.

Winnipeg's history, as Osovsky was fond of reminding his opponents, diverged from that of Montreal and the U.S. Here Reform Jews had not penetrated. In the First World War, it was the traditional Jews from Russia and Poland (*haymishe yidden*, home folk) who had organized a modest orphan home on Robinson Avenue, then moved it to Main Street and finally erected the proud edifice on Matheson.

The first superintendent of the Winnipeg Home was J. L. Greenberg, an alumnus of a Chicago orphanage under Reform auspices. He was content, said the Old Man, to exchange sabbath for Sunday, Hanukkah for Christmas and a Gentile chef for one versed in *kashrus* requirements. But Winnipeg Jews would not permit it. Greenberg was shown the door, the Jewish Orphanage of Western Canada became "a fortress of nationalist religion, of *Yiddishkeit*, and children were trained on a level of Jewish aspiration that called forth the wonder of an entire continent."

Above all, the Old Man believed in the Home as an agency for the perpetuation of "orthodox Judaism." It was a model of Jewish loyalty. To dismantle it for the sake of "progress" would be a defeat of the great tradition. But in the post-World War II years the population of the Home sharply decreased. Family and child services were taking the place of orphanages. The Old Man eventually saw his institution disintegrate. It failed but he himself was no failure. His cause had been the preservation of Jewish identity, and here he succeeded.

On a summer day in my second year at the Orphanage, when my mother was still at her job as cook—she left shortly thereafter—I came into the kitchen where the Old Man was raging. He was upset over some fault in the preparation of the evening's supper and held Mother responsible. In his anger he could become magnificently eloquent. On this occasion he invoked the sages of the Talmud and Mattathias the Hasmonean, who rose up against the tyrannical demands of the Syrio-Greeks that Jews change their diet. So long as he remained historical I stood by and held my peace. But when he lashed out at my mother with unabashed insults, my ten-year-old pride burst forth.

To her consternation I flung his castigation back at him. I, too, recalled history. I had just come from the Hebrew class where we were discussing the oppression of the Jews by Antiochus IV. "You," I piped in righteous indignation, "are like Antiochus Epimanes (the madman). You think you are Antiochus Epiphanes (the great), as he liked to call himself, but he mistook madness for greatness, and so do you. He converted the ancient Temple into a sanctuary of Jupiter and set up on the altar the image of 'the lord of heaven' which pious Jews spoke of as 'the abominable thing causing horror.' You are like him, a tyrant, making my mother cry."

I ran to my mother who held me close and herself defiant. The Old Man turned and strode out. When Mother gained control of her emotions, she insisted I go to him and apologize. Her job was at stake. He might find some pretence for ejecting my sisters and me. Reluctantly I dragged my feet to his office and entered. He was staring out the window and turned towards me as I blurted out: "My mother says I should say I'm sorry. I'm saying it, but I don't mean it." And I fled.

The incident had a strange denouement. The Old Man did not punish me. The next day he apologized to my mother and told her he was impressed that her son should have the boldness to defend her against his authority. Even more, he was proud that I should have absorbed my Hebrew lesson so well it served me in a life-situation. He did not beat me again. In the three remaining years I spent in the Home he never raised his voice or his hand against me and he took a special interest in my studies.

Although I became one of the favourites and was not beaten again, my new status was not all that enviable. I have always been innately reserved. Thus my outburst at the Old Man amazed me as much as it did him and my mother. Obviously my indignation was so immense that it vanquished fear and handed me a colossal impudence. I was scared stiff of this newly discovered capacity and felt like someone groping through a fog, blind, half deaf, choked with dark emanations.

Prior to the incident I had rarely asked a question in Hebrew class or Luxton public school, where challenges were generally permitted except on subjects like God, sex and corporal punishment. The teachers reproved me for my reticence, branding me as unsocial. In the Home the absence of questions was taken as a sign of dullness. The Old Man often quoted the Talmud to me: "The shy person does not learn." He was after me constantly to develop curiosity, to show an interest in my studies and surroundings by querying. He believed profoundly in the Socratic method, though he did not use the term. To him it was the traditional Jewish method. "Ask, ask," he would urge. "Speech may be silver and silence golden, but questions are jewels. They make the life around you shine." But I was afraid and sorry for myself. I did not want to be a questioner and draw attention to my fears. People will lean on you, I thought. They will not let you escape. To no avail. I was compelled to assume the role of interrogator if I wanted to keep the status of favourite and avoid the beatings.

The beatings for the others went on. Some of my fellow-orphans returned blow for blow, stunning the Old Man not with pain but with the audacity of their reprisals. They would have liked to beat him within an inch of his life, so great was their sense of injury. I empathized with them. Yet despite ourselves we could not help but respect him. We hated him, yet at the same time there was nothing we admired more than dedication, expert knowledge and perseverance. And that self-same Osovsky kept prompting us to increase our admiration. Alongside our resentment there emerged a wholesome respect and, what was more, a desire to emulate these qualities.

On Saturday afternoons, visiting Mother, her brother Marcus and her sister-in-law Mania, my sisters Lily and Rosie and I would divert the whole family with the laughing-stock we made of the Old Man, with our tall stories, the way we impersonated him and the faces we pulled while doing so. But one could sense on hearing our childish antics and hoots of laughter how deep down in our hearts derision was blended with esteem. We took off on others too, but we attained true histrionic farce only when we came to portraying the habits and mannerisms of the Old Man.

I would station myself in the middle of the room, one hand resting on the back of a chair, the other thrust into my shirt in the attitude of a public speaker, then stoop forward a little and start shaking my head from side to side. My brows contracted, I would squint shortsightedly at each member of my audience in turn, my lower lip limp and quivering. I would jerk out in a choked tremulous voice a series of abrupt eh-eh-ehs, which sounded half querulous, half contemplative. Then I would open my eyes wide, draw my mouth into a broad grin and articulate with drawn-out vowels: *ah-see-mee-lah-tzee-ah.*

At the outburst of laughter, however, Mother would immediately administer a sober injunction: "Don't think that he's really like that. Anybody would have gone mad having to deal with a bunch of inconsiderate little devils." Then and there she would enlarge on the harsh fate which had put the Old Man in charge of a place like the Orphanage, on the torments of having to provide himself and the staff with wages each month and where was he going to get it all from?—and at the same time see that everything ran smoothly, keep discipline well in hand and settle every squabble. "I don't envy him in the least."

Mother put her finger on the nub of Osovsky's difficulties. He was not only the inside man, as they say in the garment industry, but the outside man. He was not only an executive director, administrator, mediator, disciplinarian, preacher and teacher but a publicist, a playwright, a journalist, a drum-beater and a fundraiser. With these internal and external problems of the Home always weighing on him, he had to go out to the provinces to arouse Jews to the needs of their institution, pull at their heartstrings and move their hands to their cheque books.

The Home drew children from all four western provinces, and its sponsors felt they therefore had a right to turn to the provincial Jews for hard currency. Every year with the coming of the robins, the Old Man would be on the road, like an itinerant folk preacher, wheedling, warning, persuading and pleading. He stopped at Melville, Yorkton, Estevan, Saskatoon, Regina, Medicine Hat, Lethbridge, Calgary, Edmonton and Vancouver. No town was too small for him so long as it sheltered a few Jews, usually general merchants on the main street. He gave them not only the opportunity to perform *mitzvos*, good deeds, but provided them with the joy of listening to *a Yiddish vort*, an insight into a Jewish problem, an interpretation of an ancient text, a word of comfort concerning the Jewish future. Thus he took from the Jews of the West their cash but gave them full value in return, a reason for being what they were.

To the Old Man the Jews were a chosen people. Not for him the subtle distinction between a chosen people and a choosing people. Was it not odd of God to choose the Jews? Not a bit. He knew what He was doing. The Jews were special and never more special than when they showed compassion for homeless children.

With all his imperfections, evident to young and old, Osovsky fed the flame of an ancient people, small, oppressed, scattered but with a tradition that enriched the lives of individuals, with the will to give more than to take, with a sense of mission to the world. However far I may have strayed from his fundamentalist philosophy through the years, it is due to him, as well as to Hebrew teacher Shimon Frankel, that the flame still burns in me.

IV

Teacher

Every weekday afternoon at 4:30 I dragged my feet into the class-room in the basement of the Orphanage building, where Hebrew subjects were taught. Weekdays were long and confining. From 9 a.m. to 4 p.m. orphans attended Luxton public school. When classes were let out at four, we had half an hour for the fifteen-minute return to the Home and a snack. Then into a classroom again for an hour and a half, poring over another kind of grammar, history and literature bequeathed by ancestors who had never even heard of Canada or an American hemisphere.

A schoolboy's resentment of his school is proverbial. For an Orphanage kid the resentment was compounded by uneasiness and fear. I feared that my institutional identity might become known to the other students at Luxton. It was impossible to hide the knowledge of who I was from school authorities. Mr. Forhan, the principal, had no trouble disciplining Orphanage wards. He would point four fingers at you, the upper two separated from the lower two in the fashion of the *kohen* (priest) blessing the congregation in the synagogue, and intone: "The superintendent shall hear of this."

But if other pupils got to know of your orphanhood status, you were accorded extraordinary treatment. Since you had to conform to institutional rules, your fellow-students didn't bother arranging meetings with you outside school hours. A parented student could always cajole his mother into letting him go to the movies on a weekday, but nobody could hope for such departures from the norm in a kid from the Home. An inmate thus inspired other pupils to keep their distance. I did not take this attitude kindly, and strove to keep my identity a secret as long as possible. The effort of suppression contributed to my nervousness and irritability.

Small wonder then that by four o'clock I was mentally and physically spent and could apply myself only half-heartedly to the

demands of the Hebrew class. The other members of the class
fared no better. We were like prisoners straining at the leash. Once
we saw a film at the Metropolitan Theatre, "The Volga Boatman",
where chained men were forced to pull a ferry-boat along singing,
"Hay euch niam." We did not know what the Russian phrase
meant, but often a group of us would line up, imitate the motion
of the movie Volga boatmen and row into the Hebrew class with
the refrain, *"Hay euch niam."* Nothing more accurately expressed
the repression of our confinement. We were little time-bombs
waiting for opportunities to explode.

Handling the miniature explosives was the job of Shimon Frankel, the Hebrew teacher. His colleague, Mr. Rachlis, taught the
younger children in a neighbouring classroom, but his task was
relatively simple: the reciting aloud of *aleph-bet*, reading exercises,
nursery rhymes and songs. Frankel, on the other hand, had to
pound esoteric knowledge—Hebrew grammar with seven tenses,
the priestly mysteries of the Book of Leviticus and succession by
assassination of the ancient kings of Israel—into the skulls of his
charges. The resistance and opposition he met would have challenged a being with the combination of Samson's strength and Solomon's wisdom.

I had difficulty with Frankel at first, or rather he had problems
with me. I was simply not interested in Hebrew studies after a long
and tiring day at Luxton school. For days on end I even interrupted his lessons by singing snatches of "Roses of Picardy" un-
detected. Since he could not rivet my attention, he eventually
showed me the door. "Out, Re'uven [my Hebrew name], until you
rouse yourself. Go and meditate on your indolence and insubor-
dination!"

As I walked alone, plunged in meditation, across the wilderness
of the Orphanage yard, I had penitent thoughts: you have this
hour on your hands because you have been kicked out of Hebrew
class. What's going to be the end of it all? Surely you know by
now that you always pay for it in the end. You didn't pay attention in class. In fact you were defiant. But now you've been called
to account, you're contrite and depressed. What's it going to be?
You've got to mend your ways, that's what. It's enough to see
your mother annoyed, angry, weeping: "What's to become of you
and your father? He's now one of my children, too. I have to support him, you and your sisters. I need my job in the kitchen. If
you're going to be bad, neither you nor I nor your sisters will be
able to stay here. Where will we all go?"

I make my resolution. I'm going to do everything to make something of myself. From now on I'll study my Hebrew. No more backsliding. I'll ask questions, as the Old Man wants me to. I'll make myself a good-boy Joe. The real orphans can afford to be bad. They have only themselves to think about. I have my mother and sisters to worry over. I'll copy out even the whole of Joshua and Judges again, as I was bidden to do and refused. And I'll read books. I'll start from the top shelf in the library and read them all in order. Take yourself in hand, Reuben. After all, you've got more sense than those orphan monkeys, especially the she-monkeys who squat there in class, repeating everything after the teacher like monkeys. I'm going to show them. I can knock them all into a cocked *yarmulka* (skull-cap) if I want to. I'd start right now if I could get back into the class without the Old Man catching me.

I marvel at the indomitability of man. Frankel, the invincible, took a bunch of little upstarts, diminutive barbarians, worn to a frazzle by the pressures of a public-school day, and taught them not only fluency in Hebrew but a knowledge of the cantillation of the Torah in the synagogue and a reverence for the great mainstream of traditional Jewish ideas. This native of an obscure locality called Propoisk in Eastern Europe, born in the 1880s, attended a *yeshivah* (a Talmudical academy), migrated to Winnipeg, where other Propoiskers had preceded him, in his early twenties, tried storekeeping with his brother but quickly realized his unfitness for it, became a *melamed* (a Hebrew teacher) in Canora, Saskatchewan, for a year, returned to Winnipeg where he married, and finally found his niche in the Orphanage.

We called him Moreh, teacher or guide, and he was worthy of both titles. Of average height, he did not present an imposing appearance. He had large, but not disproportionate, facial features—a big nose, wide mouth, big ears—all with a leathery skin. His voice was loud without the subtleties of modulation, yet when he read the Torah at services it was impressive. His ability to blow the *shofar* (ram's horn) on Rosh Hashanah became an Orphanage legend. He rarely spoke of loyalty, duty and obligation, as the Old Man did, but he didn't need to. Osovsky appealed to our external devotion, Frankel to our internal attitude. He taught us gradually that everybody has an inner life, that it is thought that ultimately determines action. His love of the great tradition was obvious to his most indifferent pupil. That love, he knew, is not taught but caught.

The way Moreh taught the stories of the Bible made us partic-
ipants in them. Suppose that the angel had come a moment too
late to stop Abraham from sacrificing his son? Suppose the serpent
in the Garden of Eden had swayed Adam, not Eve, to eat the fruit
of the tree of knowledge—Moreh would emphasize that the text
didn't say apple but fruit—would Adam have succumbed as easily
as did his wife? Oh, what a go we had at that supposition! The
girls insisted that Adam was as gullible as Eve, hiding out of cow-
ardice and suddenly discovering after all that had happened that
he needed a pair of pants. What a simpleton! At least Eve was de-
cisive; you knew where she stood.

Suppose Isaac and Rebecca hadn't played favourites with their
sons, Esau and Jacob, causing a rift between the two boys and setting them to war against each other, the feud never letting up until
the present day. Our discussion led us to the system of favourites
in force at the Orphanage. Was it fair? Was it just?

Suppose Pharaoh and his chariots had not drowned in the Red
Sea but had caught up with the Israelites and hauled them back to
Egypt to become slaves again? Would Moses have tried to liberate
them once more? Or would another liberator have risen in his
place? If people want to be free, isn't that like a hunger, which
never lets up until appeased?

Or let's go back to that scene at the Red Sea, as the Bible tells it.
There were the Egyptians drowning, and there were the Israelites
on the opposite shore singing a song of victory. What kind of business is that—exulting over other people's misfortune? Isn't that
expressly forbidden: "When your enemy falls, do not rejoice!" Exactly, said Moreh, that is why we pour out drops of wine at the
Passover *seder* (feast) when we recite the ten plagues visited upon
the Egyptians, so that our cup of joy should not be full. We must
have pity for the living, whether they be friends or enemies.

These interpretations sounded rather unorthodox and risky. A
report of our free-for-all discussions reached the Old Man who
visited our classroom and stayed for most of the session to get
first-hand information on Frankel's agnosticism. Nothing came of
the visit, and no reprimand followed. Either the superintendent
must have concluded that the reports of an unconventional approach were exaggerated or Frankel must have persuaded him that
the traditional commentaries themselves challenged the text. In
any case, Moreh continued his probing pedagogy as before.

He introduced me to three basic Jewish ideas—God, Torah and

Israel. My interest in God rose out of a dispute in the synagogue one sabbath. Deuteronomy 28 was the scheduled portion of the week. The words are harsh and severe. No one likes to be called to the Torah for this section, known as *tochaha* (warnings). Since the adults refused the invitation to mount to the altar, the suggestion was made that one of the bar-mitzvah boys do so. No, countered others, why should an innocent boy be accorded such a reading?

Here is the unpopular passage: "If thou wilt not hearken unto the voice of the Lord thy God, to observe to do all his commandments and his statutes which I command you this day, that all these curses shall come upon thee and overtake thee. Cursed shalt thou be in the city and cursed shalt thou be in the field. Cursed shall be thy basket and thy kneading trough. Cursed shall be the fruit of thy body and the fruit of thy land, the increase of thy kine and the young of thy flock. . . ." The passage goes on for some fifty more verses, enumerating in detail how the sinner will be smitten with consumption, fever, inflammation, fiery heat, drought, mildew and a variety of other visitations. Who would want to be called to the Torah when such damaging whammies are being enunciated? No one, except Moreh. He mounted the altar and stood there fearlessly as the imprecations were sounded.

I found all this disconcerting, to say the least. Is our God so wrathful and vengeful a deity? Does He strike such fear into the hearts of Jews that they refuse a *mitzvoh*, a good deed, declining to go up to the altar and in effect rejecting the Torah?

Moreh did not deny that there is a terrible divine anger which comes into the world as the result of evil-doing, but, he insisted, there is an obverse as well as a reverse side to the Torah. Prior to the curses are the blessings: "If thou shalt hearken to the voice of the Lord thy God, blessed shalt thou be in the city and blessed shalt thou be in the field. Blessed shall be the fruit of thy body and the fruit of thy land and the fruit of thy cattle, the increase of thy kine and the young of thy flock. Blessed shall be thy basket and thy kneading trough. . . ."

The answer did not satisfy me. The blessings constitute only fourteen verses, but the curses amount to more than four times as many. The emphasis seems to be on God's vindictiveness not his compassion. Moreh conceded the point. There is more evil than good in the world, more pain than joy.

In later years I read Dean Milman, the nineteenth-century English historian, who confirmed Moreh's assessment: "The sublimity of the denunciations in Deuteronomy 28 surpasses anything in the oratory or poetry of the whole world. Nothing, except the real horrors of Jewish history, can approach the tremendous maledictions which warned Israel against the violations of the Law." Milman's words were prophetic. The unspeakable malefactions of the Holocaust in World War II even exceeded the Biblical execrations. Moreh lived long enough to become aware of them.

When he told me there was more evil than good in the world, I would not accept it. How I argued with him! Is God all-powerful? Yes, said Moreh. Is He present everywhere? Yes. Is He good and just? Yes. Well, if He is good and just and can do something about evil, why doesn't He? "I have been asking myself that question for more than forty years," said Moreh. "I have no answer. Nobody has the answer. Nor ever had it."

"Nobody? Not even Abraham who discovered God?"

"Not even Abraham. You remember how God told him that Sodom and Gomorrah were to be destroyed and Abraham objected? How can God destroy cities where good men may be residing? 'Shall not the judge of all the earth do justice?' " Moreh believed there must have been some good men in Sodom despite the Bible's insistence that the city was completely evil.

"And those good men perished with the bad?" I asked.

"Yes."

"Is that just? Is it fair?"

"No, but life is neither fair nor just."

"How about God? How can He be fair if He destroys the good with the bad?"

"God's ways are not our ways," said Moreh. "If God will not do his work, then we must do it for him. *A rachmonis auf die lebedige*, a pity for the living."

God was not a subject I was willing to let go easily. I kept gnawing at it with my friends. I spoke of it to Melvin Bobrin who had been through a pogrom in Europe and whose parents had perished in an organized massacre of Jews in Russia. Melvin did not believe in God. "Nonsense," he said, "if God is strong enough to prevent evil and makes no effort to do so, He's not a very good God, is He? How can you pray to such a God? He simply doesn't exist."

I put Melvin's argument to Moreh.

"Does God exist?"

"Yes."

"If so, then why doesn't He make sense out of this world? Why doesn't He punish evil men and reward good men, as the Bible claims He does?"

"You aren't the first to ask this question and will not be the last. Job asked it long ago: Why do the righteous suffer and the wicked prosper?"

"Did Job get an answer?"

"No."

"You mean he asked such a tremendous question and was content to abandon it?"

"Not exactly. He wrestled with the question, gnawed at it as you are doing, rebuked his friends because they didn't see the problem his way. Job rebelled as you do, but in the end he simply gave up. He couldn't understand. And that's the only answer. We simply don't understand how God works."

"And you want me to believe in something I don't understand?"

"There are many things in the world you won't understand, yet you will believe them. Nobody has ever explained love. We don't know what makes it work, but we believe in it."

"What do you mean 'we'? Are you saying everybody believes in God?"

"Well, many people say they don't, but they act as if they do. There are no atheists. Everybody acts as though there is a purpose in the world. Otherwise they would do as they please. They would steal and murder."

"But there are people who steal and murder!"

"Yes, they are the unbelievers. They have to be taught to believe. Otherwise they must be separated from other people, isolated until they can believe. If you are to live with other people, you have to live on the assumption that there is a purpose and a pattern to life, that you must do the work of God if He doesn't."

"In other words, God isn't really all-powerful. He depends on us."

"Correct. God has no power without us. We are his partners, as the tradition says. He works inside us; we work outside."

"Then why do we pray to God? Why do we behave as though He and no one else can help us?"

"Prayer is not just asking for help and standing.by until it comes. Prayer is a reminder of your obligations. That's what most Hebrew prayers are, reminders. '*Shema Yisrael*, Hear, O Israel, the Lord is our God, the Lord alone.' You don't ask for anything there. You're simply reminding yourself that we all have one

Father and therefore belong to the same family and must come to each other's aid."

"What you're saying, then, is that we are God. We are powerful, and we have to correct injustice and make things fair."

"In a real sense that is true. We are God. He is in us, in everybody. That is why we must respect each other, because God is in us. If we steal and murder, we are doing these things to God. We may not understand how God works, but we must believe He is in us. We may not be able to control the world outside and we can never grasp its meaning entirely, but we have power over ourselves, so we aren't entirely helpless. It isn't right that we should rely on God to do all the work. It's far better to rely on God inside us than outside us."

I have learned since my arguments with Moreh that his ideas were not orthodox doctrine. Indeed, he never used the term, although it was constantly on Old Man Osovsky's lips. Osovsky was a publicist. He needed a word, a rallying cry to fire his supporters. Frankel was a teacher in a nobler sense. He needed no slogans, no catchwords. His aim was understanding, not propaganda. How often I heard him quote the ancient fathers: "I have learned from all my teachers, but from my students more than from any of them." He learned by teaching.

Learning, for Moreh, was the highest value. "The study of Torah," he would quote, "is the supreme activity, for without study one cannot know how to behave, what to do in a particular situation." It was Moreh who suggested that David Gilman, his most brilliant student, and I study the Talmud. I wasn't quite eleven, and Talmud seemed as distant and incomprehensible as calculus.

The Talmud is a series of sixty-three treatises, divided into six general headings and containing interpretations by rabbis or teachers over a period of seven hundred years, from 200 before the beginning of the Christian calendar to the year 500. It comprises two sets of interpretations—the Mishnah, which covers the first four hundred years, and the Gemara, a commentary on the Mishnah which developed over three hundred subsequent years. It deals with every kind of subject imaginable: agriculture and laws for the poor, the sabbath and festivals, laws for marriage, divorce and inheritance, civil and criminal law, sacrifices in the ancient Temple and purity regulations. Legal discussions and debates make up much of the Talmud, together with what today's lawyers would call *obiter dicta*. What would an eleven-year-old find interesting in such voluminous and complicated material?

For centuries Jewish youngsters were introduced to the Talmud at a more tender age than I was under Moreh. In some circles boys began Talmudic studies with the tractate of *Kiddushin*, marriage laws. Because of persecutions and the fear that families would be torn asunder, boys were betrothed early, and it was incumbent on them to learn about the responsibilities of a husband though they had not yet reached the age of puberty.

Moreh tested *Kiddushin* on Gilman and me, but it didn't work. The tractate on marriage laws begins thus: "A woman is acquired in marriage in three ways. . . She is acquired by money, by deed and by intercourse." Already Moreh had a problem. How was he to explain intercourse? In an earlier age a youngster would have been told that he would understand as he grew older. But Moreh and his pupils lived in a more "enlightened age." He simply could not give such an answer. Besides, he was not that kind of teacher. His method encouraged challenge. Despite the "enlightenment" of the 1920s, sex education was not yet the norm.

We therefore turned to a less disturbing Talmudic area, *Baba Metzia*, the Middle Gate, a nearly two-hundred-and-forty-page treatise dealing with civil law on contesting claims. There are sixty-two more treatises, enough to have discouraged any eleven-year-old from the belief that he would be able to cover the Talmud in a lifetime. "It takes a lifetime," said Moreh, "and it is worth the effort."

"But, Moreh," I expostulated during study of a convoluted passage about two people who both claim to have found a particular garment, "what does an incident of two men arguing over a second-hand pair of pants have to do with me in 1925, the age of the airplane, the radio and the picture show?"

"It isn't an old pair of trousers that is the point here," Moreh countered. "It is rather that more than 2,000 years ago, at a time when the barbarians of Europe and the British Isles were painting their bodies blue, a group of men, your ancestors, were concerned about individual rights and the necessity of achieving a peaceful accommodation among men. Jewish law is not just a packet of archaic legalisms. It is an advanced moral attitude that still has something to say even to people who go up in flying machines and watch moving pictures."

"But does all of Jewish law speak to our time?"

"Some of it is outmoded. We have little use now for the regulations concerning sacrifices and purity. But we still have much to learn from the Talmud in human relations. Many point to the Bible as upholding a vindictive law: 'an eye for an eye, a tooth for a tooth, a life for a life.' To us this sounds vengeful, and it is. It was an early attempt by the Mosaic Code to correct the Babylonian practice of exacting extra penalties, such as two eyes for one. Our early Code tried to make the punishment fit the crime. But such an amendment fell short of the ethical standards of the rabbis of the Talmud, which is the supreme arbiter in our tradition. The Talmud asks: Suppose a person with a healthy eye smote another person's bad eye, would you apply the principle of an eye for an eye, a good eye for a bad one? That would be unjust, say our sages. Therefore the Biblical injunction was not taken literally. It was interpreted as compensation. And our teachers of more than two millenia ago detailed the kind of compensation that was to be paid—for the injury itself, for pain and suffering, for medical expenses, for loss of time at work, for embarrassment. The whole of the civilized world has based its law upon these ethical Talmudical foundations. Anybody who quotes the Biblical verse, 'an eye for an eye' in order to justify revenge is an ignoramus."

I can still hear the note of pride in Shimon Frankel's voice as he spoke of the great tradition. He was a proud Jew but not in the ethnic or national sense. His pride came from an attachment to a millenial striving to raise imperfect men from the morass of indolence, ignorance, materialism and greed. He was devoted to *am yisroel*, the people of Israel.

The Old Man harped on *dos Yiddishe folk*. He meant the Jewish nation, political Zionism for the most part. For Moreh the crucial word was *am* (people), the Israelite slaves who, while never ashamed of their lowly origins, had transformed themselves into a people that embraced the Torah, the crown that made them sovereign yet submissive, propelling themselves into freedom through responsibility.

"Are we special, then, a chosen people?" I would ask.

"We are special as every people is special, as every individual is unique. Too many Jews think chosen people implies a superior breed. It has never meant that. The Greeks considered themselves the élite and all others barbarians. The Romans conferred citizenship only on the most eminent. But from the beginning Jews were chosen not for privilege but for responsibility. A Jew must obey six hundred and thirteen commandments in order to fulfil his obligation, a non-Jew only seven. It is not necessary for a non-Jew to become a Jew to achieve salvation. The Jews do not hold up their way as the only way to God. But if you were born such or if you embrace Judaism voluntarily, then you must strive to set an example. You cannot be an authentic Jew and decline the responsibilities. You cannot say: I am a Jew because I am loyal to my people. You must say: I am a Jew because I am loyal to the obligations of the Torah. Once you guide your life by Jewish values, other kinds of loyalty will take care of themselves. You don't have to learn how to become a nationalist Jew, but you do have to learn —and it takes long, hard study—how to be a Jew devoted to the great tradition."

Moreh was careful to point out that Jews were just as sinful as people of other faiths. "Because of our sins we were exiled from our land," he would quote from the prayer book. What made Jews different was not that they succeeded in behaving better than others but that they were carriers of a moral and spiritual tradition. They produced an élite breed of men—prophets and Talmudical scholars—who developed a code of behaviour by which people could live in peace. It is this code, he said, that must be preserved, treasured, adapted and emulated.

Moreh was an enthusiastic student of the Midrash, the allegorical portions of the Talmud into which the ancient scholars would digress. His favourite Midrash illustrated how the great code came to the Jews. He would tell us how, before God gave Israel the Torah, he approached every tribe and nation and offered it to them. But it was refused by the children of Esau, of Lot, of Ishmael, each offended by one of the new commandments.

> Thence God went to all the other nations, who likewise rejected the Torah saying: "We cannot give up the law of our fathers. We do not want thy Torah. Give it to the people of Israel."
>
> Whereupon God came to Israel and spoke to them: "Will ye accept the Torah?" They said: "What is written therein?" He answered: "Six hundred and thirteen commandments." They said: "All that the Lord has spoken will we do and be obedient."

At this point Moreh would interpose an explanation of his own. It would seem from the Midrash so far that the Israelites simply accepted a package they had never seen before. Not so. Every group of people lived in accordance with a developing tradition, and the giving of the Torah, said Moreh, was the climax of an evolving tradition to which the Jews had already demonstrated loyalty. As the Midrash explains, Abraham, Isaac, Jacob and his sons—all had gone out of their way to observe at least one of the ten commandments; the Jews had carried the tradition long before they considered themselves its custodians. They were not simply chosen out of the blue. Instead they chose to promote a distinctive way of life. Really, the Jews are not the chosen people but a choosing people, Moreh said. It is their role today and always—to continue selecting the way of the spirit. They must set an example. As Isaiah says, they must be "a light unto the nations."

"It's hard to be a Jew, not because our path is sown with oppression and persecution, not because of the anti-Semites, but because we have to keep choosing the right way." These words of Moreh have been as wine to me. And the longer they age in me the more choice their flavour.

On the day I left him to study in the Talmudical academy, the *yeshivah*, Moreh read the following Midrash to me:

Thus said the Holy One blessed be He to Israel:
My children, what have I allowed you to lack?
What do I ask of you?
All I ask is that you love one another,
And let there be found in you neither transgression nor theft nor
    any ugly thing,
So that you never become tainted.
As it is said: "It hath been told thee, O Man, what is good . . .
    and to walk humbly with thy God." (Micah 6:8)
Do not read: "Walk humbly with thy God,"
But rather: "Walk humbly and thy God will be with thee."
As long as you are with him in humility
He will be with *you* in humility.

Moreh still walks beside me.

V

Cantor

Choir practice was usually held Saturday evening at seven, when we returned from an afternoon spent with relatives and friends. Nobody was in a mood for rehearsing. We had eaten more delicacies than were good for us. Deprived of sweets during six days of the week, we gorged ourselves on the seventh day. We were tired and melancholic. It was always difficult to return to the Home after a period of undisciplined freedom.

Sam Ostrow, the choirmaster and cantor of the Orphanage synagogue, was in no mood to negotiate his way through a bunch of urchins with negative dispositions. Choir practice was usually a war between two opposing armies—Ostrow, who fought to squeeze some kind of melodious sound out of unwilling songsters, and the orphans who fought him as a tyrant seeking to impose an alien way of life on a helpless population.

Our cantor was small in every respect but one. He had a big voice. It issued out of an abbreviated body—small, pear-shaped torso, short arms, miniature hands, undersized feet—creating an astonishing effect. One did not quite believe the voice belonged to its producer. The disbelief enhanced the quality of the sound. It was capable of dramatic crescendo and lyrical diminuendo.

Ostrow was a drawing card at the Home. His appearance on Rosh Hashanah and Yom Kippur, flanked by an aggregation of some forty orphan voices, was a celebration in itself. On ordinary sabbaths only a handful of adults from the neighbourhood would be on hand and the services were unadorned by formal song. But the festivals, starring Cantor Ostrow and his choristers, were usually events of communal significance.

How we sweated in the summer months rehearsing for the fall holidays. Orthodox services for the Days of Awe are prodigious projects. Originally Hebrew prayers in the ancient Temple at Jerusalem were modest affairs. Sacrifices were the main feature. But during the course of two and a half millenia following the Babylonian exile Jewish liturgists from Palestine, Babylon, Spain and the rest of Europe built up a mass of supplications and *piyutim* (prayer poems). Each accretion was precious to succeeding generations, and none dared to select and discard. The result was a High Holiday liturgy of considerable extent. At the Orphanage, services on Rosh Hashanah lasted from 8 a.m. until 2 p.m. and on Yom Kippur they were an all-day marathon. Long services were made longer by the melodic extensions of cantor and choir, but to complain was to question the revelation at Sinai.

In an ordinary orthodox synagogue the congregation is permitted to *daven*, that is, to recite prayers individually but not necessarily in unison. The hubbub is great, but the fervour can be awesome. In the synagogue at the Home we sang everything and gave no quarter to the congregation, made up of adults from the community. Perhaps that was the reason our religious exercises were so popular. The orphans did most of the work.

Some Winnipeg Jews could not stand the Orphanage service. It was governed by too many rules. They would say: "In my little *shul* on Lusted Street we are down to earth. No ceremonies, no fuss, no bother. If you feel like it, you can talk loud, shout at the top of your lungs, do as you please, just as God commanded. Whose affair is it if it's in place or out of place? If someone doesn't like it, let him close his eyes and stop his ears."

The Orphanage synagogue was for those who did not mind letting the cantor and choir dominate the proceedings. Ostrow never looked so grand as when he performed before a packed house. Dressed in flowing robe and prayer shawl and a tall skull-cap, he lost his diminutive appearance. With his back to the worshippers, as in the traditional synagogue, his voice combined the fervour of the Psalmist and the soaring words of the prophet. He intoned God's universal sovereignty over man and nature, and we responded with hope for the disappearance of iniquity from the earth and the coming unification of mankind. Since the prayers were in Hebrew, neither he nor we understood what we were saying.

Our ignorance occasioned a memorable outburst from the Old Man on one of his pre-holiday visits to choir rehearsal. He sat there listening to the Hebrew phrases and his face screwed up in horror.

"You're saying the words," he shouted, "but do you know what they mean?" Not a sound from the ranks of the singers. He turned to Ostrow.

"How can you teach them mechanical symbols? It's just a mish-mash. Do you think you will inspire anybody on the Days of Awe with this garbled jargon?"

Ostrow's temper was as fiery as the Old Man's, but he also had a meekness Osovsky could not match. "You're right," he said shamefacedly, "there's no beauty in singing unless we know what the words mean. Maybe we should invite the Hebrew teacher to choir practice."

"Not necessary," said the Old Man. "I'll tell you what you need to know." And he launched upon an exposition of the Hebrew liturgy, giving me my first insight into the historic development of Jewish devotional literature.

"First you must know who wrote the prayers. They didn't just fall out of the sky, nor were they given at Mount Sinai with the Ten Commandments. They were written by men of genius who understood the human soul. One of them who composed the opening paragraphs of the special portion of the New Year *Amidah* was Rav, so renowned that he was simply called by his title and not his name, which was Abba Aricha. He was a student of Rabbi Judah the Prince, the editor of the Mishnah of the second century."

Ostrow had risen from his chair and was walking up and down impatiently.

"Are you listening?" Osovsky roared at him, as if he were a lowly member of the choir.

"I'm listening, I'm listening," said the crestfallen cantor. "You're telling us about Rav."

"I'm telling you about prayers that are almost two thousand years old. You should tremble at the thought that you are in a noble tradition and that it's your job to continue it. Imagine that without Ostrow, Rav's creation would die. That's the way you have to look at the prayer in order to sing it meaningfully."

Ostrow smiled, but he was impressed, and so were we.

"To get on, Rav studied with Rabbi Judah in Palestine, but he returned to his native Babylon and founded his own school at a place called Sura, a centre of scholarship which lasted eight hundred years. Now what do you say of such a genius?"

"I'm listening, I'm listening."

"Let me quote some of the sayings of Rav so you and your *boy-*

chiklach and *meidelach* (lads and lasses) know who you're dealing
with. Rav said: 'The world is a beautiful world, and man will be
called to account for every lawful occasion on which he has deprived himself of its goodness.' He also said: 'It is well to busy oneself with study and good deeds, even when the motives for doing
so are not entirely disinterested, for the habit of right-doing will
eventually make the intention pure. Israel's redemption depends
on repentance and good deeds.'

"Now it was this great Rav who composed the prayer you are
singing: 'Now therefore, O Lord our God, impose thine awe upon
all thy works and thy dread upon all thou hast created, that all
may revere thee and prostrate themselves before thee, that they
may all form a single band to do thy will with a perfect heart.' This
means that when all men recognize one God they will form one
brotherhood."

"Did you hear that?" Ostrow said turning to us. "Those marvel-
ous words, those wonderful hopes. Let's see if we can make our
music match the magnificence of the words."

We sang our hearts out—Robbie Robbins, Bobby Moss, Bennie
Ackerman, Georgie Ackerman, Morris Gilman, Bobby Gelfand,
Flora Loewy, Esther Fink, my sisters Lily and Rosie and all the
rest. The Old Man was about to leave, but Ostrow held him back.
"You've done such a good job with the *Amidah*. Now help us with
our *pièce de resistance, Unesanetokef.*"

The Old Man's chest heaved with pride. He had scored. "*Unesanetokef!* 'We will observe the mighty holiness of this day.' Every
Jew who has *dos pintele Yid*, the tiniest Jewish essence, in him,
cannot help but be stirred by this poem. It was written by Rabbi
Amnon of Mayence, Germany, in the eighteenth century. That
was a time of severe persecution for our people. There were many
such times. Rabbi Amnon himself was tortured by church authorities.

"In this poem he makes us feel the reality of Rosh Hashanah, the
day of judgment, when God opens the Book of Life in which each
of us has a page in our own handwriting, recording our deeds of
the past year. One by one, as a shepherd counts his sheep, He re-
views the record. He misses no one, not even the littlest lamb.
Everybody is counted and remembered. Everybody is important."

Knowing that he had us in the palm of his hand, the Old Man
built on the picture. "As sheep our lives are precarious. We are like
a consumed cloud, a vanishing dream . . . our origin is dust and

we return to dust." A pause. "But the poet does not allow himself the luxury of despair. He makes a triumphant declaration of faith: 'Thou art our ever-living God and King.' By repentance, prayer and good deeds, we can rescue ourselves from the pain and uncertainty of the world. Faith gives meaning and dignity, hope and purpose to our lives. When we link ourselves to the doing of God's work we become a spark of the divine."

The choristers were mesmerized. We began to sing as if in a dream. Georgie Ackerman sang his solo about the sheep so sweetly we almost sobbed. Choir practice usually took an hour and a half. The session lasted nearly three hours, and time flew.

Osovsky and Ostrow introduced me to the glory of Jewish liturgy, a beauty I have never ceased to bask in. Set prayers can become a deadening habit. But if one knows the *nusach*, the prescribed recitative for all occasions, the prayers can never become mechanical. They take on the character of the occasion and season and one lives in accordance with a liturgical rhythm. The theme changes though the liturgical framework and content are essentially the same. They are old friends always in new garb, always comforting, and they still arouse in me the essential message—that I am a Jew only because I recognize my kinship in the human family, which inhabits a single planet.

Singing was as much part of our life-pattern as eating and sleeping. We chanted prayers at meals and bedtime. We gave vent to earthy ditties on picnics. Dressed in our sabbath best, we fancied ourselves veritable troubadors welcoming the Sabbath Bride, the Queen of the Days, before supper on a Friday evening. With the dining-room tables set festively, decorated with flowers from our own gardens, the girls standing in a row against one wall, the boys against an opposite one, our voices blending in two-part harmony or sounding antiphonally, the call to worship would soar: "O come let us sing before the Lord, let us shout for joy to the Rock of our salvation."

Ostrow would not lead us on the sabbath eve. His duties encompassed only special sabbaths, festivals and high holidays. It was the Old Man, grandly and ostentatiously, who would conduct our sabbath musical offerings. His arms would swing vigorously when commanding *forte*, the forefinger and thumb coming together when eliciting *pianissimo*.

The flavour of the sabbath was sweet and tender to us, not just because of the special meal of gefilte fish and fruit compôte but because of our radiant joy in the music we were able to make. Our singing taught us more of life's goodness than all the well-intentioned words and warnings that came through the didactic exercises of the superintendent and his assistants.

As an occasion for song, the Passover *seder* was a highlight of our annual cycle. It was also an event filled with appetizing foods. We looked forward to the *kneidlach, matzoh* balls, with mouth-watering expectancy, but we also knew there was to be fun chanting the boisterous *seder* ditties. "Who can speak and who can tell? Oy vay, chiri biri bim bom. Who knows one?"

"I know one," came the roaring response from the mob of orphans. "One is our God in heaven and earth."

"Who knows two?"

"I know two. Two are the tablets of the covenant. One is our God in heaven and earth."

"Who knows three?"

"I know three. Three are the patriarchs, two the tablets, one our God in heaven and earth."

On and on it went. "Four are the matriarchs, five the books of the Torah, six the sections of the Mishnah, seven the days of the week, eight the days before circumcision, nine the months of childbirth, ten the Commandments, eleven the stars in Joseph's dream, twelve the tribes of Israel." All year long we would hunt for events and objects in the traditional sources to match the numbers. In my last year at the Home we reached twenty, a record.

The *seder* songs were tailor-made for orphan consumption, simple, repetitive and folksy. "*Had Gadya*, one little goat, one little goat, my father bought for two zuzim. Then came a cat and ate the goat that father bought for two zuzim. Then came a dog that bit the cat that ate the goat my father bought for two zuzim." This chant could have gone on endlessly too. But the top of the totem pole was usually reached when we mentioned the supreme authority: "Then came the holy One blessed be He and slew the angel of death that killed the *shohet* that slaughtered the ox that drank the water that quenched the fire that burned the stick that beat the dog that bit the cat that ate the goat my father bought for two zuzim. One little goat, one little goat."

Singing was not always fun, and choirmaster Ostrow, who on occasion was a man of high spirits and light heart, could literally wield a big stick. He usually conducted the choir with a slat from one of the folding chairs in the auditorium-synagogue where practice sessions were held. That slat not only kept time; it was the instrument of the conductor's wrath, signalling a wrong note, prodding a chorister to sing out and expressing the plain cussedness of the choirmaster. Rarely did Ostrow apply the stick for specific reasons. Rather it was for a general principle. Almost everybody had to feel the crack of the slat at least once during rehearsal. Otherwise, from the conductor's view, the session was a lyrical failure.

One particular night we were rehearsing in the well of the auditorium because alterations and repainting had made the stage at the altar unavailable. The boys sat in two rows facing the girls in a similar arrangement. We were going over Psalm 117: *"Halelu es hashem kol goyim*, Praise the Lord all ye nations." It was a bright melody, but on this occasion it came out with little zest. Again and again Ostrow urged more energy. "Sing, you lazy louts, sing or you'll feel the sting of the stick."

At last we were launched into the composition. The music took on a bouncy syncopation as it progressed. Suddenly one of the boys chimed: "Beat me, daddy, eight to the bar." Ostrow froze, thunderstruck. Slowly he found his voice. "Who said that?" Not a sound from anyone. He turned to the boys; it was a male voice that had desecrated the psalm. "Who was it? Reuben, Dave, Harris, Roy, Bobby? Identify yourself or I call Mr. Osovsky." No response. With blood in his eye and menace in his demeanour, Sammy Ostrow grasped the slat and, passing down the front row, hit every male member as rhythmically as if he were still conducting. Still no answer from anyone.

Somewhat relieved, Ostrow resumed rehearsal. Once more we swung into *"Halelu*, Praise the Lord all ye nations," and when we reached the syncopation every blessed voice in that heroic choir roared: "Beat me, daddy, eight to the bar." Ostrow went white, then purple. He made for the door, bellowing: "Osovsky, Osovsky, it's murder here!"

We learned a useful lesson from that incident, that we possessed power. United, pressed by a common enemy, bearing a collective vindictiveness and determination, we discovered we could make a stand even against authority from which there was no appeal. Mahatma Gandhi would have called our demonstration *satyagraha*, non-violent resistance.

Harsh and temperamental as he sometimes was, our choirmaster was nonetheless a talented and dedicated musician. Since the choir consisted only of altos and sopranos, he had to reduce four-part

compositions to two-part harmony. His job was further complicated by our inability to read music at sight. He fed us melodies
phrase by phrase to the accompaniment of his slat, often beating
time on an unlucky head or shoulder.

His was a self-consuming job at modest recompense. He re-
ceived $50 a month with a bonus of $300 for the High Holidays.
But Sam Ostrow found his reward in other ways. Winnipeg's Jew-
ish community drew the renowned American cantors of the day—
Yossele Rosenblatt, Zeidele Rovner, Mordecai Herschman and
Leibele Glanz—all of whom made the obligatory stopover at the
Home to listen to its choir and to heap praise on its director.
Ostrow also found his reward in his disciple, Georgie Ackerman,
who was inspired by the master's devotion to become a cantor
himself.

When Ostrow was not pounding music down our throats so that
we could regurgitate it, he relaxed with us. Sometimes he would
break into a Yiddish song just for the joy of it. Ostrow had large
appetites which he demonstrated for all to see. Following choir
practice he would hasten to the kitchen where my mother offered
him some of his favourite delicacies: herring with large tomato and
onion slices and corn on the cob soaked in butter and sprinkled liberally with salt, all of it washed down with several glasses of tea
and lemon. Sated, he would sit with hands clasped over his belly,
eyes half closed, and sing a ditty, for all the world as content, as
the Yiddish goes, as God in Paris. Afterwards he picked his teeth
with a shaved match, sucking the remnants of his meal noisily
through the gaps.

He was the only one among our trainers and teachers to show us
the inner man, and remarkably candid he proved to be. While he
was paid for his work at the Home, his living came from his calling
as an itinerant salesman or manufacturer's agent. He travelled
through Western Canada and brought back stories of his sexual
exploits. Much of this chatter may have been pure bluster, but it
was entertaining, and Sammy made the most of it. He would look
at a pretty girl and say: "See, there is my downfall."

His gaze focussed particularly on Flora Loewy, the leading girl
singer. Flora was "the queen," virtually an officially recognized institution. For Osovsky, Ostrow, the nurses and everybody else she
seemed the acme of perfection. She was popular with girl-
friends—was usually surrounded by a coterie of them—barring
some inevitable jealousy and resentment. She was a favourite even

of Frankel, who ordinarily maintained academic objectivity. She was in high favour with the boys and seemed to select Bennie Ackerman as her foil.

Very keen on being queen, she was clever enough not to let on. She was a winsome girl, a girl whose eyes sparkled with wisdom, whose hair was tidy and her dresses spotless. She was soft-spoken with gentle manners and always walked with dignity. The boys would indulge in chivalrous dreams about her, and the girls would hide their envy and eagerly seek her company. Ostrow would gaze at her sadly as she got up with a flourish from her chair at choir practice and murmur: "That's my downfall. A girl like that melts me down. She'll grow up a dangerous one, I'm telling you. She's going to be dangerous, that one."

It was Flora's slacks that sent the choirmaster clean out of his mind. No one could fathom where she got them. Perhaps she had sewed them herself with material provided by the Ladies Society, which rarely missed a Tuesday afternoon darning and designing dresses for the girls. It was just before Passover and she was the first and only girl to appear in this get-up. The slacks were of fine material, well ironed, dainty and trim, bespeaking lightness and ease with every movement of the thigh. Ostrow, following her longingly with his eyes, must have thought the whole world his for sure.

VI

Bandmaster

Nobody seemed to know the bandmaster's first name or initial. He was always Cocking or Mr. Cocking. Nor did we have a nickname for him. His dignity and reserve aroused our caution and deference.

The old master musician, a product of England's Kneller Hall, where men who made music for the armed services learned their craft, was deft-fingered, skilful not only at his job as band leader but at anything that called for fastidiousness and the capacity to see things through. Strangers might have thought him misanthropic, for he was always withdrawn and sparing of speech, but his friendship with me ripened, especially when he began teaching me the violin, constantly revealing more and more of his good nature, his consideration for others and an honesty devoid of pride or self-interest.

Occasionally he would wear a kerchief around his neck on account of a throat ailment that seemed to trouble him winter and summer. He coughed a great deal. I suspected he was a smoker, since an acrid smell of tobacco hovered over him, but he never smoked in our presence.

His appearance was always immaculate, shoulders back and straight in a well-fitting jacket, trousers pressed to a knife edge, shoes, usually brown, polished to such a high shine that they would reflect the overhead lights whenever his foot tapped to the rhythm of the music. There was nothing superfluous about him, every detail merging with the whole personality in the most natural manner.

He treated the Old Man with the diffidence of a person of high breeding who knew his place, who gave full value for his stipend and would brook no nonsense if his dignity were offended or his position misunderstood. Osovsky was reduced to almost silent politeness in his presence. One felt the Old Man had no experience in handling a stiff Anglo-Saxon who never raised his voice to adults and gave to them and demanded from them the most correct behaviour. Yet Cocking could keep time with his stick on the fingers of one of his errant little novices who hadn't a clue to music's mysteries, making him cower with his demolishing epithet: "Duffer!"

At all events Cocking served me as a model. I liked his Anglo-Saxon reticence, a contrast to those Jews who were given to letting their emotions fly in any direction. I did not hesitate to try to imitate his dress and mannerisms, discovering that by applying a few drops of water on my own sabbath shoes I could bring them to a high bandmaster gloss, and sometimes affecting a handkerchief around my neck à la Cocking.

He knew the fingering for every band instrument—cornets or trumpets, B-flat and E-flat clarinets, saxophone, oboe, flute, piccolo, trombone, French horn or alto horn, euphonium or baritone, tuba or bass. He could even handle a mean set of drums. At rehearsals Sunday mornings we would be seated in an arc and he would stand between the two ends of the arc waving his stick and listening for a wrong note. Once he detected a culprit, he would leave his accustomed position and stand behind the sinning instrumentalist, beating his stick against the music stand and singing out the notes in his hoarse, throaty voice. If he caught the sinner with an F natural instead of an F sharp, bang would come the stick on the knuckles and out would come the expletive, "Look sharp, you duffer!" The agony of trying to make music under the threat of knuckle pain and that searing ejaculation contributed to many an orphan's nightmares.

We played marches by Sousa, medleys from *Carmen*, *The Mikado*, Offenbach's *La Périchole* and overtures from a variety of obscure composers. Cocking had an imperialist strain, accentuated by his role as conductor of Winnipeg's Princess Pat Military Band. He was addicted to such pieces as "Under the Double Eagle" and "United Empire March." He was unabashedly patriotic, whatever the brand. We produced approximations of "The Maple Leaf Forever," "Rule Britannia," and of course "O Canada," "God Save the King" and "Hatikvah," the Zionist national anthem. Our bandmaster was no expert in Jewish music, but he managed to orchestrate the Hebrew anthem, since it was based on Smetana's *"Die Moldau."* It was always a puzzle why Osovsky did not demand that the band play the songs of the Jewish pioneers of Palestine, for the 1920s was the decade of rising Zionist aspirations. Perhaps he did make such demands, but they were impossible to fulfil. It would have meant custom-made musical arrangements, an expense the Orphanage Board would have rejected.

Though I loved music, I was an indifferent instrumentalist. I trod a hard path from French horn to euphonium to trombone and finally, at the insistence of my mother, to the violin, but what I achieved in versatility I lost in virtuosity. The violin, of course, was not part of the band. Yet it seemed to the members of the Board and the Ladies Society to be a more "Jewish" instrument. After all, neither Jascha Heifetz nor Mischa Elman played the euphonium. Cocking performed on the violin with great feeling, but he never seemed to transmit enthusiasm for it to his charges. And the dreams of the Orphanage directors of producing at least one Mischa Elman faded with the phasing out of the strings.

However, Cocking's efforts did produce at least three professional musicians. Robbie Robbins became a singer-drummer for an orchestra on the Pacific coast; Annie Serkis, adept at piano and trumpet, was engaged by a girls' orchestra that travelled through Western Canada; and saxophonist Dave Ackerman managed a comfortable living with popular orchestras in Toronto.

The band, though it served no purpose in cultivating Jewish consciousness, was important to the Old Man as a public relations medium. We were in demand by the Zionists for their cultural affairs, by the Talmud Torah for its fund-raising bazaars and by the Winnipeg municipality for civic celebrations. When Manitoba celebrated its golden jubilee as a province and ethnic groups sponsored floats in the parade, the Jews presented the band on a gaily decorated truck with a proud sign: "Jewish Orphanage and Children's Aid of Western Canada." We were not a marching band. That would have meant uniforms and special lessons in coordination, training the budget could ill afford. So we were crowded into the back of a truck, reinforced by a railing, where we produced passably synchronized sounds to the delectation of enthusiastic Jewish citizens who lined the streets to cheer us on.

For a fat donation to Orphanage coffers the band could also be hired by local tradesmen for promotional purposes. We played once at the opening of a hardware store at Dufferin Avenue and Main Street. The proprietors were supporters of the Home and, as befitted solid citizens who shared their good fortune with the less prosperous, arranged for the orphans to entertain the crowds. In the days before television such an event was a big attraction, and the neighbours spilled into the streets.

The affair had a carnival air. There were free refreshments and souvenirs. Special delicacies were prepared for the orphans— corned beef, wieners and all the fixings. Cocking was present, viewing the proceedings with a faint air of distaste. He led us through much of our repertoire and the special compositions rehearsed for the occasion—the "Light Cavalry Overture" by Franz von Suppé, "I Love You Truly" and "Let Me Call You Sweetheart." On principle our bandmaster could not stomach jazz, which was all the rage at the time, but some Victorian instinct in him yielded to unsyncopated popular love songs.

During one of the breaks we were invited to gorge ourselves on the smoked meats and salads. Cocking kept his distance in the background. But he could not escape the notice of the proprietress who brought "a special plate for the music teacher." It was piled high with thick delicatessen creations, baloney, wieners, plump and juicy, beans and dill pickles. The alumnus of Kneller Hall blanched as he accepted the abundant offering. He held it away from him. There was no way he could bite into the sandwiches with delicacy. He sniffed the provender as if it were a foreign concoction invading his cultivated sense of propriety. Gradually he eased himself out of view and disposed of the kosher viands behind something or other. It was but one indication of Cocking's discomfort in an atmosphere dominated by Jewish taste and custom.

There were others. He would on occasion feel it his duty to deliver a lecture on the relation of music to life. Such homilies may have been the practice at Kneller Hall, and Cocking probably believed it to be good for orphans, too. One must play one's instrument accurately, he would say, and always in harmony with the rest of the players. That meant individual responsibility plus co-operation. A good band member understood both, a good citizen strove to achieve both.

Once Osovsky entered the auditorium as Cocking was addressing us; it was the Old Man's custom to visit all training sessions. Cocking reddened a little, but plodded determinedly on, with the Old Man betraying no hint of what he thought of the indoctrination. Suddenly the gentleman from "over 'ome" said: "You are of the Jewish race. Stand for it. Be its witness." Osovsky started. Did the Old Man think the bandmaster had over-reached himself, was intruding on his territory? Did the Judaic pedagogue resent the infusion of Anglo-Saxon virtues into the orphans, though admittedly clothed in Jewish overtones?

The puzzle became clear some days later when Osovsky entered the yard and motioned us to him. He liked to stand among his charges and carry on an exchange. This time he opened the discussion with a question: "What do you think about the term 'the Jewish race'?" Nobody reacted.

"Mr. Cocking used it last Sunday morning during band practice. Didn't you wonder why?"

"It didn't bother me especially," an orphan offered. "He just meant the Jews, didn't he?"

"Yes, of course. But 'Jewish race' is not a term a self-respecting Jew would use." Now we understood.

"Have you been reading the newspaper lately?" The Winnipeg *Free Press* was regularly on the rack in the library, but most of us limited our perusal of it to the funnies.

"Hasn't anyone been reading about the National Socialists in Germany?" Nobody had.

"They are called Nazis for short. They believe that mankind is divided into colour groups called races, that of all the groups the white race is greatest and others inferior. Within the white race are further subdivisions. The Semites, who include the Jews and Arabs, are the lowest. The Aryans, who include the Greeks, the Romans, the French and the Germans, are the highest. But even within the Aryan family there are various levels. The noblest and most exalted Aryans are the Nordics whose representatives are the blond Scandinavians and the Germans. The Nazis say it is their duty to purify these Nordics from the corrupting influence of intermarriage with lower-caste whites like the Jews. Now do you understand what race is?"

Osovsky presented the Aryan race theory rather simplistically. For one thing, he was speaking to eleven- and twelve-year-olds. For another, this was before the Nazis had to modify their hierarchy of values to make room for Mussolini and his Italians and for the Japanese who, as Mongolians, did not even rate within the white race. The Nazi propagandists were nothing if not ingenious. They created the honorific title of "yellow Aryans." As for the Palestiniaṅ Arabs, whom they later sought to rouse against Britain and the Jews, they failed to designate them as "Arab Aryans" but discreetly omitted references to their Semitic character in Nazi propaganda intended for their consumption.

We were somewhat bewildered by the torrent of information. We knew there were anti-Semites in the world who hated the Jews without cause. But that they were a political party with a kind of religion based on Jew-hatred seemed incredible.

"Is it true the Jews are the lowest race?"

Osovsky eyed the questioner with the patience reserved for the irredeemable ignoramus. "How can Jews, who gave the Ten Commandments to the world, be the dregs of humanity?" We all fixed on the offending orphan our righteous indignation. The question was not as irrelevant as we thought. In later years I discovered Jews who accepted as fact anti-Semitic perceptions. Believing themselves to be what the haters insisted they were, they became self-haters and tried to escape their identity. I met Jews who were assimilationists not because of indifference but because of a deliberate attempt to disengage from what they despised.

"Then Mr. Cocking shouldn't have used the words 'Jewish race,' " said an orphan addicted to logic.

"No, but you must excuse him. A Gentile is not so sensitive to such offensive language as a Jew would be. It is important that you remember."

After this conference in the yard Cocking never addressed us formally during rehearsals again. Perhaps he was told to stick to his last. But for me that was not the last of the discussions on Jewish race. I had learned a phrase that touched me deeply and was determined to pursue it.

I turned to my favourite resource person, Shimon Frankel, the Hebrew teacher. With Moreh my shyness evaporated. On a sabbath after the service, on my way to my aunt's house on Burroughs Avenue, I accompanied Moreh to his Alfred Avenue domicile.

"What is the Jewish race, Moreh?"

"There is no Jewish race, only the human race."

"But people use the words, don't they?"

"Yes, Reform Jews found it a convenient term, since they gave up the idea of the Jews as a national group. But it isn't popular even among them."

"Mr. Osovsky says it's a favourite phrase of Jew-haters."

"Ah, he must have been talking about those noisy German National Socialists. Actually they're not original even in their anti-Semitism. About seventy years ago a misanthropic Frenchman, Arthur de Gobineau, wrote his essay on 'The Inequality of the Human Races' and a renegade Englishman, Houston Stewart Chamberlain, who has been a long-standing Jew-hater, published—now what did he call it? Oh, yes—'The Foundations of the Twentieth Century.' The Nazis must be drawing their ideas from these false prophets."

"How do we know they are false prophets? They wrote books and people read them. They must make some sense."

"They are false because they divide people and sow animosity. Ideas and actions that separate human beings are wrong. Ideas that make people aware of their common origins are right. The Midrash is right. It asks: 'Why did God create only one man, Adam, in the beginning? In his omnipotence He could have created millions.' Its answer is good and wise: 'So that no one should be able to say, my ancestor was greater than yours.' A man's blood does not make him superior."

"But surely blood means something?" I cut in quickly. "King George V is of royal blood, isn't he?"

"That's nonsense. Nobody has royal blood. That's Nazi talk. They believe the specific traits of each race are in the blood, and that nothing is more disastrous than the loss of blood purity through the intermarriage of Aryan and Semite. Could anything be more absurd?" Moreh suddenly stopped in the middle of the sidewalk and looked at me in astonishment, so nonsensical did the idea seem to him.

It was ridiculous to him because the Nazis had not yet come to power. Several years later, in 1933, the elimination of Semitic blood, even to fractions of one-eighth, became one of the chief domestic occupations of the Third Reich. Moreh and I were innocents, deep in a theoretical discussion at a time when the most fertile imagination could not foresee the savage consequences of the blood theory in concentration camps and death factories.

"Purity of blood is a fraud," Moreh continued vehemently. "Every people in Europe is a composite of several types. The Germans themselves, although the Nazis deny it, are the result of an interesting mixture—Celts, Teutonic tribes, a sprinkling of Roman settlers and a considerable contribution of Slavic blood."

"How about the English? They seem to keep to themselves, off on an island. They have barons and lords who marry their own kind. Isn't their blood pure?"

Moreh was almost contemptuous. "The English are the most composite people in Europe. During their first thousand years they drew on Celtic, Roman, Germanic, Danish, Norman and French stock. And in the last few hundred years the English have been the recipients of steady accretions from all over the world. You can say the same for Spain and Italy. If there is a 'pure race' in this world it must be a group of savages in some jungle or desert region, cut off from all other human beings."

"Well, how about the Jews? We don't marry everybody. Aren't there Jewish laws against intermarriage? Bob, Alfie and Georgie Harrison have a Jewish mother and a Gentile father, and some of the kids say they are not really Jewish."

"The Harrison boys are Jewish because they have a Jewish mother. But you're right. There are deep-seated objections to intermarriage. Still that didn't stop the Jews from racial intermingling. The ancient Israelites were descendants of at least three groups: the Arameans whom the Hebrews found in Palestine as part of the Canaanites, short with round faces and skulls and thick noses; the Bedouins who dwelt in the desert, tall and straight-nosed with elongated skulls; and the Philistines, Israel's long-standing enemies, who were absorbed by conquest and intermarriage. You remember how Samson wooed Delilah, the Philistine. You and I may be descendants of Philistines. Who knows?" Moreh's lips puckered into a smile.

"Are Jews then permitted to marry Gentiles?" The question was very important to me. My oldest sister, who had moved to Chicago, was rumoured to be accepting "dates" from Gentiles, causing my mother severe anguish. For her, marriage with a *goy* was identical to apostasy.

Abhorrent as intermarriage was to Jews in the 1920s, it was then only a marginal problem. The percentage of Jews who married non-Jews was almost negligible. Today the intermarriage rate is more than 50 per cent. Today's Jewish parents may not be as extreme in their opposition as was my mother, but their objection is still real. They can do nothing to prevent such a marriage, however, once a son or daughter is determined to enter it, despite warnings and condemnations. Even in self-contained orthodox communities, young Jews find a way of breaking out of the stric-

tures against intermarriage. Perhaps Moreh's answer might have
been more stringent had he been able to foresee the forest-fire
proportions of its spread. As it was, his words had a reasonable
and lenient tone.

"Opposition to marrying non-Jews," said Moreh, carefully
choosing his words, "has fluctuated over the centuries. It is true
that the Bible is filled with warnings against intermarriage with
neighbouring peoples, but why so many warnings if the practice
wasn't prevalent? Indeed in the entire Bible Ezra and Nehemiah are
the only figures to carry on a campaign against intermarriage. In
Deuteronomy there is a prohibition against marriages with Am-
monites and Moabites, but the Talmud virtually nullifies it. It
properly says that racial stocks are so mixed up that the law can no
longer be applied."

"So we can marry Gentiles!" I interjected triumphantly.

"Now don't go so fast," Moreh countered reprovingly. "In most
periods of our history converts were welcomed. We cannot ex-
clude *goyim* from embracing Judaism just because they were born
Gentiles. That would be imitating the Nazis. If non-Jews become
Jews through an affirmative act, they are as validly members of
the Jewish people as those born of a Jewish mother. But marrying
Gentiles who are not converts is another matter."

By this time we had reached Moreh's house, a typical Winnipeg
bungalow where he lived with his wife, his mother-in-law and two
children. He invited me inside for *kiddush*, the blessing over the
sabbath wine. I eagerly accepted, knowing there would also be
lekah, honey cake. Mrs. Frankel made a great fuss over me. She
loved visits by her husband's pupils. It indicated that Moreh's influence extended beyond the classroom. Besides, I gave her the
chance to indulge an Orphanage kid.

"My," said Mrs. Frankel, "Reuben is so eager. We must make a
rabbi of him."

"I don't know about that," I blurted out, "but I would like to be
as learned as Moreh." He reddened, but his pleasure was evident. I
think Frankel would have taught us even if he had not received a
salary. He was a natural pedagogue with a love for the tradition
that he never ceased to plumb for wisdom. His joy in it was con-
tagious.

"As I was saying," he interjected, eager to turn the subject away
from himself, "our authorities always welcomed proselytes and
said they should count as natives. Leviticus, for example, and

Isaiah and Ezekiel. What is not so familiar," said Moreh, "is the attitude of the Talmud. Many people think that the scholars of the Talmudic period built a 'hedge around the Torah,' freezing out non-Jews. This is simply not true. They pointed to Biblical heroes as converts: Abraham, Judaism's first convert; Tamar, Judah's wife; Job, who is said to have been converted by Dinah, Jacob's daughter; Jethro, the father-in-law of Moses. Even the Greek and Roman historians speak of converts to Judaism. In the fourth century the king of Yemen and his subjects converted. So did the well-known Khazars and their king of the eighth century. Large numbers of Christians in Hungary in the sixteenth century went over to Judaism to escape the attacks of Suleiman, the so-called Magnificent. Conversion was an accepted part of Jewish living. To be sure, there are a few Talmudic opinions opposing conversion, but this is because converts are usually more observant and thereby expose the waywardness of other Jews."

"If all this is true, why are Jews so obstinate in opposing Gentiles even when they become Jews? Why is marriage even to a convert such a tragedy?"

"We must understand, Re'uven, that persecution has made Jews defensive. Many of us have come to believe that every Gentile is a potential anti-Semite. We have been disillusioned too many times. We have come to feel that a Gentile can always revert to his former status though he embraces Judaism, but a born Jew will always be what he is."

I nodded my head, but I didn't really understand. I was impatient with what I considered a narrow attitude of suspicion and resentment.

"In any case," said Moreh, "you can now see how effectively Jewish history disposes of the theory that the Jew is a separate race. On the contrary, like other vital peoples, the Jewish people represents a mixture of many racial stocks, some of which are known, many of which can only be guessed."

Thanks to Mr. Cocking I had learned a valuable lesson. But I still gnawed on the problem. If we are not a race, not united by blood, why are there Jewish features, like our noses, for example? Why does the audience at the Orpheum vaudeville theatre immediately recognize Potash and Perlmutter, the comedians, as Jewish? How can we at the Home tell instantly a Jew from a non-Jew? Isn't it because of their Jewish physical peculiarities?

It took time to find answers. Not until I was a student at the
Seminary in New York, listening to Professor Franz Boas, did I
discover that Jews do not really look "Jewish." He showed that
even height, usually regarded as a trait transmitted by the chromo-
somes, is subject to change because of the environment. His prime
examples were the American-born children of Jewish and Italian
immigrants, regularly taller than their parents. The arched, so-
called Jewish nose exists among less than 25 per cent of Jews, while
more than 60 per cent have straight or Greek noses and a few have
even the snub variety. Dark hair may predominate among Jews,
but some 30 per cent are blond, as I was as a child, and Davey
Favor and Ben Skrupka, Orphanage kids, were red-heads. So why
was it easy for us at the Home to recognize a Jew? Probably
because of his gestures and mannerisms unconsciously caught
from contact with other Jews. With each generation the Jew looks
less "Jewish," blending into the Anglo-Saxon mode of facial immobility and reserve. All this, however, became clear long after I left
the Home.

In the Home I simply accepted Moreh's positive assertion that
there is no Jewish race in spite of my confusion about "looking
Jewish." Still questions assailed me. If we are not a race, how
should we refer to ourselves? As a religion? As a nation? The Old
Man seemed the logical source for answers, but he was not as ap-
proachable as Moreh. He was a man of moods and made us
acutely aware of them. Before approaching him for anything—a
concession or information—one had to determine whether he was
receptive. It took months for me to catch him in a state of mellow-
ness, after a Hanukkah celebration in which members of the Board
and guests participated. He had been in fine fettle that evening. His
speech drew an eloquent parallel between the indefatigable Maccabees, who fought their enemies against great odds, and the courage and endurance of the supporters of the Home, who fought the
massive enemies called indifference and apathy. The Old Man was
always good at rousing enthusiasm. When it was all over and
everyone had left, he sat quietly drinking a glass of tea and lemon,
humming a tune. I approached.

"The Maccabees you spoke about tonight, what did they fight
for, their right to practise the Jewish religion?"

"Of course. Don't you remember I said they marched to Jerusalem and dedicated the Temple to the worship of God?"

"But is that all they won, the right to pray in the Temple? They lived in their own land, Palestine. This made them like a nation. Wouldn't you say Jews are more like a nation than a religion? Lots of Jews do not come to *shul*. You yourself said a great many Jews don't believe in God. Why are they still Jews?"

"Excellent question. How long have you been chewing on this?"

"Ever since you told us it's wrong to say the Jews are a race. If we are not a race, and Moreh agrees we aren't, then we must be a religion. But then why do we still call people Jewish when they don't believe in our religion?"

"A question worthy of a Solomon. The fact is we are a nation."

"But a nation has a land and a government and an army. We don't have any of these things."

"We hope to have one day."

"You mean we'll all settle in Palestine?"

"Yes, under the Zionist flag."

"But until then are we a nation or a religion wanting to be a nation?"

"We are a nation with a religion but lacking certain characteristics of nationhood. We had them before and we shall have them again. You must believe that."

I hadn't the wit at the time to ask whether if we are a nation of Jews and also belong to a nation called Canada, we are not in a fundamental contradiction. I took the Old Man's definition on faith and it stayed with me until I studied under Mordecai Kaplan, professor of homiletics at the Seminary. He defined the Jews not so much as a nation with political trappings but as a "people" with a common history and a common sense of destiny, expressing itself through a religio-cultural tradition. A Jew remains within the fold so long as he does not repudiate that tradition. Describing Canada or the U.S.A. as a nation and the Jews as a people helped me face up to the problem of dual loyalties. But no one has yet truly resolved the contradiction.

I owe Canada the obligations of a native son and citizen. I owe the Jewish people, of which the state of Israel is only a part, my spiritual values. Neither Canada nor Israel compels my absolute loyalty. In the event of war between Israel and a friend of Canada or between Canada and Israel itself I would choose on the basis of values: which nation is closer to my obligations as a member of the human race? Neither Canada nor Israel occupies the supreme position in my hierarchy of values. Each is a modern state which considers its own interests as paramount. They are both secondary to me. My values are tied in with the interests of mankind, as I learned from Moreh. Each deserves my loyalty to the extent that it serves this overriding goal. It was a long road from Cocking's "Jewish race" to Mordecai Kaplan's "peoplehood."

VII

Jesus

Hannah Lerman was dead. She was a quiet little girl of seven, pretty, even-tempered, exuding innocent charm. Her voice had a lilt, and her presence usually brought out smiles. She was a favourite of the nurses and other higher authorities, but none of her peers seemed to mind. When she was stricken with a mastoid and taken to Children's Hospital somewhere east of Main Street, everyone seemed sad and spoke of the illness in hushed tones. Then suddenly she was gone. The infection of the mastoid had entered her brain.

Death for the first time had loomed over us. Death was an intruder and we resented him. Most of the orphans had never experienced having someone taken inexorably away. Their parents had died when they were too young to grasp the meaning of dying. But Hannah was alive and well one day and dead and cold the next, and we hated the trespasser. Death was not only incomprehensible but cruel. Mean, we said. Tragic, the ladies of the sewing circle said. Unjust, the rabbi said at the funeral.

It was cold the day Hannah was buried. Prairie cold has a power unknown to the rest of the world.

In winter we were always fretting with flushed cheeks, sore throats and congested chests, which the volunteer doctors were valiantly battling. The Winnipeg winter is hard. Snows come down in blinding blizzards and pile in drifts along the roads and the hollows. They choke the lanes and heap themselves against the doors of houses. They freeze hard and winds whip the powder off them, leaving exposed the ridges of ice like ripples on a dead white sea.

There must be colder places, to be sure, like the Arctic tundra where frigidity is reminiscent of paralysis. Prairie cold burns. It glows to a white intensity. When the temperature plummets to 40° below zero Fahrenheit, the cheeks turn creamy. The remedy in the

1920s was to rub snow into the affected parts, but the after-burn would remain for some time. On such a glacial day Hannah's funeral was held.

The hearse parked in front of the Orphanage entrance. We could see the forbidding little coffin through windows on either side of the car. The snow-covered lawn was, as the Yiddish saying goes, black with people. Winnipeg Jews were possessive about their orphans, and the death of one was a shared tragedy. The Ladies Society was out en masse, keening. Mrs. Rafalsky, foremost as a party-maker, also headed the group of mourners. She flung herself at the hearse sobbing: "*teibele* (little dove), *malechel* (little angel)."

The Orphanage choir, arrayed on the entrance steps, accompanied Sam Ostrow as he chanted the memorial prayer. The cold, the sadness, the sorrowful multitude put a strain on our voices, but we carried the melody, such as it was. Ostrow intoned: "O God, filled with compassion. . ." The words sounded incongruous. Everybody recognized the Hebrew word *rahamim*. Pity? Where was the mighty God's pity? It set the women off on a new wave of wailing and stunned us, the orphans. We sobbed our hearts out as did Cantor "Sammy", finishing the prayer in a series of convulsive sighs: "Thou who dwellest on high . . . grant perfect rest beneath the sheltering wings of thy presence . . . amidst the holy and pure . . . who shine as the brightness of the firmament . . . unto the soul of Hannah, daughter of Abraham . . . who has gone unto eternity. . . ."

As the sobbing subsided, Rabbi Kahanovitch mounted the steps, turned to the audience and spoke, the frosty vapour issuing from his lips in clouds: "I hear a voice from that little black box telling us that life is fragile. It begins with painful birth and ends with painful death, and its fabric in between has dark threads running through. Life is like a fleeting dream, floating dust.

"You ask why God takes an innocent little soul. What has she done to deserve such a fate? In seven years a little girl hasn't had time to sin. What does God want from her? Aren't there other blacker souls in this world to appease his wrath?

"Why?—the voice from the black box asks. Give us an answer! But, my friends, there is no answer. God is mysterious in his ways. He judges us according to his own standards. We cannot understand, as Abraham our father failed to understand and hurled his protest at the Lord: 'Shall the judge of all the earth not do justice?'

But whose justice are we talking about? His or ours? If ours, then we are inconsolable. If his, then we must be silent. God in his wisdom has got right." The rabbi's rolling baritone reached tenor levels.

He came down a few decibels. "We must take comfort from our Torah, the core of our tradition. We are not the first to lose a *neshamale*, a little soul." The voice became soft and didactic. He was now calling on the wisdom of the great tradition.

"Our sages, may their name be a blessing, say that one sabbath day when Rabbi Meir was at the house of study addressing the people, his two sons, who were of uncommon beauty and already learned in the Torah, died. Beruriah, their mother, carried them to the bedchamber, laid them on the bed and covered them with a sheet. As the sun set, Rabbi Meir returned and asked for his sons that he might bless them. 'They are not far off,' said Beruriah. She served him wine over which he made the special prayer at the going out of the sabbath, and food. 'Where are my sons that they may drink from the cup of blessing?' he asked. 'They will be here anon,' said Beruriah. The rabbi ate and thanked God for sustaining all living things. Then Beruriah said: 'My husband, I would fain ask thee a question.' 'Ask it, my love.' 'A few years ago someone gave me two jewels to keep for him. Now he wants them back. Shall I return them?' 'This is a question my wife should not have thought necessary to ask. Would you keep from a person what is his own?' 'No,' replied Beruriah, 'but I thought it best to acquaint thee therewith before I returned them.' She then led him to the bedchamber and removed the sheet. 'My sons, my sons,' cried Rabbi Meir. And Beruriah said: 'Didst thou not teach me that we must return to each his own? See, the Lord gave, the Lord taketh away, blessed be the name of the Lord.'

"We have been given Hannahle for a little while. Now the Lender wants his precious jewel back. We have no choice, of course, but we must do it with a full heart, knowing that we savoured a gift of love. We must be grateful for God's gift, for his mercy endureth forever."

Kahanovitch's words were balm to the multitude. The women dried their tears, the men blew their noses. All was quiet again. The sun sparkled on the snow. The cold did not burn any more. It gave way to a kind of inner heat. The hearse drove off, a line of cars following. We knew there was an interment service at the cemetery, but we were not permitted to go.

My sister Lily was Hannah's monitor. She took the little girl's death hard, as did the rest of the Orphanage population. For me, the real shock came not so much from Hannah's ineluctable departure as from the sudden awareness that nobody seemed able to do anything about it. There's an end to life, and it could come to anybody at any time. Or maybe death isn't the end. Then what comes after?

I asked my mother on one of my visits to the kitchen when I knew the Old Man was in town somewhere: "What happens to us when we die?"

"You shouldn't be thinking of such things. It's not healthy. Here, have a frozen apple." Mother was a *Yiddishe mameh*. She solved problems by giving you something to eat.

I asked Miss Rose, the nurse. She said: "If I had the answer to your question, I'd market it, make millions out of it and retire so I wouldn't have to sort out boys' underwear any more."

I asked the Old Man. He said: "Don't bother me with your pilpulistic questions. Haven't we enough problems staying alive? Let the philosophers worry about death." Evidently he was in the wrong mood.

As usual Moreh came to the rescue. It was uncanny how he would come out with the right words: "We don't have all the answers. How could we? We haven't died yet."

I poured out all the secret questions of my heart: "What is it like in the grave? Is the ground dark? Do bodies decay?"

"Yes," said Moreh, "it's dark like Sheol in the Bible. And our bodies change. They change in life. They always grow older and weaker. And they change in death. Change is a part of life."

"But everybody is so afraid of change. See how they cry at a funeral. There were more than a hundred people around Hannah's hearse and every one of them had tears for her."

"Since life is uncertain it's natural for people to be afraid. But there's no shame in crying. Tears have a function. They give us release. They enrich our joy. Be glad that you belong to a people that knows how to weep. Instead of being bottled up inside we can be outgoing and compassionate."

"Do you cry, Moreh?"

"Yes."

"Why, because you're not sure of what's going to happen to you?"

"Partly. I cry mostly because I can't help myself. I am moved by sorrow and pain as other people are. But that doesn't mean I am entirely without hope. I'm inclined to believe the rabbi who says a thousand years in the next world are not worth an hour in this one. It's a good world we live in. The Jew is an incurable optimist. We have always believed the world is a blessing. At the same time, there may be something to the idea that life goes on even after death. There are things that never die. Memory, for example. When I die, I hope you will remember me. If you do, I will live. Don't underestimate memory. The Jews have good memories. That's why the Jewish people has lived for thousands of years. Our memories keep us alive."

Moreh was suddenly remote as if the subject had become irrelevant. I was quiet for a moment, sensing his mood. Then I said brusquely with the off-handedness of youth:

"That reminds me, Moreh . . . the rabbi's speech. He said God has pity. I wonder why nobody interrupted him. Did God pity Hannah? Either He has no pity or He isn't much of a god or He simply isn't there."

Moreh's voice was deliberately patient, as if he had given his answer many times. "How shall I prove to you that there is a God, Re'uven? By painting a picture of him? God never sat for his photograph. Distrust anybody who thinks he has a photograph of him, although people have been trying to picture him from the very beginning. . . .

"First our ancestors pictured God walking in the garden in the cool of day and hunting for Adam under the trees. Then they thought He lived on a mountain, Sinai, where He spoke with Moses. The centuries passed. Now He was no longer on a distant mountain but in Palestine, which is so small you can hide it in a corner of Manitoba. But He filled the land of Israel. The idea of him had grown. More centuries passed. The Jews could not keep God geographically limited. World-wide lines of communication opened up. Now God was Lord of all the earth. 'It is He that sitteth above the circle of the earth,' said Isaiah, 'and the inhabitants thereof are as grasshoppers.' The Jews would not let God stay little. They continued to expand their idea of him: 'If I ascend up to the heaven, thou art there; if I take the wings of the morning and dwell in the uttermost parts of the sea, even there shall thy hand lead me.' How's that for a picture? The Psalmist wrote that. That is probably the most magnificent enlargement of the idea of God in history."

Moreh paused and fixed a kindly eye on me. "That's about as far as you can go with a picture. But it doesn't really matter what kind of a picture of God you have. What is important is how you behave toward others, observing the law. A Hasidic rabbi once said people should act as though they were atheists, as if there were no God and everything depended on them to save the world and put some sanity into it. That's what really counts."

Moreh kept warming to his subject. It was hard to stop him. "God is so great and vast that we can only think of him in symbolic terms. But I suppose you can say He has a near end, which we touch whenever we serve each other. At Hannah's funeral God was there. We were a mass of people pitying each other in a great sorrow we shared. A little girl brought us together as a compassionate fraternity. She made God real for us."

I was still unconvinced. "What you say sounds wonderful, Moreh, but you haven't yet given me a single bit of proof that there is a God. If He were doing his job, He would have saved Hannah. Give me proof that I can see."

"You remind me of Frederick the Great who put the same question to his physician-in-ordinary: 'Zimmerman, can you give me one single proof that God exists?' The doctor's answer left the king speechless: 'The Jews, your majesty.' There is a hard fact. The existence of the Jewish people today proves there is a God."

More than a decade later, in 1938, I discovered that Frankel had anticipated the Christian theologian Karl Barth. That was the year the brown-shirted S.A. men were sending German synagogues up in flames. It was the year when Barth wrote: "If anyone wants a proof of God, something visible and tangible that no one can deny and that is displayed for everyone to see, he must turn to the Jews."

"Yes, the Jews," said Moreh to his eleven-year-old pupil. "According to the rules they should no longer exist. Where is ancient Rome? Its legions crushed the Jewish state and Jews were driven out to all parts of the world. Yet Rome perished and Israel lives. After Rome the Jews endured for the next two thousand years without a state and an army. They were scattered around the world in small groups, despised, persecuted, rejected, exposed to attempts at conversion by Islam and the Christian churches and always on the verge of annihilation. But they survived and preserved their identity. If I were choosing a symbol for the Jews, it would not be the military shield of David, which the Zionists have chosen, but the burning bush that is in flames but is not consumed.

Other nations were forced to pull up stakes and find new settle-
ments, but they vanished. The wandering Jews alone remained
Jews. That is the unique feature of their history and destiny."

"But Moreh, Moreh, what is their secret?"

"To that question I can give you a sure answer. Old vanished
cultures have left memorials to their existence in the form of
material objects. We know and study them through clay tablets,
tombs, sculptures and coins unearthed by archaeologists. Jewish
life in ancient times has left very few traces of that kind. The most
important heritage the ancient Jews left does not exist in stone and
bronze but lives in thoughts, visions and ideas. Peoples over
whom proud monuments stand as memorials perished and disappeared. The Jews bequeathed their ideas, and they still live. There
you have the secret, and for me the proof that God exists. He lives
in the invisible idea."

I felt like shouting hurray. At last, something to hang on to,
even though I would have liked it better if I could see God as a picture. This whole planet, I later realized, could freeze over and it
would mean nothing . . . nothing at all. . . . But if there is a God,
whether He is a personal Being or a Force, everything becomes
enormously important . . . every life . . . every death. . . .

The day after Hannah's funeral I returned to Luxton public school.
The question came up of whether the orphans should be kept
home to observe *shiva*, the seven-day mourning period, since
Hannah was our "sister," a member of the Orphanage family. It
was decided, however, that the sooner we got back to the routine
the more rapidly our grief would be assuaged. My eighth-grade
teacher, Miss Stevens, aware of how deeply Hannah's death had
affected the orphans, expanded the morning prayers with a passage from the New Testament and the hymn "Jesus Loves Me."
She was a very Christian lady and meant well but had little understanding of how sensitive even young Jews were to Christological
exercises. I approached her after school.

"Miss Stevens, we don't believe in Jesus."

"But Jesus believes in you, Reuben. He loves you and dear little
Hannah. If you could understand that, your heart would be at
peace knowing that she is in heaven with all the other angels."

"You mean Jesus is looking after her, Miss Stevens?"

"Oh, yes. He looks after us all. How much happier you would
be if you believed."

"Yes, Miss Stevens." It was useless to argue. That look she gave me through her pince-nez was fixed, unalterable. I had learned not to oppose it.

Later that day after Hebrew class I asked Moreh: "Why don't Jews believe in Jesus?"

His jaw dropped. "Now what set you on to that line?"

"Miss Stevens says Jesus has the answers to all my questions about Hannah."

Moreh was not one to run from a delicate subject. "Miss Stevens is a Christian and perhaps does not know that Jews do not believe in *Yeshua Ha-Notzri*." He used the Hebrew equivalent for the name of the Nazarene in order to soften the reference. To many Jews of the 1920s, who had emigrated from Eastern Europe, the very name of Jesus was associated with persecution and pogroms and pronounced with dread.

"But why don't we believe in him?" I persisted.

Moreh was beyond his depth. "I'll have an answer for you tomorrow." It was obvious that he wanted to confer with the Old Man. I had created an incident that touched on Christian-Jewish relations. What should be done? Protest to Miss Stevens' principal, to the board of education? Should it be made into a *cause célèbre*? That might be unwise and a threat to the Jews. Prayers in the public schools were an accepted practice. No one dared challenge them, and Jews acquiesced because they had no recourse.

The next day I was called into Osovsky's office. "Reuben, you handled your teacher wisely. In future you must do the same. When she mentions Jesus you are to be silent. This is the twentieth century and we do not engage in Christian-Jewish disputations. There is no point to them, especially since Jews do not usually come out winners."

"All right, Mr. Osovsky, I won't discuss the subject with Miss Stevens any more. But I'd like to discuss it with you. What about Jesus? Does he have any answers? And why don't Jews accept him?"

"I'm ahead of you. You're entitled to answers. Mr. Frankel thinks so. At first I disagreed. There are times when you have to accept the assurances of your elders that a thing is so. I thought your questions about Jesus were *hutzpah*, but your Hebrew teacher convinced me otherwise. I have made an appointment for you with Rabbi Samuel of Shaarey Zedek. He is a learned man in these things. If anyone can help you, he will. Be respectful. Put on your sabbath clothes. Here's your street-car fare."

I was dumbfounded. Rabbi Herbert J. Samuel was a noted communal personality. He was a native of Glasgow, Scotland, and a "reverend" of the Anglo-Jewish school. On official occasions he even wore a turned collar as British rabbis did, imitating the priests of the Anglican church. He participated in civic functions, often addressed non-Jewish audiences and occasionally made the newspapers. That the Old Man should turn to him surprised me, because he sometimes referred to him as an assimilationist.

I prepared for the appointment in awe and with great care, finishing off my shoe-shine with drops of water à la Cocking and even asking permission to take a mid-week bath, an unheard-of procedure. I got off the street-car at William Avenue. Shaarey Zedek had gone through a number of mergers with other congregations and name changes until it assumed the character of what we would today call modern orthodox.

Inside, the building did not carry the same carbolic odour I was used to at the Home but a musty smell of prayer books and prayer shawls. I passed the sanctuary with its impressive Ark, a far cry from the simple repository for the Torah scrolls at the Orphanage. Rabbi Samuel was at the telephone when I entered his book-lined study. He had the look of Theodor Herzl, the founder of political Zionism, whom I remembered from a picture in the Old Man's office. A Van Dyke beard bobbed up and down as he spoke into the receiver. There was the turned collar I had heard so much about, and it gave me the eerie feeling that I was not so much in the presence of a rabbi as of a priest. But he soon put me at ease. He lifted the cosy from a tea-pot on the sideboard, opened a cupboard and brought out a plate of cookies.

"Do you like cookies, Reuben? I shall call you that, since you bear a proud name, that of Israel's eldest son. Do you know the *berochoh* (blessing) for cookies?" I nodded and recited it.

"Amen. Now I shall be mother," he said in what I later learned was an Oxford accent, though the burr still came through. First he poured milk into the cups and then added the tea in the British fashion. I always remembered that sequence, because it gave the tea a special flavour.

"Now then," he said leaning back, "Mr. Osovsky tells me that ever since he told you that you learn only by questioning you have been an inveterate challenger and your questions never cease. How did you get interested in the subject of Jesus?" He had no difficulty with the name. It tripped off his tongue as easily as if he had said Moses.

I told him about Miss Stevens.

"Well, now, we must have many teachers in our public schools who fancy themselves evangelists with a sacred mission. One day we shall banish the church from our schools and the country will be a more convivial place for all. Do you know what the Bible is?"

"It is the *Tanach*—Torah, *Nevi'im* and *Kesuvim* (Five Books of Moses, Prophets and Writings)."

"Excellent. Now you should know that for Christians a whole section is added to the Bible, not as large as the Hebrew Bible but very important to them. They call it the New Testament. It is the story of Jesus."

"Should I read the New Testament?"

"No," said Rabbi Samuel decisively. "Jews shouldn't read the New Testament until they are thoroughly familiar with what Christians call the Old Testament, our Bible. Since we don't recognize the New one, there's no necessity of calling ours the Old one. It is simply *Tanach*, as you said."

"Is there something wrong in reading the New Testament?"

"They told me you gnaw on a bone like a puppy. Of course not. But what's the point of seeking other people's treasures before discovering the gems in our own heritage? You have a mother. You must know her and love her first. Then you may seek to know what your friend's mother is like."

"But isn't it possible that I might appreciate my own mother better by getting to know my friend's mother?"

"You don't let go, do you? All right, I'll save you the trouble of reading the New Testament. I'll tell you what it says about Jesus." He spoke confidently and with what seemed to me remarkable familiarity with the composition of the Christian book or, more properly, books.

"Although all twenty-seven books of the New Testament mention Jesus, they tell us very little about him. We don't know for sure in what year he was born or if he is an historical figure, since what we do know is only what the New Testament tells us."

"But not everybody in the Hebrew Bible is historical either, according to Mr. Frankel."

"Nobody is certain about the complete historicity of the Hebrew Bible unless you accept the truth of every jot and tittle of it. Most Jews do, just as most Christians believe that Jesus actually lived. Let's agree that we are talking about people who are not legendary. We've got to get on."

I detected a certain impatience in Rabbi Samuel. I was afraid I might anger him and get into trouble. I decided to put a brake on my tongue for a while. It wasn't hard to do. My natural inclination was to keep silent.

"The principal material about Jesus," said the rabbi, "is in the four Gospels. Each is named for an alleged author: Matthew, Mark, Luke and John. The first three contain duplicating material. John is different in content and style from the other three. It doesn't divide the career of Jesus, as do the other three, into a period in Galilee in northern Palestine, a journey to Jerusalem and the last fateful visit to the Jewish capital. Instead Jesus moves freely from Galilee to Jerusalem and back. In John the trial and death of Jesus take place on the day before Passover. In the other three the crucifixion is on the first day of Passover. This is out of character with Judaism, of course. If the Jews were handling the execution, they would never schedule it on the holiday or even on the eve of one. Everything clear so far?"

"You're going very fast, but I'm following." Actually it was too fast for me and I determined then and there to read the New Testament for myself, since Rabbi Samuel said it wasn't wrong to read it, only that I shouldn't.

"Now," said Rabbi Samuel, always indicating a turn in the argument with the word Now. "We know only vaguely the condition of the times in which Jesus lived. He may have lived to thirty, according to Luke, or less than fifty, according to John. Palestine had become a Roman province in 63 B.C. and in 4 B.C. was divided into three parts. The Romans loved to divide and rule. In 6 A.D. they deposed the king of one part, Judea, and banished him to Gaul. Procurators or governors then ruled Judea from 6 to 38 A.D. In the lifetime of Jesus oppression by Roman soldiers and Jewish resistance was an ordinary experience. During this period Jews turned to their sacred literature for comfort and encouragement. . . . Would you like more tea?"

I shook my head.

"Another cookie?" I nodded and he passed the plate.

"Now. . ." I prepared for another turn in the argument. "The Bible, through such prophets as Ezekiel, told the Jews that oppression was not destined to be eternal or misfortune unending. Through God's help evil times would turn to good, and a descendant of David would occupy the throne of Judea. In Palestine the ceremony of making a man king was not to crown him, but to anoint him with oil. The Hebrew word for anointed is *mashiah*. In

English it is pronounced messiah. The word messiah translated into Greek is *christos* which in English is shortened to Christ. Nothing in the word Christ relates it to Jesus. Understood?"

I permitted myself one word: "Understood." But I was shocked at his use of the word Christ. I had never heard a Jew pronounce it before.

"And so. . ." (The rabbi took me by surprise; I thought he was going to say Now) ". . . oppression and adversity intensified Jewish yearning for the Messiah. It was believed that he would destroy the foreigners occupying the country. Since Jews were at that time already spread throughout the civilized world, the Messiah would miraculously gather the exiled back to Palestine to the proper Davidic kingdom. Some believed the Messiah would usher in the awaited 'last judgment.' Some thought that all men would be resurrected, raised from the dead, and then stand judgment. Others thought that all men would stand trial and only those judged innocent would be resurrected. Jews did not agree with each other on many questions. Resurrection provided one of the disputes between the two camps, the Pharisees and the Sadducees. When Jesus came upon the scene there were disagreements over him. Some accepted him. Most did not, because their expectations didn't materialize. The power of Rome was not broken. The Davidic line was not restored."

I sensed that it was safe to ask a question: "So there were Jews who accepted Jesus. Why do Christians say the Jews rejected him? Not all Jews did."

"The Christians are right. As a whole we did reject him, certainly later on. We did not accept that he died on a cross and was quickly resurrected and then ascended to heaven, there to await the appropriate time for his second coming. We did not and do not believe that he was the Messiah. We do not call him Lord. We cannot agree to a view about any man which raises him above the level of a man and makes him God."

That seemed very logical to me. So when I came out with an explosive "I agree," the rabbi was taken off guard.

"Oh, so you're not such a protester any more! You're coming around. In that case, let me lead you to some understanding of the difference between Jewish and Christian ideas that surround Jesus. Jews understand sin as an act, something done. By and large, Christians understand sin as a state, a condition of man. Thus a Jew believes he can atone for his sin, his act, on his own. He can turn to God and ask for forgiveness. It's a matter between him and

God. A Christian believes that a man is by nature a sinner, so he
has to change his nature. He therefore cannot do it alone. He can
only do it through the Christ who died to redeem everybody from
their sinfulness. That is why your Miss Stevens said Jesus cares for
Hannah and for you."

I was silent again, but this time because light was glimmering. I
relaxed and helped myself to another cookie.

Rabbi Samuel was encouraged by my silence which he took as
acquiescence. "Christians ask: 'What shall a man believe?' Jews
ask: 'What shall a man do?' The Christian holds that belief will
bring a man to action. The Jew insists that when a man performs
an act, though he doesn't understand fully its import, it will lead to
understanding and faith. Christians usually convene a council of
authorized persons to determine and vote on what the proper
belief should be. Not once in their history have Jews called together an assembly to decide some article of faith. In Jewish
history our heroes are men who codified the *halachah* which tells
what we should do."

The telephone rang, and the rabbi answered. "No," he said to
the caller, "I can't see you now. I have a very important guest." He
looked me in the eye. "A young man from the Orphanage." After
a moment he added: "I agree. The Home comes first in all our af-
fections." He replaced the receiver with a big smile. "Everybody
loves our Orphanage." I smiled back and reached for a third
cookie, really a fourth, but who was counting?

"O.K., Rabbi Samuel," I said. "You've explained the difference
between the two religions. Which is the true one? Miss Stevens
says Christianity is and therefore everybody must accept Jesus."

"You're only eleven," said the rabbi looking into my eyes as if he
were reaching for my soul, "but I'm going to say something I hope
you will remember for the rest of your days. No religion possesses
the truth. Every religion searches for it. The search itself is what is
important. Truth comes from a clash of opinion and belief, a
peaceful clash, of course. The Talmud says steel sharpens steel.
That is why the Talmud preserves every opinion, because the minority opinion of one generation may become the majority decision of the next. Judaism does not require everybody to be Jewish.
You can be non-Jewish and observe only the seven laws of Noah
and still achieve salvation. It's a pity that Christianity insists it has
the truth and there is no road to God except through Jesus. Keep
your mind open, Reuben, concentrate on your behaviour and
understanding and wisdom will come.

"Well, have I helped you?" I had been told to be effusive in my thanks, to make the rabbi feel his time had been well spent.

"Thank you, Rabbi Samuel," I said in a little speech I had rehearsed. "I shall think very deeply on what you said and will remember it for many years to come."

On my way home I stopped at the branch library on Machray Avenue and took out a copy of the New Testament. I always carried my library card for such emergencies. Arriving at the Home, I reported to the Old Man as instructed and gave him a glowing account of my visit, hiding the New Testament under my coat. That evening I didn't do much homework.

As I plunged into the Gospel According to St. Matthew, I expected a grand statement similar to the one that begins the Hebrew Bible: "In the beginning God created heaven and earth." Instead a series of "begats" greeted me, just like the "begats" in Genesis which bored me to tears. Nonetheless I plodded on and the feeling came over me that the account makes too much fuss over Jesus' credentials. I would have been more impressed with a categorical declaration: "Jesus, the Son of God, brought peace and love into the world."

It didn't get any better as I read on. Matthew Chapter 27 horrified me. Here were the Jews telling Pontius Pilate to free Barabbas and crucify Jesus. "And with one voice the people cried, 'His blood be upon us and our children!' " Unbelievable! Why would a multitude of Jews take such blame on themselves and implicate their children for generations to come. It was simply out of character. Besides, didn't this contradict the prophet who said that the parents may eat sour grapes but the teeth of the children will not be set on edge? Moreh said this meant the sins of the fathers would not be visited on the children. You can't hold children responsible for what their parents do. "This is an anti-Jewish book," I decided, and read no more.

It was not until I studied under a wise professor of English at the university, who suggested I read the New Testament as "literature," that I went back to the Gospels of Matthew, Mark, Luke and John, and went on to Paul's First Letter to the Corinthians, Chapter 13, perhaps the most sublime essay on ethics ever written. Miss Stevens would be pleased that I can appreciate parts of the New Testament and accept them.

From Hannah Lerman to Miss Stevens to Jesus to Rabbi Samuel—it was not such a tortuous path after all.

VIII

Christ-killer

Picnics were our favourite pastime. They meant freedom from the oppressive routine and the perpetual rules, a welcome change of diet, gifts and prizes. The Ladies Society would prepare the sandwiches, mix gallons of lemonade and purchase wholesale huge cans of ice cream packed in ice. The Girls Auxiliary would arrange the races and award the prizes. Usually we would be taken in cars or by street-car to Kildonan Park, several miles north of the Orphanage. Occasionally we would be treated to an outing in Assiniboine Park in the south end, where a visit to the zoo constituted bonus entertainment.

Outside agencies would also sponsor picnics. The fraternal order of Elks organized an annual outing for the orphans of the city's institutions, Protestant and Roman Catholic, but we were not included. Then one summer an invitation came. No one knew why, and nobody asked. It was enough that the barrier was breached.

The Elks really went to town for their charity project. The children of each institution were to compete in races according to age, in a choral contest and in stage presentations. We were to sing "O Canada," and prepare an original dramatic skit. The song was easily mastered. We had been singing it for years under the direction of Sam Ostrow as a composition in two-part harmony. As for the skit, we decided to present a minstrel show. The girls sewed costumes, begging and borrowing straw boaters and other accessories. Collectively we scoured the joke books for popular vaudeville dialogue. The Old Man gave us no help. Black-faced minstrels were not a Jewish theme and beyond his province.

The day of the picnic arrived, and we set out for Assiniboine Park in cars provided by the Elks. We bubbled over with self-confidence. Our runners had been training for weeks. Ostrow had put us through our paces vocally, and we were ready to render "O

Canada" with the same fervour as we gave to the High Holiday
service. At a dress rehearsal of the minstrel show the night before
we wowed the staff with our high jinks and jokes. We were determined to win every event.

We almost did. None of the other choirs could touch our musical polish. After all, theirs were aggregations organized for the occasion. We had regular rehearsals the year round. Our racers ran
away with every prize in every category. But we failed miserably
as minstrels. The judges were far more impressed with the offering
of a Protestant children's home in which girls and boys carried
milk pails and sang sweetly of the joys of living on the land. Truth
to tell, they deserved the prize. Our show was not very compli-
mentary to blacks, and as members of a minority we should have
been taught better and known better. We were children of our
time, just as filled with prejudice as members of the majority.

We proved to be bad losers. Complacent and superior in our
other victories, we bit our nails over defeat in the drama depart-
ment. The judges said we were too sophisticated and chose a
theme unsuited to our age level. We did not accept the judgment
graciously and darkly hinted at bias, even anti-Semitism. The latter charge was impossible to substantiate. But since the drama contest was last and the Jews had won everything else, it was argued
that the *goyim* were determined to bring us down a few pegs.

Whatever the case, the day was generally not a happy one. Announcement was made that several Elks, carrying batches of dollar
bills, would be circulating among the orphans and if approached
with the question, "Hey, Bill, are you a bill?" would hand a dollar
to the lucky questioner. The complaint arose that non-Jewish orphans were waving dollar bills all over the park but not a single
Jewish child was favoured with one. The real altercation occurred
among the adults. One Elk was reported to have said to a group
defending the Jewish orphans: "Jews! A good boot in the seat of
the pants, that's what they need. Trouble wherever they go. No
satisfying them. Give them a hand, and they'll snatch the arm,
too. And argue with you about it." Several orphans said that when
they asked a man in Elk's costume, "Are you a bill?" they got the
answer, "Yes, but not for a kikey kid."

It was the last time the Jewish Orphanage was invited to an Elks'
outing and my first brush with charges and counter-charges of
anti-Semitism. Most Jewish children in those days had such experiences earlier.

Of course, I was aware of anti-Jewish feeling long before the fateful Elks' picnic. At Luxton public school it was the custom among non-Jewish pupils to address an inmate of the Home as "Abie," regardless of his real name. On one occasion a substitute nurse had been engaged for the girls' side and my sister Rosie became involved in an altercation with her. In the exchange, according to Rosie's testimony, the nurse called her "a dirty Jew." The Old Man was brought in to mediate, but he was the soul of reason. He said to Rosie and her indignant friends: "We can't expect to, be loved by the whole world."

Shortly after the Elks' picnic, an Orphanage soft-ball team played a team of grade eight pupils in Luxton school yard. The non-Jews were short a player, and the orphans magnanimously volunteered my less than adequate talents. With me on the opposing team they felt certain of victory. Just to prove their error, I played my heart out, even batting in a runner with a two-base hit. But the joy of my new-found allies turned to consternation when I was tagged out running for third. The captain accused me of conspiring with the Jews to "throw" the game. "You lousy little Christ-killer," he spat at me. I was thunderstruck.

The accusation of treachery brought before me the New Testament scene. There were the Jews screaming, "Crucify him, crucify him! His blood be on us and our children," and I was one of those children. The Gospel According to St. Matthew Chapter 27 was alive and well and living in the Luxton-St. Cross neighbourhood. Where did that boy get the Christ-killer expletive? From his parents, his priest? He must have been taught, carefully taught.

My first reaction was like that of the Jewish boy who comes crying to his mother: "Johnny says I killed Christ. Honest I didn't." Then I thought of turning to Moreh who usually helped me with my inner struggles. But Moreh always blanched when I mentioned the name Jesus, and coupling it with Christ actually made him squirm. He must have had terrible experiences in his East European *stetl* with the protagonists of the Nazarene. I resolved to do some investigation on my own.

Books. Moreh said the wisdom of the ages was in a book, that Jews were *am hasefer*, people of the book. Why couldn't I read them on my own? Surely some Jews somewhere had something to say about Jews and Jesus and who killed him.

The librarian at the Machray Avenue lending branch was helpful. I asked for books on the crucifixion of Jesus, especially by Jewish authors. Why only Jewish writers? Well, maybe non-Jewish, too. She assumed I was writing a school essay. A catalogue search produced Joseph Jacobs' *As Others Saw Him*, Claude G. Montefiore's *The Religious Teachings of Jesus* and H. G. Enelow's *A Jewish View of Jesus*.

Jacobs, Montefiore and Enelow revealed many things to me— that crucifixion was a form of capital punishment common among the ancient Greeks and Romans but not among Jews; that nailing or tying the hands and feet of a convicted person to a cross of wood and leaving him there until he expires is unknown in Jewish law; that Jews had their own forms of capital punishment if they had wanted to execute Jesus: stoning, burning, beheading and strangulation. The sources at the main library, which I visited the following Saturday afternoon, added more facts. The crucifixion was clearly in accordance with Roman law. The procedure—the crown of thorns, flagellation, bearing of the cross—was typical of Rome's punishment of political rebels. Besides, Jewish courts, under the Roman conquerors, had no power to inflict capital punishment. All this is borne out by the inscription, "Jesus of Nazareth, king of the Jews," signifying not a heretic but a rebel against the Roman state.

With each bit of information my excitement grew. I discovered a statement by R. Travers Herford, an Anglican priest, in his book *The Pharisees*, that the account in the New Testament is unreliable. Who could stand in the face of such solid evidence? I sensed, however, that for multitudes of Christians the New Testament was a holy book and that no outside arguments or proofs, powerful as they might be, could contradict it. As I was led from reference to reference it became clear that the captain of the Luxton soft-ball team *had* been taught. For two thousand years Christian teachers, including the official church, had taught that Jews were demons, devils, the incarnation of malevolence. The teaching was repeated so often that it became part of the mentality of Christians. Oh, Moreh, no wonder a dread came over you when I gave utterance to the name of Jesus Christ!

Moreh must have known the history of the centuries following the crucifixion, how Jews were not considered human enough to deserve justice. Late in the fourth century, for example, the flourishing synagogue of Callinicum, Mesopotamia, was burned down at the instigation of St. Ambrose, the influential bishop of Milan. The emperor Theodosius ordered the synagogue to be rebuilt and the guilty punished. Bishop Ambrose protested: Jews are enemies of Christ and beyond the protection of the law. When Theodosius persisted in the cause of law and order, the powerful ecclesiastical authority threatened him with excommunication. To help Jews would be the same as opposing Christ himself.

The record got worse as I went from history to words spoken from Christian pulpits. St. John Chrysostom, also of the fourth century, was a vehement preacher against Jews: "I know that a great number of the faithful have for the Jews a certain respect and hold their ceremonies in reverence. This leads me to refute such an opinion. I have already stated that the synagogue is worth no more than the theatre. Here is what the prophet says, and the prophets are more to be respected than the Jews: 'But because you have a harlot's brow you refused to blush' (Jeremiah 3:3). But the place where the harlot is prostituted is the brothel. The synagogue therefore is not only a theatre but a place of prostitution; it is a den of thieves and a hiding-place of wild animals . . . of impure beasts. We read: 'I abandon my house, cast off my heritage' (Jeremiah 12:7). Now if God has abandoned them, what hope of salvation have they left? They say that they too worship God, but this is not so. None of the Jews, not one of them, is a worshipper of God. . . . (The synagogue) is simply a house of idolatry. . . . The Jews live for their bellies, they crave the goods of the world. In shamelessness and greed they surpass even pigs and goats. . . The Jews are possessed by demons, they are delivered to impure spirits. Instead of greeting them and addressing to them as much as a word, you should turn away from them as from the pest and a plague of the human race."

I found these sentiments in a book of "Servants of God" canonized by the Roman Catholic Church. That Chrysostom should be called a saint, who, by definition, is one extraordinarily charitable and patient, seemed incredible. As a boy I had no context in which to place these words which were as painful as physical torture. I had no way of measuring them against the mentality and moral insensibility of the age of the Church Fathers. I took them at face value, and they were monstrous.

But that wasn't the end of the story of the canonized servants of God. The book told of St. Dominique du Val who was born in Saragossa, Spain, and lived from 1237 to 1250. Why was a boy of only thirteen made a saint? Because he defended the Christian faith by standing up to the Jews. They struck back, according to the account, by using his blood in the mixing of unleavened bread for Passover. Young Dominique had made a specialty of visiting the Jewish quarter where he protested against their malevolent chantings with hymns to the Virgin and the saints. The Jews greeted his sacred songs with threatening fists and cries of vengeance.

One day, while in the street of the Jews, Dominique was spirited away by a usurer, one Mose Albayucet, whose beak of a nose gave an impression of a bird of prey and whose eyes were dulled by the constant, greedy contemplation of gold. He kept the boy in a cage until the time came for the bloody rite. That night the cage with its precious cargo was taken to the home of a prince of the synagogue, where the rabbis convened, all of them with long beards, hooked noses, swollen bellies and eyes gleaming with malice. Dominique took hold of the crucifix, which hung from his neck, for protection.

"Trample the Christ with your feet," said a whining voice.

"Never," replied Dominique, "he is my God." And the boy prayed.

"Let us get on with the ceremonies," said the evil ones. Dominique's temples were circled with a crown of thorns. Mose Albayucet produced a hammer and nailed his soft hands to the wall. Blood was drawn from his veins until the flasks and cups in the hands of the rabbis were full. Albayucet removed the boy's body from the wall, mutilated it, kept the head and hands and returned the trunk to the box. Quickly the bloodstains were removed from the wall and floor. The rabbis washed and returned to their homes at the stroke of midnight.

Later two little pierced hands and a head crowned with thorns were found at the bottom of a well. The maimed trunk was discovered by some fishermen as they came ashore.

Albayucet confessed, was baptized and hanged on the gallows in the marketplace. It was the year of grace 1250.

This story, here condensed, appeared in a book that bore the *nihil obstat* and was written for the edification of the masses. It must have burned into the minds of Christian children for generations.

This folk tale filled me with disbelief, loathing and revulsion. Jews using the blood of a Christian child in the making of *matzah*? What abysmal ignorance and calumny! One simply had to open the story of the Exodus from Egypt, which Jews have been reading for more than two thousand years at Passover, to realize what compassion moved them in their concern for humanity: "This is the bread of affliction which our forefathers ate in the land of Egypt. All who are hungry, let them come and eat. All who are needy, let them come and celebrate the Passover with us. . . . Now we are slaves; next year may we be free men." This invocation opens the *seder*, the joyous, loving family feast.

The emphasis is on all the children of God. All need to be fed. All need to be free. Our *matzah* is pure, mixed with the tears of children who are hungry and oppressed. To tell Christians that this sublime unleavened bread is foul and abominable is a lie that denies earth and heaven!

Times change. A generation goes and another comes. Eleven-year-olds in the 1980s do not confront the problems of their counterparts in the 1920s. Christian writers, Protestant and Catholic, have become aware of the injury done by the savage myths of the past. Jewish-Christian dialogues abound. Catechisms and preaching have been purified of language that might offend. But the scars remain. You can take the boy out of the 1920s, but it's hard to take the 1920s out of the boy.

Anti-Semitism, I learned from my role as "Abie" at Luxton school, and confirmed by later experience and study, is different from other prejudices. It is pervasive, universal and seemingly timeless, apparently immune to any cure. It has had a long and dishonorable history. It has swept every continent, infected every land and found adherents under every form of government and in every social order.

Other prejudices are either rational or irrational. Anti-Semitism is both, and each has a Biblical model. One is the Egyptian enslavement of the Israelites; the other the Amalekite assault on them. "There arose a new king over Egypt who knew not Joseph," says the Book of Exodus. "And he said unto the people: 'Behold the children of Israel are too many and too mighty for us. Come let us deal wisely with them lest they multiply and it come to pass that, when there befalleth us any war, they also join themselves unto our enemies and get them up out of the land.' " It is possible to understand the Egyptian treatment of the Israelites even while condemning it on moral grounds. The Amalekite attack, on the other hand, was not only immoral; it was motivated by sadistic impulses. It was unprovoked aggression against the weak and helpless among the children of Israel.

The rational, gentlemanly type of anti-Semitism has lasted well into the twentieth century. It is exemplified by such writers as H. G. Wells. In his autobiography he acknowledges that he resisted attempts by his friends to interest him in the Jewish problem. Later on he concluded that the cause of anti-Semitism lies in the fact that Jews are much too preoccupied with their problem, that it is largely a figment of the imagination or a result of supersensitiveness, a trait to which Jews are notoriously addicted.

As for the irrational views of anti-Jewish antagonism, they early infected the Greek sophist Apion, who lived in Alexandria during the first century and proposed "objective" theories to justify hatred of the Jews. He declared that leprosy was a disease indigenous to the Jews. He said that the vaunted Exodus was only the escape of a leper band under Moses. As lepers the Israelites lacked any gift for government or the arts. Their laws were full of hatred for non-Jews, annually sacrificing a Greek youth in the Temple at Jerusalem and worshipping the head of an ass in the holy of holies. Apion's views anticipate practically every aspect of Nazi anti-Semitism, its racism, its denial of Jewish creativity and its vilification of the Jewish religion. The line of descent from Amalek to Apion to the Christian promoters of St. Dominique to the Luxton school soft-ball captain is plain and direct.

What I did not know as a child was that religion is capable of enforcing irrational anti-Semitism. There is, it seems, something in human nature that makes us hate those who have done us good. The Jew has given the Western world its religion, and it seems that he has never been forgiven for it. Why? Evidently because he remained loyal to his own faith after having made his contribution to Christianity.

The Jews produced Jesus, Paul and the Apostles, gave Christianity its scriptures and moral code and influenced its basic institutions and rituals, but steadfastly refused to accept this new religion which insisted on calling itself the new Israel. Thus the New Testament, on almost every page, reflects the pain and anger of the early Christian Church at the Jewish refusal to accept the new creed.

The chief contribution of the New Testament to anti-Semitism, the critical one that kept anti-Jewishness alive in the heart of the Western world, is the account of the crucifixion, which focuses on the Jews as the cause of the death of the Son of God. The story simply does not make sense. But logic has no part in Christian anti-Semitism. There is more than a little truth in Israel Zangwill's acid observation that "many Christians who do not believe that Jesus ever lived are sure that the Jews killed him." As a result of the Christ-killer myth a staggering burden of misery and pain has been imposed upon the Jew through the centuries.

And so when the Luxton school captain hurled that imprecation at me, though I did not know it, mine was the pain of more than sixty generations of my people. I could have hit back but I was too shocked to move and uncertain but that he might have been right. What I did was far more significant. I went to the books, as Jews have traditionally done, and found my comfort in ideas.

In the years since then the Church has begun to see the disastrous implications of the myth. Following the Second World War the Roman Catholic Church realized at last the direct connection between the preachments of its representatives and the nefarious program of the Nazis. At Vatican II, therefore, a special resolution absolved the Jews of any complicity in the crucifixion. Many Jews received this belated declaration, with its implied remorse, in a spirit of contempt. But I welcomed Vatican II's efforts to redress this wrong.

My belief concerning the direct responsibility of the Church in fomenting anti-Semitism has undergone change in recent years. In the post-World War II years I had no doubts that the Church had indirectly provided the Nazis with the label and content of their anti-Jewishness. As French educator Jules Isaac wrote in the 1950s: "Christian anti-Semitism is the powerful, milleniary and strongly rooted trunk upon which all other varieties of anti-Semitism are grafted, even those of a most anti-Christian nature." It was, however, Hannah Arendt, the brilliant interpreter of the Nazi era, who, without absolving the Church of its part in anti-Semitism, made me realize, at times with discomfiting vehemence, the contribution of the Jews themselves to this scourge of the ages. In the early Christian centuries the hostility between Synagogue and Church was not a one-sided creation. Jewish leaders, regarding themselves as intellectually superior to Gentile Christians on Biblical subjects and not entirely forgiving toward the practice of Christian proselytizing, might have incurred less antagonism had they reacted less sharply. In any case, to charge the Church of today with culpability for the persecutions of the Jews by Christian ancestors is to fall into the same error committed by the anti-Semites against the Jews. As Father Edward Flannery has said: "The guilt of Christian or Jew is neither collective nor retroactive."

What we need today is to exercise sensitive care in language, teaching and ceremonials. Jews need to understand that prejudice against *goyim* is a failure of Jewish faith, and Christians need to recognize that anti-Semitism is a denial of Christian love.

More than six months after the incidents at the Elks' picnic, on the festival of Purim, the Old Man delivered a talk on anti-Semitism. It was a sombre speech, out of tune with the occasion.

Purim is a merry holiday on which custom usually permits authority to retreat from severity. During the recitation of the *megillah*, the Book of Esther, we were given noisemakers, greggers, which were sounded whenever the name of Haman was read. In the Talmudical academies of Eastern Europe rabbinical students would be allowed to ape their instructors and preach farcical sermons, but at the Home such a suspension of the rules was unthinkable. Even Purim had its serious lesson, and the conveyor was Aaron Osovsky. His Purim speech dealt with Jew-hatred as a stubborn and complicated disease.

In a country like Canada, he said, few come out openly and point a finger at the Jews. They generally deny they are anti-Semitic, as the Biblical Haman did. Haman, the first political anti-Semite, admitted nothing of his personal antipathy for Mordecai the Jew. It was as a loyal and far-sighted statesman, interested in the welfare of the state, that he demanded the annihilation of the Jews: "Their laws are diverse from those of every people. Neither keep they the king's laws. Therefore it profiteth not the king to suffer them."

The Old Man also made the point that anti-Semitism is often so convoluted that Jews tend to blame themselves for having caused it and engage in apologetics.

After the service we drank tea and milk and consumed the savoury *hamantaschen* (three-cornered tarts shaped like Haman's supposed hat and filled with poppy seeds or prunes). Over the noise of the greggers which some of the younger children were still twirling, I posed a question:

"Mr. Osovsky, if it's true, as you say, that anti-Semites usually put on a front and that we must beware, won't we be looking for anti-Semites everywhere?"

"We have no choice. We must be on our guard."

"But that means we could be spending most of our time hunting the anti-Semites and have no time for anything else!" I had heard Moreh use this argument.

"We should spend time hunting and fighting them. Some of our leaders have this as their main function. Of course, most of our time should be spent in constructive activity."

"Is it true that every Gentile has some anti-Semitism in him?" I had heard this from Rabbi Samuel of Shaarey Zedek synagogue.

"It is true that every Gentile who has come into contact with the anti-Jewish myths in the New Testament will probably harbour antagonism toward Jews. That would certainly encompass most Gentiles in countries where Christianity dominates."

"That means," I said, "we will always have to suspect our Gentile neighbours. It will be hard making friends."

"It has always been hard to leap the barriers that separate Jews from Gentiles. In the old country Jews and Gentiles rarely fraternized. We were an isolated community, a state within a state. We were regarded as aliens. Here in Canada it is easier. While there is no official anti-Semitism, it still lurks in the byways and in the hearts of our fellow-citizens. There are still hotels and pensions in Winnipeg Beach and Gimli and other resorts where Jews are not welcome. I am afraid that even in this land of freedom easy friendship between Jews and *goyim* will not be achieved for a long time, perhaps not in my lifetime or yours." The greggers were going again, but he went on determinedly:

"Like Job in the face of a higher adversary," he went on, "intelligent Jews facing their relentless foes know that the truth will not help them: 'I shall be condemned; why do I labour in vain? If I wash myself with snow and make my hands ever so clean, yet wilt thou plunge me into the ditch!' Apologetics, as I said, are useless. The anti-Semite has the Jew coming and going. He is a capitalist . . . and a communist. He's lazy and doesn't work . . . and he steals the jobs of Canadians. He mixes with Christians . . . and sticks too much to his own people. He desires and foments war . . . and is a pacifist and refuses to fight. And of course out of one side of his mouth the anti-Semite says: 'Canada is the best country in the world, richer, happier and healthier than any other.' And on the other: 'The Jews are too powerful in Canada and we must get rid of them.' "

Bob Rodos interrupted. "Isn't it true, though, that when Jews misbehave they give the whole Jewish people a bad name?"

"Enough with the greggers already," said the Old Man. He continued. "We must remember that we are representatives of an ancient people with a great moral code which has proved its worth

over the centuries. I have to admit we've got our share of Jewish
criminals and they bring us anguish. But any secret hope that
fewer Jewish criminals will mean less anti-Semitism is doomed to
frustration. In any case, anyone who assigns a single cause or even
a group of causes to anti-Semitism is on the wrong beam. It is a
deeply rooted complex which has persisted under different social
and religious systems. It is incredibly stubborn."

"What can we do about it?" This from a chorus of voices, mixed
with gregger sounds.

"As far as the anti-Semite is concerned, nothing. He is immersed
in prejudice of which he himself is often unaware. For this reason
information and factual replies are useless. Fortunately the majority of Canadians have not yet surrendered to ill will. Their minds
have not yet been closed by the preachers of hatred. They are just
uninformed. Therein lies the opportunity for disseminating the
truth. Effective and dignified rejoinders must be made through
newspapers, radio, that new miracle of communication, and the
lecture platform. That is why I speak to Gentile audiences as often
as I can."

"Suppose this went on for twenty years," Bob Rodos asked,
"would all anti-Semitism be removed then?"

"Education is a long process, and the most effective campaign
will not banish anti-Jewish prejudice in my lifetime or in yours. As
well as educating people we need to work hard to preserve the
rights of all people, not only those of the Jews. Jews must be in the
forefront of progressive laws that will improve the economic and
social lot of masses of people. For when people are in need, they
look for scapegoats and Jews are easy to spot and blame. However, nobody has mentioned the best way of fighting anti-
Semitism."

We were silent. Not a gregger was heard.

"After all my speeches and your Hebrew studies, you still don't
know? Let me stress it again and don't you forget it. The best way
of resisting anti-Semitism is to strengthen the victims. How do we
do that? By building up their muscles and giving them guns, so
they can fight back? Some day we will have a government of our
own, and we will fight for our rights. Meanwhile we have to be
strong in our loyalty to Jewish values and grow in our understanding and love for the Jewish heritage. The Jew lived for four thousand years because he stood for something fine and noble. The
anti-Semites attacked, but they fell back before the spiritual

strength of the Jew who survived in spite of them. The Jew who is aware of the greatness of his religion, of his irresistible history and culture can stand up to his foes. The Jew who is ignorant of his past is an easy prey for the shafts of prejudice. Apply yourselves to your Jewish studies as well as to your public school subjects and you will build your own self-respect, your own mental health and hope for the future."

The Old Man was smart. He knew how to bring the argument around to our own responsibilities.

IX

Zion

In 1925 the Hebrew University opened in Jerusalem, and joy burst forth on Matheson Avenue. The joy sprang mainly from Old Man Osovsky. At last something tangible in the Promised Land to which the Jews of the Diaspora could cling as their hope and pride. "See," said the Old Man when he made the announcement to the orphans at meal time, "that's how Jews begin to build a country. They establish a centre of learning first."

Actually draining the malarial swamps, farming, making a living from undeveloped Palestine came first. But it was true that the pioneers of the *Yishuv* (Settlement) had it in their minds as a priority to erect a school of modern and traditional knowledge which would act as a cultural hub for the Jews of the world and humanity itself. And it was true that Jews had throughout their history stressed learning as indispensable to living. It had been so even in the ghettoes of Europe.

"Here they are building the old-new land on the foundation of the old wisdom," said the Old Man. "Rejoice, rejoice," he chanted.

To an eleven-year-old the news was not as exciting as he made out. Palestine was at the other end of the world, and a university, where students spent exacting and lonely hours studying, did not appear as something to dance in the streets about. But as plans for a local celebration began to materialize I was caught up in the delirium.

There was to be a splendid celebration in the Talmud Torah hall at Charles and Flora, and the Orphanage choir and band would perform. Mr. Cocking put the band through its entire repertoire at rehearsals. We prepared the overtures, the marches and the popular love songs. The only Jewish composition we knew was *Hatikvah*, the Zionist anthem. But it didn't really matter what we played. The trumpets and the drums always roused the crowd.

The choir, on the other hand, had much to contribute to the

Zionist mood. We knew the songs of the Palestine pioneers—*Yoh-hai-lee-lee amolee* and Bialik's *nigun* (tune) to which there were no words, only melody and enthusiasm. We were specialists with Psalm 103: "Praise the Lord with clear-toned cymbals. Praise him with loud-sounding cymbals. Let everything that hath breath praise the Lord. *Halleluyah!*"

"Sing out, you rascals," cried Cantor Sam Ostrow. "Sing or you don't get ice cream and cake at the big party." We sang our hearts out.

"What's all the fuss about a university?" I asked Moreh.

"Listen to the boy," said Moreh in astonishment. "Only a university! The last time we had a real academic centre in the Holy Land was two thousand years ago when Rabbi Yohanan ben Zakkai founded his school at Yavneh. Sure we have had great academies in Babylon, Spain and all over Eastern Europe and wherever there was a handful of Jews clustered into a community there was a school for Torah. But those were schools for traditional learning. The Hebrew University is not only for the study of Talmud and other traditional subjects and not only for Jews. It will have departments in the humanities and the sciences—history, archaeology, sociology, physics, chemistry, law, medicine and architecture. The university will lay the basis for the society and government of a twentieth-century nation. And the results of its study and research will radiate around the world. Then the words of Isaiah the prophet will be fulfilled: 'For out of Zion will go forth the teaching.' Then will we truly be 'a light unto the nations.' "

My jaw must have dropped. "Don't look so dumbfounded," said Moreh. "I have just painted a dream, a vision, but it will come to pass, believe me. We Jews have a genius for making dreams come true."

It still seemed astonishing, even after Moreh's explanation, that people should get so delirious about a school—until the day of the celebration. The Talmud Torah hall had never seen such a crowd. Only a few hundred lucky ones were seated. The greater number were massed around the walls, standing in the aisles, in the vestibule and spilling into the street. Bunting decorated the outside and inside of the building. Zionist flags flanked large portraits of Theodor Herzl, the founder of political Zionism, and Lord Balfour, the British foreign minister who in 1917 issued his declaration recognizing the right of the Jewish people to a homeland in Palestine. The band's marches raised audience enthusiasm to fever pitch and when the choir sang the songs of Zion, people stamped and cheered. All because a university was opening its doors.

The speeches were endless. The president of the Talmud Torah introduced the president of the Zionist Organization who presented the chairman of the meeting. They all said the same things. What a glorious moment! How fortunate we are to be of this generation, to be able to witness the blossoming of a land and its spirit!

After a time the audience, somewhat bored, began to provide its own entertainment. People were calling to one another across the hall. The conversational hum threatened to drown out the speakers. Finally the chairman announced that the moment had arrived for the featured speech. It was to be delivered by that great orator and communal worker, the superintendent of our beloved Orphanage, Aaron Osovksy.

The Old Man walked slowly to the dais from his seat on the platform. He was an experienced hand at enticing and holding audiences. Silently, with four fingers in his jacket pocket and thumb sticking out, he surveyed the hall until all was quiet. He began slowly and softly, building to a crescendo. He told the Jews what they wanted to hear; at first he was florid and deferential, then commanding. For the first time I heard an exposition of Zionism. The word had always been part of the environmental vocabulary. Now, as the Old Man spoke, I began to understand why it engendered such passion.

"We are an abnormal people," he said, "because we have no land. We are scattered over the world, dependent upon the nations who harbour us. We keep apart from others and keep together, for only thus can we hope to preserve our individuality. Because we are a national minority that has lost its historic homeland we are bound to stir up feelings of dislike and hostility. At best we are tolerated, for the most part maltreated and persecuted."

The Old Man's hearers settled down. He was talking their language, describing their experiences.

"In the Middle Ages the Jews were despised because it was believed their ancestors had repudiated and executed the Redeemer of mankind. According to the teachings of the Church, we are condemned by the will of God to lead the life of an 'eternal wanderer' with the mark of Cain on his forehead.

"In the course of time, as the Renaissance and Enlightenment weakened the authority of the Church, the medieval religious theory became untenable, but the feeling itself survived. The growth of economic and cultural influence in the nineteenth century intensified Jew-hatred. Anti-Semitism, which soon spread to most countries of the Diaspora, had manifold and disastrous effects: in Eastern Europe bloodthirsty pogroms, in Western Europe a vigorous social, cultural and political campaign against the Jews.

"What has anti-Semitism done to us? It has robbed us of our nearest and dearest. But more. It has plunged us into a state of degradation from which nothing will rescue us except the dignity of independence on our own land."

The cheers were deafening. This was Zionist passion in its pristine beginning, before the emergence of a Jewish state rendered it a conventional assumption. The Old Man continued, buoyed by the applause.

"We have a land, a small strip of territory from which we were expelled two thousand years ago but which we have never let go. The intrinsic connection between the Jewish people and Palestine has never been broken. The enduring attachment of the Jews to their ancient homeland is one of the most remarkable facts of history. Jews have neither forgotten the land of Israel nor ceased to look forward to their return to it. Every Passover, at our feast of freedom, every Yom Kippur as we end the fast, we give voice to our yearning and aspiration: *'L'shonoh habo'o b'yerusholayim.'* 'Next year in Jerusalem.' "

The audience took it up as a chant. On and on it rose like a wave. Osovsky let it roll for a while, then held up his hand and a hush ensued.

"There are those who say that other lands would do just as well, Uganda or perhaps an island off the coast of Africa, or maybe, as one British politician has suggested, Egypt. Surely we don't want to go back to Egypt. We've been there before." How the audience roared and clapped at that!

"No, Palestine, the land of Israel, and only Palestine is ours."

The cheers rose again, but this time the Old Man let them go on until they subsided. Then he proceeded to give a remarkable summary of three thousand years of Jewish history, telescoping the centuries, showing how the Jews had defeated time in their tenacious devotion to and yearning for the land of their fathers. Always they had proclaimed: "If I forget thee, O Jerusalem, let my right hand wither."

"We have an historic claim to Palestine," he shouted to cheers.

"There are those who deny historic rights to a land because geo-
graphical and political conditions of the past are not in themselves
sufficient ground for a national claim under entirely different circumstances today. I concede there is no reason why old frontiers
should be restored simply because they existed centuries ago. Wars
of conquest and territorial annexation by reference to historic
rights are vain and invalid."

The Old Man was repeating the conventional wisdom of those
days. This was more than four decades before the Six Day War of
1967, when the state of Israel conquered the West Bank and later
retained it on the grounds of historic right. In the 1920s, however,
Zionists argued that the Jews did not come into Palestine as conquerors but as inheritors of the prophetic tradition and the representatives of the civilized West bringing blessings to the under-
developed Near East.

Thus he went on: "We are not in Palestine because a certain area
was once part of our distinct national territory but because of the
abiding spiritual connection between us and our historic homeland. Real historic right comes not from a mere external event or
from a factual situation belonging to the past but from historically
significant cultural achievements that become permanent factors
of national life. Only creative activity is the real source of right
either for an individual or for a social group or for a national community. We have a just connection with Palestine because we are a
creative factor in it, a permanent element of economic, cultural
and spiritual development in the history of the country."

The Old Man arrived at his peroration: "The word Zion has
three meanings. First, it denotes the strong citadel of Jerusalem
stormed by King David. It is also used as a poetic name for Jerusalem, the Temple and for the whole of the Holy Land. Finally, it
is the symbol of the Jewish past and future, associated with the
most precious memories and sacred hopes of our nation, with its
religious ideals and messianic aspirations.

"Let us make real the three meanings. In our devotion to Zion,
let us render the *Yishuv* a strong citadel, able to defend itself
against all foes. Let us lay the foundations of a modern national
culture upon which the classic Jewish genius can develop. This we
can do through the Hebrew University. Finally, let us break the
last fetters of our spiritual ghetto and turn our face to the world as
once again we send out prophets and sages to beat swords into
ploughshares and teach humanity itself the ways of peace and
justice."

The audience was delirious. A group of young men stormed the platform, raised the Old Man shoulder high and carried him into the street singing: "We will go up to our land with song and joy."

Osovsky had delivered the kind of speech that appealed to every brand of Zionism—Labour on the left, General in the middle and Revisionist on the right. Though he carried the label of General Zionist, he inclined toward the maximalist position of Vladimir Jabotinsky, founder of the Revisionist party. In 1917 Jabotinsky had organized the Jewish battalions that took part in the conquest of Palestine under General Allenby. A call went out for Jewish volunteers of the Diaspora to join Jabotinsky's legion. In Winnipeg the Old Man had beaten the drum for enlistments. His oldest son Sam had answered the call, as did my oldest brother Maurice. My parents were incensed that a lad of barely eighteen should have been induced to fight thousands of miles away. They blamed Osovsky for influencing him to embark on what they considered a dangerous and futile adventure—all this years before the Old Man became superintendent of the Orphanage.

While his Zionism had shifted somewhat to the centre as World War I receded into history, he retained his admiration for Jabotinsky, who was later to number among his followers an Irgun extremist by the name of Menachem Begin.

The man who understood Osovsky's Zionism best was Moreh who openly disagreed with his "boss." Moreh was a follower of Ahad Ha'am, vigorous opponent of Theodor Herzl's political philosophy and spiritual leader of the "Lovers of Zion." I was once treated to a passionate debate between my two mentors. As I recall this debate, it is startling to realize that almost sixty years later their arguments have not been resolved. Even the reality of the Jewish state has not lessened the dialectics between ethnic Zionists, represented by Osovsky, and spiritual Zionists, typified by Frankel. The debate occurred during the Talmud class when the Old Man came to inspect. Moreh was explaining a passage in connection with ownership of real estate in ancient Judea. The discussion excited the Old Man who drew our attention to the question of possession of land in modern Palestine.

This prompted a question from me: "In your speech at the Talmud Torah, Mr. Osovsky, you hardly mentioned the Arabs. What about their rights to the land?" I had heard Moreh wonder aloud why the Arabs were practically ignored.

The Old Man looked down at the back of his hands spread like spiders on the desk where he was sitting. "The Arabs figure very little in the history of Palestine," he replied. "In the twelve centuries after the Arab conquest Palestine virtually dropped out of history. It made no contribution to the realm of thought in science or in literature. It occupied a marginal place in the world as the modern age dawned. The country was almost derelict as World War I broke out. The Arab population eked out a precarious existence mainly in the hills."

Moreh intervened in a quiet voice: "Yet at the end of the nineteenth century Palestine had about two hundred thousand inhabitants, of whom only some forty thousand were Jews. The Arabs were there. Surely we can't behave as if they didn't exist?"

"But at the end of the nineteenth century," countered the Old Man, "the Arab population was in decline. Things have changed radically with Jewish mass immigration and colonization in the twentieth century. In twenty-five years the population has steadily increased, all due to the efforts of the Jews who are now counted in the hundreds of thousands."

The argument was now well launched. Dave, Georgie and I looked at one another, uncertain how to react. We were entangled in the emotions of two grown-ups, our teachers, who seemed to have forgotten our presence.

"You're discounting a fact," said Moreh to the Old Man. "Poor and neglected though it was, to Arabs who lived in it Palestine was still their country, their home, the land in which their people had lived for centuries and where they left their graves. We have rights, but so do they."

Moreh supported the movement known as *Ihud* (Unity) which advocated a bi-national state for Arabs and Jews in Palestine. To the Old Man *Ihud* was anathema. Mention of rights for Arabs agitated him. His smile at Moreh was a bland insult.

"Arabs deny us our rights," he said defensively. "Arab opposition to Zionism did not exist before the First World War. Let me remind you that the Arab representatives at the peace conference accepted the Balfour Declaration. One of them, Feisal, later King Feisal, entered into an agreement with Chaim Weizmann in January 1919 concerning relations between the future Arab state and Jewish Palestine. It pledged the parties to the fulfilment of the Declaration, to cordial co-operation between the two peoples and to the encouragement of immigration of Jews into Palestine on a large scale. Then the Arab representatives changed their minds.

Why? Because they were jealous of the rapid progress of Jewish colonization. Jealousy and the perfidy of the British Colonial Office have been working against us. The British were wrong to deny the Revisionists the restoration of the Jewish Legion in Palestine. It's time to transform our defensive Zionist policy to an offensive one. The ultimate aim of Zionism must openly be proclaimed as the creation of a Jewish state with a Jewish majority within the historic boundaries of Palestine, that is, on both sides of the Jordan River."

Moreh was shocked. The Old Man had always given himself out as a moderate, and here he was spouting pure Revisionism. The Balfour Declaration had pointed to a home for the Jews in Palestine, but only Jabotinsky saw statehood as an immediate feature of nationality.

Suddenly Moreh became aware of his three students. "Perhaps we should continue this discussion at some other time, Mr. Osovsky," he said. "The boys seem bewildered by our disagreement."

"No," said the Old Man to his everlasting credit, "let them know early that Jews have never agreed, nor do they agree today, about the wisest course to ensure our future. Let them be exposed to differing opinions. Judaism isn't a faith like Roman Catholicism where the shepherd issues the dogma for the sheep. Each has a right to his argument. Let the arguments clash, and the sparks that fall will be the truth."

"I agree," said Moreh. "Well, then, what is all this about a state? And embracing Trans-Jordan yet? The thing that matters most in the life of the Jews is the preservation and unfolding of the inner capacities which are the mainsprings of our cultural creativeness. The essence of our nationality is in the ideas, institutions and habits that constitute our culture. Our ultimate worth is in what we can contribute to the spiritual development of humanity. Statehood in itself is not an essential element of nationality, although it must be considered as an important factor in furthering Jewish unity and strengthening its power of resistance against assimilation. The Jewish problem cannot be dealt with merely by political methods. As Ahad Ha'am said: 'The salvation of Israel will come by prophets not by diplomats.' We must not regard the present colonization of Palestine and the creation of an autonomous Jewish community as ends in themselves. They are simply means for the revival of the national spirit and for its maintenance in the whole of world Jewry."

The Old Man's face reddened. We could always tell when his emotions were bottled up, struggling to get out. He would sputter and stutter. He got up and walked up and down the classroom aisles as he spoke. Moreh also walked up and down the aisles, and it was a miracle they did not collide.

"All this prattling about the national spirit will get us nowhere," said the Old Man angrily. "A nation must be a state or it is an illusion." He stopped pacing and looked hard at Moreh as if at someone who was pitiable and needed help. "And it isn't only for a strong Jewish entity that we need the state. We require it as an instrument against the Arabs. So long as the goal of a state is not attained it is useless to attempt to settle Arab-Jewish differences. Only when a Jewish majority exists in Palestine, only then will mutual understanding between Jews and Arabs be achieved. Even today's colonization can't be successfully carried out except by political means; it needs a strongly centralized political power. You quote Ahad Ha'am. Let me quote Jabotinsky: 'Ninety-nine per cent of all activity is economic and practical, and only one per cent is political, but the one per cent is the beginning of the whole sequence.' "

The three members of the Talmud class—Dave, Georgie and I—looked on in discomfort. I speculated on what the relationship between Moreh and the Old Man would be hereafter. Would Moreh have to leave? I had the feeling in the days that followed that each was trying to win the argument through his influence on us. Osovsky delivered more miniature lectures at mealtimes on events in Palestine, with constant references to the hoped-for Jewish state. Moreh, not so pointedly but nonetheless effectively, sought to give us an understanding of what he meant by the Jewish spirit.

His opportunity came on Tu Bishevat, designated in the Hebrew calendar as Arbour Day. The Zionists of the city prepared for that day with projects for planting trees in Palestine. One enterprising official devised a sales campaign with the slogan: "Buy a tree for an orphan." I was proud, of course, to receive a certificate with my name inserted in the proper line as owner of a tree in the Holy Land. On Tu Bishevat itself, in addition to the awarding of certificates, each orphan was given a paper bag filled with the fruits of Palestine: *boxer* (carob or St. John's bread), figs, dates, nuts, raisins and an orange, a particularly expensive delicacy in winter. The last half hour of the Hebrew class was devoted to the ceremony, the treats and a speech by Moreh. I sensed that he had prepared his talk carefully.

"These fruits and the trees the good people of Winnipeg have planted in our names remind us of the land that has been sacred to us since the time when Abraham settled in Canaan, the soil of Israel. For many centuries, except for the sojourn in Egypt and a brief period in Babylon, the Jews lived and created in that land. Then they were dispersed around the world. During the centuries of exile the unity of the Jews has been maintained by a common faith, a common tradition and a common way of life. This unity was able to withstand the pressure of alien and hostile cultures so long as the Jews lived in political and economic segregation, with a special status of their own."

Moreh cleared his throat, expecting questions, but we were silent, unaccustomed to a formal speech from this man who usually treated us informally. He continued:

"Spiritual bonds linked the Jewish communities of various countries and created a channel of communication and co-operation. The spiritual achievements of one community sooner or later became the property of the whole people. Sometimes the Jewry of a certain country became for a while a spiritual centre, radiating its light all over the Diaspora. Persia and Babylonia were such centres from the third to the ninth centuries; Spain from the tenth to the thirteenth centuries; France, Germany and Poland in the latter half of the Middle Ages."

Moreh's voice was even and vibrant. He did not have the fervour of the Old Man, but he did possess warmth and a gentle conviction. The Old Man impressed us when he spoke; Frankel embraced us.

"In the late eighteenth century," said Moreh, changing his tone, "a change took place in the status of the Jews of Western Europe. They were emancipated. The gates of the ghettoes were opened, and the Jews were admitted into the societies around them. With closer ties to non-Jews many Jews were assimilated into non-Jewish culture. In Eastern Europe, however, intolerance and persecution counteracted emancipation and slowed the process of assimilation. This difference between East and West created a gulf between the old-fashioned and modern Jew and caused a disruption in the cultural unity of the Jewish communities."

I interrupted: "Is that the way things are now?"

Moreh smiled. At last he had elicited a question. "Yes, that is the present predicament of Judaism. Today, in the advanced year of 1926, only one thing can unite world Jewry—the land of Israel. An autonomous Jewish community in Palestine will be able to give new expression to the essential characteristics of Jewish culture, our literature, philosophy, law and religion. Thus will the Palestine community become the heart of a rejuvenated Judaism and a centre of inspiration for all the other Jewish communities. But that is not all. . ."

Moreh held up his hand like a traffic policeman. It was his way of indicating that he was coming to the final point, the ultimate lesson. "The Zionist spiritual hope, proclaimed by Ahad Ha'am, is not confined to the Jewish nation alone. It is set upon a wider, universal ideal. Zionism is not an end in itself. Jewish nationalism is only a means. The homeland will radiate spiritual influences both to the Jews outside and gradually to the world at large. For what is good for the world is good for the Jews, not what is good for the Jews is good for the world. From Palestine ethical and religious gifts, in the broadest sense of those two words, will be given to all humanity for its enrichment and purification."

We applauded Moreh, an unusual occurrence in the classroom, but this was a holiday. Moreh smiled. Whether he had succeeded in defining his opposition to the Old Man's viewpoint, with its emphasis on the creation of a Jewish state as soon as possible, was questionable. We were drawn to Moreh's argument primarily because of his gentler behaviour toward us. When he administered punishment, it was never, as was the case with the Old Man, a savage beating. I sensed as never before a decided difference between the two men. The Old Man stressed power and force. Moreh believed in the inevitable victory of the spirit and intellect. Who was the more authentic Jew? Who the realist and who the dreamer?

The Old Man, of course, looked upon Moreh as a naive romantic. Historical evolution, according to Osovsky, obeys its own laws and depends upon social and political realities. One does not "wish" for mass migration; it is determined by economic motives. The successful colonization of a barren and derelict country by a tiny people, politically divided and dispersed across the world, needs power and the force of an army to back it.

But for Moreh the sceptic was the dreamer, recognizing nothing but tangible facts and refusing to acknowledge the effectiveness with which common aspirations had kept the Jew alive and helped him outlive all the power centres of four thousand years—Egypt, Assyria, Babylonia, Persia, Greece, Rome and the Ottoman Empire.

History proved both men to be wrong . . . and right. The Old Man's state had to be trimmed. Jordan and the West Bank were surrendered for the sake of independence, but an abbreviated state did materialize. Moreh's patient conviction that cultural values would ultimately produce the political structure did not come to pass. Force and power exploded, and the free and independent state of Israel emerged, in 1948, through war and bloodshed.

Yet Moreh was right. A state can come into the world through force, but it cannot maintain itself on power alone. Spiritual values must come into play. Exclusive, selfish and aggressive nationalism does not work. Democratic nationalism, based on the idea of a free humanity, must be the foundation of a state if it is to live. A just solution of Arab-Jewish differences and the fruitful collaboration of both peoples are necessary conditions for the healthy development of today's Israel and the whole of the Middle East.

Zionist policy in the 1980s must follow Moreh as a disciple of Ahad Ha'am. The settlement of Arab-Jewish differences requires appreciation of the claims and needs of both the Jewish and the Arab nations. The right of the Jews to possess what was once called Palestine as its national homeland is clear. But Moreh's insight is irrefutable. The Arabs cannot be ignored.

Many Zionists today argue, as did Osovsky in the 1920s, that the Muslims and Christians speaking Arabic who lay claim to Palestine cannot be considered as a distinct nation with a historical heritage of their own. Furthermore, it is said the Arabs cannot point to any economic or cultural achievements that closely link their history to the history of Palestine, since the country had remained almost a desert for hundreds of years until the beginning of Jewish resettlement at the end of the nineteenth century.

The fact is that the economic contribution of the Arabs to Palestine has traditionally been underestimated. Palestine had always been an important producer of key agricultural commodities and was in the midst of a significant expansion of agriculture and allied manufactured goods at least two generations before the arrival of the first Jewish settlers from Eastern Europe. Throughout the sixteenth, seventeenth and eighteenth centuries, substantial shipments of cotton and grain had been exported from·the ports of Sidon and Acre by European merchants residing in the area.

The rights and vital needs of both the Jewish and Arab peoples must be compared and weighed in relation to each other. Stirrings of modern national identity came to both peoples at about the same time in history. Justice must be done to permanent and vital national interests on both sides. It must be based neither on the one-sided view of a selfish nationalism, nor on considerations of political opportunism; neither on the present balance of power in international relations, nor on an imperialistic policy of domination by one side or the other. It can be achieved neither by mere violence nor by methods of appeasement which disregard the demands of justice, but only on the basis of impartial and equitable judgment.

Moreh, in his devotion to Ahad Ha'am, encompassed such considerations. The Old Man, in his adherence to the philosophy of Jabotinsky, did not. Ah, Moreh, that thy spirit might prevail!

X

Israelites

The Old Man loved to write and direct plays, and he had a ready-made pool of actors to draw from, the orphans. A play served two purposes. It provided constructive activity for the inmates of the Home and created another channel of communication with the community. The orphans had communal connections in several fields. Distinguished guests, writers and poets on speaking tours, would visit the Hebrew classes and listen to our declamations. The choir sang for famous visiting American cantors. The Orphanage band played for civic affairs. As if all this were insufficient, we were also in a constant series of rehearsals for the legitimate stage.

The local Yiddish repertory company, which performed at the Queen's Theatre on Selkirk Avenue near Main Street, turned to the Home when in need of a child to fill a role. I once played the boy in a presentation of *Akedas Yitzhok (The Binding of Isaac)*, in which the Shumsky husband and wife team, the repertory stars, were Abraham and Sarah. Old Man Osovsky kept me up hours past the bedtime bell for weeks prior to the performance until my lines were not only letter perfect but adorned with the proper inflection. The Shumskys were ecstatic over his insights and suggestions, considering him a dramatist of high order. I do not recall receiving any remuneration for my performance, but no doubt a contribution was made to the Home's treasury. The Shumskys belonged to the florid school of acting. The voice had to be sonorous and cadenced. Electronic devices have considerably changed acting styles since those days, but there were advantages without them. Vocal clarity and good habits in enunciation and projection were imperative.

Under sponsorship of the local Zionist organization Osovsky wrote and directed a play, called *The Penny Comes To Life*, about a little boy who dropped a coin in the Jewish National Fund box for the purchase of land in Palestine. He dreamed that the copper sprang to life and guided him through the Holy Land, showing him the accomplishments of the Jewish pioneers. Again I played the boy with Madam Shumsky as my mother.

Sometimes we presented plays on our own without the aid of Osovsky, but they did not attract communal audiences because they were in English. Osovsky's Yiddish dramas drew the masses. For Winnipeg Jews *mameh-loshen*, though not as sacred as Hebrew, was like a pair of old slippers, relaxing. They flocked to the Queen's Theatre for that reason.

In my ninth year, when I first entered the Home, Yiddish had no appeal for me. I had to speak it to communicate with my mother and when I appeared in the Old Man's dramas, but I was uncomfortable with what seemed to me its alien sing-song. Hebrew, I thought, was far more dignified. It was not only the language of the Bible, sacred to the Jews, but of prayer, of Jewish literature after the Bible and of Jewish scholars everywhere. The essential character of Hebrew, like that of the Jewish people, Moreh said, is unique, having remained unchanged for millenia. It bears the majesty of the ages. How could that upstart Yiddish compare with the antiquity and authority of *Ivris*? Moreh, who spoke Yiddish with great care and enthusiasm, conceded it was a "bastard" language with a hybrid vocabulary and a non-existent grammar and syntax. Even the Yiddishists themselves called it a "jargon" with emphasis on the last syllable. The Hebraists, including Moreh, although they loved it, viewed it as uncivilized cant.

I found Yiddish expressions exaggerated and extreme, although I used them liberally. Yiddish, I thought, was much too adept at name-calling. My mother had at least nine denominations for a simpleton: *nebech*, *Chaim Yankel* (lummox), *kuni lemmel* (dunderhead), *shlemiel* (a fellow who spills coffee on somebody else's pants), *shlimazel* (the fellow who got his pants wet), *shmendrik* (thick-wit), *shnook* (moron), *klotz* (dolt) and *yold* (imbecile). With the exception of *nebech*, these terms seemed needlessly acerbic, out of character with what Jews were supposed to be. Mother and Miss Rose, both kindly souls, did not hesitate to hurl these epithets at any child who displeased them. Sometimes a blow would have been preferable.

To hear the Yiddishists of the 1920s tell it, any Jew who did not speak *mameh-loshen* was a *goy*, a Gentile in a pejorative sense. They seemed to be unaware that masses of Jews, the Sephardim of

Arab countries, for example, had never heard a Yiddish word. Many Near Eastern Jews speak Ladino, a form of Spanish written in Hebrew characters, as Yiddish is a form of German written in Hebrew characters. In those days a *kultur-kampf* raged in Palestine between the Hebraists and Yiddishists, the latter maintaining that their language should be given official recognition. A story of the time told of a little boy on a Tel Aviv bus speaking Hebrew to his grandmother. She answered in Yiddish. So it went for some time, the boy and his Hebrew, the grandmother and her Yiddish. Another passenger remonstrated with the old woman: "Why don't you answer him in Hebrew?" "Because," she replied, "I don't want him to forget he is a Jew." In Winnipeg, Judaism and Yiddish were almost synonymous, as they must have been to millions of other Yiddish-speaking Jews of the U.S., Europe, South America, South Africa and Australia.

One cannot be neutral about Yiddish. One either despises it or has a passion for it. The devotees seem to find in it all that is holy. As the history of the Jews goes, it came late, only about seven hundred years ago. Jews who settled in the Rhineland and spoke Hebrew, Old French and the German dialects were invited into Poland to fill the hiatus between the nobility and the serfs as traders and entrepreneurs. They found Jews there who had migrated on their own and spoke Slavic. Though the Polish Jews absorbed the Germanic Jews, the former adopted the latter's language. Yiddish, as the language of tradesmen, became an amalgam of German, Hebrew, Polish, Czech, Russian, Old French and Old Italian. The linguistic mélange struck out on its own, abandoning German structure, pronunciation, grammar and spelling, and developed its own character. Women seized on it, since they were denied the formal Talmudic and Hebraic education reserved for men.

Thus Yiddish became *mameh-loshen* with a vengeance. Its temperament was further fashioned by the persecutions that flowed from the Black Death, the Crusades and the ghettoes established by the Lateran Councils of the twelfth and thirteenth centuries. Yiddish became the language of Jewish misery, an undaunted anguish that enabled the Jew to laugh at himself in spite of oppression. It helped to preserve his humanity.

It was when I discovered Mendele Mocher Seforim (Mendele the Book Peddler), the pseudonym of Sholem Jacob Abromovitch who was born in the Lithuanian town of Koplyn in the 1820s, that I fell in love with Yiddish. I heard Mendele's stories first when they were read by Harry Steinberg, the overalls manufacturer, Orphanage supporter and public declaimer extraordinary.

Steinberg carried copies of Sholom Aleichem and Mendele on his person and would whip them out if anyone showed the least sign of interest. After one of his performances I asked him where I could get a copy of Mendele's works. Steinberg became "broader than longer," as the Yiddish saying goes. His brush moustache quivered with emotion as he reached into his side pocket.

"Here, take this, *Dos Klayneh Menschele (The Little Man)*, meanwhile, and I'll bring you others." He was as good as his word. Each time he came to a meeting he would ask for me and hand me a volume, until the Old Man cautioned him to let up.

Mendele taught me that Yiddish was the language of Jewish pain, poverty and compassion. It was when I read him that I began to understand why those who laboured for the Orphanage loved his language. It was the only medium that could express their pity for the living.

When Mendele wrote, the fortunes of the Jews had hit rock bottom. They were weighed down by so many repressions that one wonders how they ever subsisted. They were forbidden to buy land and prohibited from joining artisan and merchant guilds. How did they make a living? Perhaps, as my father used to say of his own Russo-Polish town of Slonim, "The shoemaker lived off the tailor who lived off the carpenter who lived off the candle-maker—and the *yeshivah* student lived off all of them."

As the nineteenth century wore on, the condition of the Jews, which was never any good, turned worse. In Russia Czar Nicholas II tried to solve the Jewish problem through a process of Russification. He imposed conscription laws which forced ten Jews out of every thousand into the army for a thirty-year period starting at the age of twelve. Children were torn from their parents and transported thousands of miles. Forced baptisms were common.

The dislocation was not confined to children. Their parents were constantly being driven from areas designated as forbidden to Jews and resettled in other regions. The misery of the Russian peasant was proverbial, but at least he had his black bread and cabbages. The Jews had their gnawing hunger.

They were oppressed by the government, the feudal lords and, as a bonus, their own Jewish bureaucracy, the *kahal*, which performed the government's dirty work, collecting its taxes and piling on Jewish taxes for every communal activity. *Kahal* officials, like bureaucrats universally, could also be unscrupulous and corrupt, favouring the children of the rich who were excused from military service and kidnapping orphans and sons of the poor to fill the Czar's quotas.

Poor in material things, the children of Abraham were nevertheless rich in societies. Charitable organizations flourished, in Mendele's phrase, as weeds on a dung-heap. There were societies for burying the dead, visiting the sick, educating the children and supervising kosher food. They were all supported through kopeks from the masses.

This was the soil in which Yiddish grew. It was the language of the oppressed and the miserable, who are constantly asking questions but rarely get answers. That is why Yiddish puts more stress on the question than the answer. The Jew is forever asking: *Vos iz de hochmeh?* "What is the catch?"

While Yiddish grew in an atmosphere of submission, it compensated by exhibiting *hutzpah*, which English critic Kenneth Tynan defined as "cool nerve and outrageous effrontery combined," and the late Dorothy Thompson interpreted as referring to a man who shoots his mother and father and pleads clemency on the grounds that he is an orphan.

In no other language, said the Old Man, could sadness be so eloquently rendered. How else could a descendant of the patriarchs groan except by uttering "Oy!" Yiddish was a kind of refuge for the Old Man. He used to say: "What you're embarrassed to say in Yiddish, you say in Hebrew." Hebrew is a language only *in extremis*. It is Yiddish to which you turn for comfort and solace.

The Old Man contended that a whole pattern of Jewish traditional values was transmitted through his beloved Yiddish. Countless learned phrases seeped into the language from classical Hebrew texts and scholarly commentaries. In Yiddish the phrase *mer shochtim vi hiner* (more ritual slaughterers than chickens) expressed the idea of more chiefs than Indians. According to Talmudic legend, the entire people of Israel, past as well as future, witnessed the giving of the Torah, and someone short on Jewish loyalty is considered as "coming late to Mount Sinai." Sharp contrasts, such as Mutt and Jeff or Laurel and Hardy, are denoted as *shabes hagodl un kurtz freitik*, the Great Sabbath (in the spring before Passover) and the short Friday of mid-winter. A half-hearted refusal is indicated by the phrase *vayemo'en mit a shalshelet*. It is based on the Biblical exchange between Potiphar's

wife and Joseph in Genesis 39: "She said, 'Lie with me,' but he
refused." The last word, "but he refused," is marked by a *shalshelet*, the most elaborate of the vocal symbols, which occurs in-
frequently in the Five Books of Moses. Joseph apparently gave an
ornamented musical response to indicate his inner turmoil, the
clash of sexual desire and moral restraint. Hence, a half-hearted
refusal. Embedded in Yiddish, the Old Man argued, were the millenial tradition and wit of an ancient people.

Yiddish has been a major factor in my attachment to Jews. My
first grounding in it came from my parents before my ninth year.
My mother's speech had a Russian inflection—she was born in
Yekaterinislav; my father's a Lithuanian one, the kind spoken in
the *yeshivos*, the academies. When I went to the *yeshivah* in
Chicago in my fourteenth year, the Lithuanian character of my
Yiddish deepened. Osovsky was a Russian Jew, but his Yiddish
was adorned by the poetic garb of the great nineteenth-century
writers. I had never heard Yiddish spoken with such grace until the
Old Man came into my life.

Before I heard him I felt it was unworthy to be considered a
language of the Jews. How could this foundling, this patois, this
grammarless gibberish, this language of the despised and the dis-
possessed be compared to Hebrew or even to English? But through
his plays and speeches the Old Man made a boy understand that in
Yiddish the Jew could laugh at his misery, defy his pain, acclaim
his Torah and rise to indomitable faith.

The Old Man set out to prove all this in his *magnum opus, Dor
Hamidbor (The Generation of the Wilderness)*, a play about the
Israelites in the Sinai desert, about Moses, Aaron and the golden
calf.

The Old Man saw the sin of the golden calf as the perpetual
problem of the Jews, always hankering after strange gods, always
yearning for the fleshpots of other peoples, imitating their ways,
bowing down to their idols. The calf of gold symbolized the inclination to assimilation which plagued the Jews in every generation.
The Old Man accepted literally the Talmudic commentary that
through the worship of the golden calf the Israelites had lost the
gift of everlasting life, given by God when they accepted the
Torah. "As punishment they were doomed to study the Torah in
suffering and bondage, in exile and unrest, until in the messianic
time God will compensate them for all their sufferings."

This Midrash summed up for the Old Man his philosophy of history and the meaning of Jewish suffering. No medium could convey these things better than Yiddish, the language of misery and glory, laughter and tears, despair and hope, submission and unquenchable faith.

Thus the emphasis in the play was not on Moses delivering the Commandments or on the mission of the Jews to mankind, but on the error of the masses. Coupled with this theme was the dilemma of the high priest Aaron. How could he, the brother of Moses, one of the two leaders who had risked their all to bring the Israelites out of bondage, have reverted to paganism?

For answers the Old Man turned again to the Midrash. In their wrath, says the Talmudic allegory, the people threatened Aaron: "If thou wilt make us a god, it is well. If not, we will dispose of thee." Aaron, according to the account, had no fear for his life, but he thought: "If Israel were to commit so terrible a sin as to slay their priest and prophet, God would never forgive them." He was willing rather to take a sin upon himself than to cast the burden of so wicked a deed upon the people. He therefore acceded to their wish to make them a god, but he did it in such a way that the thing might still not come to pass: he demanded from them not their own ornaments for the fashioning of the idol, but the ornaments of their wives and children, thinking that the women would refuse to give them up. The women did refuse at first, but the men were so determined that they drew off their own earrings, which they wore in Arab fashion, and gave these to Aaron.

The Old Man made Aaron's inner struggle central to his play. It was with the high priest's monologue that he intended to bring down the house.

One evening, as supper came to a close, the Old Man announced that he would be casting for *Dor Hamidbor*. Practically everybody turned out, even the six-and-seven-year-olds. All nine and under were dismissed, however. Those aged ten and eleven were given minor parts. Georgie Ackerman, while under age, was awarded a major role because of his beautiful singing voice. Though *Dor Hamidbor* was a drama, there was nothing incongruous about breaking into song in the middle of the action. The Shumskys did it all the time at the Queen's Theatre. Even melodrama could tolerate song if it could provide contrast and relieve dramatic tension.

My role was that of Shammua ben Zaccur of the tribe of

Reuben, one of the unsavoury spies who brought evil reports of the land of Canaan to dissuade the people from settling there. Originally the Old Man wanted to give me the fat part of Aaron the high priest, but he was advised against it since I was barely twelve. Although it was planned to fix me with a long white beard, I was thought incapable of simulating an old man's voice. A squeal issuing from a pipsqueak was deemed too incongruous. The part was therefore given to Dorothy, the Old Man's daughter, some years my senior, who was able to sob much more convincingly as she grieved over having to make a hard decision. Nobody seemed to mind that Aaron thus became female.

As Shammua, I filled the function of cheerleader. I seemed to be repeating an incessant line in connection with almost every character in the play: "*Es lebe Aharon hakohen*. Long live Aaron the priest." "*Es lebe Moshe Rabeinu*. Long live Moses our teacher." The refrain seemed endless: "Long live Miriam the prophetess, Caleb the son of Jephunneh, Joshua the son of Nun," and on and on. I was always good for a stopgap in case of a missed cue.

The rehearsals were onerous. The Old Man was worn to a frazzle. Not only did he have to transcribe each part and help the players with their lines but he was his own speech coach, producer, scenic designer, costume designer, overall director and producer.

The day of the dress rehearsal at the Walker Theatre, Winnipeg's foremost legitimate house, he even had to plan the menu for lunch and supper, since we spent all day on stage.

When we broke for lunch, the actors lined up for sandwiches, tea and milk. I had never eaten yellow cheese before and discovered one must develop a taste for it, as for olives. With my mouth full of the unaccustomed viands that stuck to the upper palate, I emitted the expletive, "Rats!" This was too much for the Old Man who grabbed me by the scruff of the neck, then seeing who it was, let go. Suddenly he was contrite, embracing me, fondling me, asking a thousand pardons, quoting a few lines from the Yom Kippur confessional and even shedding a tear. I was embarrassed but knew enough to attribute his over-reaction to his cracked nerves. He was so concerned about the smooth running of the play that he forgot he was the all-powerful and I merely a little cog that would have submitted humbly to a wallop, a slap or a push. So overjoyed was I that the Old Man's hand was laid upon me in a caress rather than a beating that I cried out: "*Es lebe* Aaron Osovsky!"

The Old Man laughed, and this time the tears cascaded down his face in glorious mirth. His confidence was restored.

At the last minute he decided that the band was to play as part of the business of wandering in the wilderness. He had all our instruments transported to the theatre in a truck—the cornets, clarinets, oboes, flutes, piccolos, trombones, French and alto horns, euphoniums, tubas and drums. We were to play them as we marched in our flowing robes and beards, off the stage, up one aisle, down another and on to the stage again. The sound was ragged and patchy since the beard hair got into mouthpieces, the long robes kept tripping us up and we had to pause mounting the stairs to get on and off the stage. Even we understood the huge anachronism of Israelites playing modern instruments and producing a Sousa march. But the Old Man was adamant. We were to display our talents regardless of the un-historicity of trombones.

Opening night arrived. Everybody was nervous and excited except Osovsky. He seemed to have developed nerves of steel. He answered a myriad questions calmly and clearly. He examined all the props, the costumes and stage positions and stationed himself strategically in the wings with the script firmly in his hand.

The curtain rises and the play proceeds smoothly. Everyone knows his lines and machine-guns them at the audience. The Israelites complain that Moses is tarrying on the mountain. A discussion arises between two factions. Moses has vanished and will not return, say some. O ye of little faith, say others. Moses has retired to bring the most sacred code of law known to man, a code that could bring peace, justice and prosperity to humankind.

The scene shifts and a sub-plot involving twelve spies takes over. Ten of the spies stand against the other two, the pious Joshua and Caleb. As they argue I cheer the disputants. First, *"Es lebe Palti ben Raphu."* Then, *"Es lebe Yehoshua bin Nun."* Back to: *"Es lebe Gaddiel ben Sodi."* Finally, "Long live Yigal ben Joseph." Each cheer is punctuated by the roar of the mob: *"Hedad, hedad."* "Hurrah, hurrah." The issue is not resolved. In the midst of the rebellion and confusion Georgie Ackerman comes out of the wings to sing, *"Die velt is ful mit soides.* The world is filled with mystery." It seems an appropriate song, since all is confusion anyway. The audience applauds with much gusto.

Again a shift of scene. Aaron is besieged by the Israelites to fashion a calf of gold. He (that is, she) argues. He gets an argument in return. The people threaten him. He steps to stage front. The curtain falls behind him, and Aaron drops to his knees to deliver his anguished monologue:

"Why do you put upon me this burden, O Lord? This is your world and you can take care of it. Why roll on me the responsibility of this insane business? I am tired and cynical and out of heart and want to rest. . . . The Lord God, merciful and gracious, long-suffering and abundant in goodness and truth. . . Thou who art Father and Lord, forgive me for what I must do!"

The curtain opens again, and the climactic scene unfolds. The children of Israel are stripping their bracelets, earrings and rings and dropping them into a great tub. There is tumult, shouting and singing. Half-sorrowfully Aaron orders two men to lift the gold and silver and carry the collection out to the wings. The dancing and singing intensify. The people call for their god: "*Egel hazohov!* The golden calf!" At this point several Israelites are to pull the idol by a rope on to the stage. It is stuck. With a great heave-ho it comes unstuck, but instead of head first it emerges rear-end forward. We heave again. It is impossible to turn the figure around.

The Old Man's dispassion cracks. He shouts at me from the wings: "Reuben, start cheering." I cry: "*Es lebe Moshe Rabeinu!*"

"*Hedad!*" shout the Israelites.

"*Es lebe Yehoshua bin Nun!*"

"*Hedad!*"

"*Es lebe Caleb ben Yephunneh!*"

Again, "*Hedad!*"

I am running out of heroes and have to start on the villains.

"*Es lebe Nahbi ben Vophsi!*"

"*Hedad!*"

"*Es lebe Shaphat ben Hori!*" Now I am running out of villains. The idol still will not budge. Aaron's son Elazar must lower his head and kiss its forehead, but the head is far from him and he can't get near it because of the crush of traffic. Resignedly he bends and plants a kiss. Let it fall where it may.

"Look," hisses Lobey Harris, one of the Israelites, in a stage whisper, "he's kissing the cow's ass."

The actors stop dead in their tracks. The audience is in paralysis. Suddenly a titter sounds at the rear of the balcony. It is answered by a giggle in the orchestra. An antiphony of cachinnation is heard. Sniggers become cackles. Chortles grow into guffaws. The audience roars, screams and finally shrieks. At last the very intensity of the convulsion induces its own reaction. Hushing and shushing take over. An irrepressible quiet reigns. But it is not to last long. The play continues, punctuated by chuckles and titters and an occasional whoop until it comes mercifully to a close.

In its weekly edition the Israelite Press began its review of *Dor Hamidbor*: "Last Sunday evening children of the Jewish Orphanage presented a unique version of the wandering Israelites in the wilderness." Unique was the right word.

The lead paragraph was tongue in cheek, under necessity of having to recognize the imperfections of the presentation. But then the writer switched to praise of the Old Man as a teacher of history. He had brought the twelfth century B.C. into the twentieth and made it real. He had bridged the millenia, had demonstrated the undying quality of a spiritual heritage.

Apart from the side benefit of getting accustomed to facing an audience, Osovsky's plays gave me a sense of history. I relived the lives of my forefathers. Wilderness bedouins, judges in Canaan, kings of Israel, exiles in Babylon, Maccabees, Talmudic scholars, Rashi, Judah Halevi, Maimonides, the false messiahs Shabbetai Zvi and Jacob Frank, the sixteenth-century redactors of the law, the Hasidic Baal Shem Tov, the Gaon of Vilno and the Zionist Herzl—they were far more real to me than Mackenzie King and Calvin Coolidge or even Charles Lindbergh who, in my last year at the Orphanage, flew the Atlantic. It was this sense of the past that enabled me to feel the Jewish momentum, the pulse of the eternal Jew.

Today much of this perspective has disappeared from the Jewish community. Too many Jews have been trapped into seeing the Holocaust of World War II and the subsequent establishment of the state of Israel as the central events of post-Biblical Judaism. They make the mistake, an understandable but tragic one, of magnifying events of their own time into the be-all and end-all of Jewish existence. Often the Holocaust theme intrudes into other areas of Jewish life so as to crowd out factors and meanings that make for survival.

In the past Jews were able to consider the episodes of the moment in the light of an overall view. Heinrich Graetz, the nineteenth-century historian and the first to undertake a critical study of the Jewish past, stresses in his eleven-volume history two basic themes: martyrdom *and* ideas. It is one thing to look at the history of the Jews as a record of martyrdom and another as a history of ideas.

To look at suffering alone is to see only the external. Graetz believed that inner history, i.e. the history of thought and ideas, needs to be studied on the same level. To keep emphasizing the Holocaust without stressing the second theme is to view Jewish history lopsidedly. The contemporary historian Salo Baron has termed this approach "the lachrymose view of Jewish history."

People like Elie Wiesel, the poet of the concentration camps, continue to predict another Holocaust, which is understandable because of an obsession with the trauma of experience in the Nazi death factories. But Jews must refrain from using the argument of the Holocaust to justify whatever they may do. Nahum Goldmann, late president of the World Jewish Congress and the World Zionist Organization, said that to use that argument "as an excuse for bombing the Lebanon, for instance, as Menachem Begin does, is a kind of *hillul hashem*, a banalization of the Holocaust, which must not be misused to justify politically doubtful and morally indefensible policies."

I concede that the Nazi Holocaust was unique in character, since it was an attempt at genocide without benefit to the perpetrators, pursued with scientific efficiency strictly out of hatred for the victims. The Holocaust has no parallel even in the unspeakable treatment of other victims of the Nazis; no parallel in Hiroshima, Wounded Knee or My Lai, where the circumstances and intentions of the perpetrators were different in kind as well as degree. It is important to confront the Holocaust as a warning that it is possible for human beings to drain out of themselves every ounce of pity for the living. There is much to be said for the contention that the Holocaust shows the bankruptcy of Western culture, that in the words of Wiesel, "at Auschwitz not only man died but also the idea of man," the conception of man in Western humanistic tradition.

Yet even in the face of this unencompassable calamity it is necessary to recognize that every brand of persecution was unique. When in 1648 Chmelnicki's Cossacks ripped open the bellies of Jewish women, placed live cats inside and sewed them up again, that was unique. When at the destruction of the second Temple one-third of the three million Jews were slaughtered, another million enslaved and the remainder exiled, that was unique. At least the Holocaust of our century, enormous in its savagery, still left ten million Jews alive in affluent lands.

In every generation the Jews have suffered, and each experience had something terribly different about it. Without perspective we are without reason, and without reason we are lost. We are then driven to think of the six million in Hitler's time as going to their deaths passively. This arouses extreme reaction—slogans of "never again"—leading to immoderate behaviour on all matters affecting Jewish security. It is not true that the Jews went to their deaths as meek lambs. That maligns the men and women of Minsk, Vilno, Bialistok and numerous smaller ghettoes, as well as the Jews of Warsaw, the countless thousands who fought with the Partisans, those with great spiritual courage who risked their lives to observe the ancient traditions even in the camps and bore themselves with dignity, refusing to imitate their oppressors.

We ought to make special efforts to present the Holocaust with a sense of history and not simply as protest. As the Holocaust of the sixth century B.C. produced the synagogue and the Bible and the one in the first century resulted in the Talmud and the traditional Jewish school, so we must strive to build out of the destruction of European Jewish communities in our century a spiritual power that will overcome the temptation toward requiting violence with violence. The purpose of Jewish existence is not to fight enemies or to support the government of Israel at all cost. It is to reduce suffering in the world.

Some Jews—Elie Wiesel, Manes Sperber, Arnold Schoenberg and others—have reacted to the Holocaust with pride in the heroism and dignity of the victims. Some have responded in mournful affliction. But too many Jews today recoil only in shame and wrath. The phrases that invariably return in conversation are: "We were exterminated like vermin. They killed us like rats. Never again!" Too many stand in Yad Vashem, the Jerusalem memorial museum to the six million, with clenched fists and spiteful faces. Shame and wrath are surely understandable, even respectable. But they themselves are inveterate killers. They keep renewing themselves to become collective vindictiveness handed down from one generation to the next. Only the spiritual rebound—tears of compassion, a pity for the living and the will not to imitate the persecutors—only the spirit becomes part of the great tradition.

Thus a sense of history argues against a short-sighted view of tragic events and for perspective. I am one of the lucky Jews of my time, in part through Osovsky's plays, which bound past and present into one continuous vista. In the Orphanage I was taught to see tragedy, pain and persecution in historical and spiritual terms, as part of the upward human struggle toward justice and peace.

XI

Bar-mitzvah

It was Moreh Frankel's responsibility to prepare the orphans for bar-mitzvah, a task not entirely to his liking. He was fond of his students and loved his craft, but he was not enamoured of the bar-mitzvah ceremony. In the Talmud, he said, bar-mitzvah is simply a description applied to every grown Israelite and refers to the age of responsibility in religious matters with no ceremony or institution in mind.

Bar-mitzvah, as an institution, is only about six hundred years old, said Moreh, and its recent origin made it suspect, especially so since by the 1920s it had degenerated into a parrot-like recitation that had no connection with a boy's previous training or his post-bar-mitzvah studies. Moreh recalled that when he was bar-mitzvah, as a student at an East European *yeshivah*, he was simply called to the Torah on a Monday morning without a party or any other fuss. He became aware at that moment that he was a "son of a commandment," which is what bar-mitzvah means, and was expected to assume responsibility for six hundred and twelve additional commandments. Bar-mitzvah for him meant a lifetime devotion to the precepts and practices of Judaism.

In the 1920s bar-mitzvah had already become more "bar" than *mitzvah*, more partying than studying. A boy of twelve memorized the blessings over the Torah, rehearsed a portion from the Prophets and recited a set speech. Moreh used to parody the typical speech to demonstrate what it should not be:

"My dear parents, relatives and friends! I want to thank you for all you have taught me, that I might live intelligently as a Jew and as a Canadian. May you be granted long life, prosperity and peace. I pray that I may be granted understanding that I may ever be a devoted son, loyal to my people, my community and my country. May God send blessings upon our beloved rabbi, my teachers, the officers and members of this congregation and all who are gathered here to honour me and share the joy of this occasion with me and my family. Amen!"

All fine sentiments, said Moreh, but as superficial as the flotsam and jetsam on the sea surface. A bar-mitzvah must be anchored in the great tradition. His studies should begin seven years before his thirteenth year, and what he says on the sabbath when he is called to the Torah should reflect his learning and be geared to years of study after bar-mitzvah. Moreh did not succeed with all the orphans in long-term training, but he did leave all of them with standards toward which they could yearn and aspire.

A typical Canadian "son of the commandment" today would find Moreh's standards an intolerable burden, for only the exceptional boy reads Hebrew fluently, is familiar with the basics of cantillation and continues Hebrew studies after his thirteenth year. For most contemporary youngsters the bar-mitzvah ceremony is a graduation exercise, although it was intended to be only a beginning to a life of devotion to the ideas and precepts of the Torah.

One of the problems of bar-mitzvah celebrations in the Home was the absence of a parental role. A father has a special part to play in the traditional proceedings, preceding his son to the Torah and reciting a benediction: "*Boruch shepetorani*. Blessed be He who has freed me from the responsibility of this young man's conduct." This blessing is the signal that a "son of the commandment" must start developing an awareness of the consequences of his behaviour.

At one point Moreh thought that since the Old Man was our surrogate father it might be appropriate for him to say *Boruch shepetorani*. But while the Old Man supervised, disciplined, trained and taught, he did not engage in parenting. Nor did we feel that if there were a fault in our responsibility he would cover for us. *Boruch shepetorani* was not an element in Orphanage bar-mitzvah ceremonies.

Instead Moreh would bear down on the moral and religious responsibilities each boy himself carried even before bar-mitzvah. On his twelfth birthday he would begin putting on the *tephillin*, the phylacteries, every morning. Just prior to the exercise Moreh would teach him to say: "Let a man strengthen himself like a lion and arise in the early morn to render service to his Creator." Since an orphan had no father to watch over him, said Moreh, he had to be strong as a lion, morally and spiritually, the kind of strength that requires rubbing the sleep out of one's eyes and applying oneself to one's studies.

"Moreh, what is *tephillin*?"

"It is the Hebrew plural for *tephillah*, prayer."

"But the *tephillin* are really leather containers, and there is a transparent section underneath through which I can see pieces of parchment."

"The parchments contain the four most important passages in the Torah—the *shema Yisroel*, that God is one; that we must fulfil his commandments and thereby be good human beings; that He redeemed us from Egypt and desires every person to be free; and that there are consequences to every action, good or bad."

"Why do we put the *tephillin* on the arm and on the head?"

"We lay the *tephillin* on the arm, opposite the heart, to indicate the duty of subjecting the longings and designs of our heart to the service of God and man, and upon the head near the brain, thereby teaching that the mind together with all the senses and faculties is to be subject to his service."

Mostly I learned about the *tephillin* not by questioning but by imitation. I watched Moreh as he stood and put them on reverently and with appropriate benedictions, according to the proper ritual procedure. For Moreh this constituted a wedding ceremony performed every morning—a daily marriage to justice, mercy and lovingkindness. As one does not interrupt a marriage ceremony by conversation, so one must be silent and reverent while "laying on the *tephillin*—visible symbols of the obligations of heart and mind."

Long before I put on the *tephillin* Moreh began to prepare me for bar-mitzvah and beyond. I had entered the Home in my ninth year and been introduced almost immediately to the cantillation of the Torah, which goes back to the fifth century before the common era.

This cantillation system consists of some twenty-five little signs which appear above and below the words of the Biblical text. They are called *te'amim* or *neginot*, accents or melodies. European Jews called them *trope*. Each accent is not a single note but a musical phrase. *Te'amim* serve the same purpose as neumes or notations in the language of musical history, based on the Hebrew word *ne'imah*, a tune. Moreh was as innocent of neumes and musical

notations as a rock musician would be of Torah cantillation. Yet
he had a fine ear, and when he sang the *trope* on sabbaths and
festivals one could almost absorb the meaning of the words with
the music he made. For the cantillation can determine the proper
phrasing of the Biblical verses, thereby clarifying the Hebrew syntax, and Moreh was a master of cantillation and accentuation.

At the age of nine I became so familiar with the twenty-five little
signs above and below the Biblical words that I could chant them
on sight as I read the text. Without warning Moreh would often
call upon me to recite the *haftarah*, the portion from the Prophets,
at the sabbath service. By the time my bar-mitzvah arrived,
therefore, it required little preparation to read the *haftarah* of my
sabbath, an honour accorded every thirteen-year-old celebrant.

Moreh also taught me to be proficient in the reading of the entire
sabbath Torah portion or *sidroh*. Since the Torah scroll is written
without vowels and accents, I had to memorize these details, a
rather considerable feat, but one I had accomplished so frequently
it was no prodigious task to perform it the day I became bar-
mitzvah. I was not the only expert in cantillation; there were
others like David Gilman and Georgie Ackerman.

Thus Moreh had no need to prepare his charges for bar-mitzvah
in the usual fashion. They could easily prepare themselves. However, he did require understanding from his students, and this en-
tailed careful examination and study of the text.

My *sidroh* or Torah portion was *Pikudey*, taken from Exodus,
Chapters 38 to 40. The subject matter is not especially exciting. It
discusses the building of the first house of worship for the Israelites
in the wilderness of Sinai. Since they were wandering bedouins, it
had to be portable, easily put up and taken down. The *sidroh* lists
the construction materials in great detail, even as to their worth.
All the gold talents and silver shekels donated by the people would
probably have been worth up to a million dollars in 1927 terms,
said Moreh. *Sidroh Pikudey* is also expansive in the description of
the garments of the high priest Aaron.

It took four months for all the work to be completed, says Scripture, and on the first anniversary of the Exodus from Egypt the
first house of prayer was dedicated. With this description the Book
of Exodus ends. All this, I felt, might be of interest to an anti-
quarian or even a historian, but to a Canadian thirteen-year-old it
did not provide much inspiration.

About a month before I was due to be called to the Torah,

Moreh wanted to check my progress in the cantillation of *sidroh Pikudey*. We climbed the three flights of stairs to the auditorium where the Torah scrolls were kept in the Ark.

Moreh drew aside the curtain and pulled open the doors to reveal three "dressed" scrolls. It was a resplendent sight, when I viewed them standing side by side as if nothing in the world could move them. Each scroll was encased in a velvet mantle embroidered in gold thread. Through the top of the mantle protruded two staves, called *atzei chayim*, trees of life. Mounted on the staves were two finials called *rimmonim*.

Moreh embraced the centre scroll, which he had rolled to the desired portion beforehand, and laid it on the reading desk which was covered by an embroidered cloth. He removed the finials, raised the scroll at an angle so I could "undress" it by removing the mantle. He untied a cloth binder, and there was the beautiful script written with pious care, with a quill pen. Metal was forbidden because it was a symbol of war and violence.

"Now," said Moreh handing me the pointer, "begin the *sidroh*."

"But, Moreh, I have learned it, and it makes no sense to me. Don't shut me out. Help me to understand."

"Well, if you don't understand there's no use just making a jumble of sounds, is there? You have to put it all in perspective. Consider the whole of the book and the book that precedes it. Genesis is the story of the creation of mankind. It ends with the biographies of a few personalities: Abraham, Isaac, Jacob, Joseph. But the Book of Exodus is no longer the story of personalities. It is the story of a people, the beginning of the career of the Jewish people."

"What a strange thing to say," I countered. "An individual has a career. But how can a whole people have a career?"

"If you think about it," said Moreh, "many modern nations have a sense of world career. The soldiers of Napoleon, for example, believed they were bringing liberty to the world and thereby made France a great nation. The English in Victorian days, or even as far back as Queen Elizabeth, felt they had a 'white man's burden' to carry, to bring order and civilized behaviour to the world. This mission made England great. The United States from the very beginning felt that its democracy was something to teach the world. The Jews are interesting because they are the first people in the story of man that had a sense of mission toward the rest of mankind. We were the first career-people in the world."

"If we were the first, then we must be the grandest and most important people in history." A boy has no trouble being a chauvinist. I wanted to believe with all my heart that the Jews are superior to everyone else.

"Now don't go jumping to conclusions. Our history is not the most important or even the grandest, but it is the longest continuous story. Other peoples may be as old as we, the Babylonians and the Egyptians, but there is no continuity from the history of the first settlers in Mesopotamia or the Nile down to their present descendants. Our history is the longest unbroken tradition in the annals of mankind."

"Well, that's something to be proud of, too, isn't it?" I was determined to defend the Jews come what may.

"Yes, it is," said Moreh softly. "And what event would you say has left the deepest impress on the Jews?"

It was easy to sense where Moreh was leading. When I said, "The Exodus from Egypt," he was jubilant.

"Yes, the Exodus, the deliverance! So great has been its impact that we have been remembering it every sabbath and every festival in our homes for millenia."

I watched Moreh in wonder as the love of the great tradition poured out of him, the magic of devotion to an ideal. He took the pointer from me, and began to beat it on the palm of his hand to mark the rhythm of his words.

"The Jews not only carried the vision of freedom," he continued. "They wove it into the fabric of their group attitudes and law. When our ancient teachers taught kindness to strangers, they based the argument on the Exodus: 'Remember you, too, were strangers in the land of Egypt.' When the laws governing slavery were promulgated, they provided that a slave serve only six years, and ours was the first community to abolish permanent slavery."

"But where does our career come in, Moreh?"

"Our career was an inspiration to others. When the feudal system began to crumble, where did the serfs turn for assurance in rebelling against the barons? To the Book of Exodus. They drew their encouragement from the breaking of the yoke of Pharaoh. When the first settlers to North America fled from the tyranny of the old country, the seal they proposed for an independent state depicted the Atlantic ocean as if it were the Red Sea which they crossed with the Israelites. When William Wilberforce fought the slave trade and the black slaves themselves needed hope to sustain them until the day of liberation, they sang: 'Go down, Moses, way down in Egypt land/tell ol' Pharaoh/Let my people go.' Thus was the love of liberty written into our history and the history of mankind by the first event in the Book of Exodus, your book, Re'uven."

Moreh had laid the pointer on the desk, and I picked it up to emphasize my questions.

"Well, if it is my book, I should be able to understand all of it. Yet there are things in it I just can't understand or accept. The miracles, for example." I waved the pointer. "The plagues, the opening of the Red Sea, the pillar of cloud and flame. How can I believe all this?" Moreh took the pointer from my hands for fear I would spear myself with it.

"I find it hard to believe, too," said my honest teacher who kept nothing from me. "Modern people are uneasy when the Bible speaks of miracles. We feel we are too enlightened to believe in them. But are we? We are always hoping for miracles when we fall sick of a disease for which there is no cure. Besides, miracles do occur. People who should have died are cured. We reject miracles because they are a suspension of nature and nothing can happen outside natural law. But let's not be too superior to the people of three thousand years ago who explained natural conundrums as miracles. They were dumbfounded. Miracle was the only way they could describe them. Actually the greatest miracle was not any of the ten plagues or the parting of the Red Sea, but the recognition of one God at Sinai. How do you explain the fact that a small group of ex-slaves developed the concept of a spiritual God? Here were half-scared creatures wandering through the desert, complaining step by step, wishing they were back in Egypt. How did it happen that they thought of a universal God?

"And why did the recognition of a pure God without the superstition and miseries of paganism come to this people, our people? You can be sure it was too much for them. Before long they made idols. But they were also the first people to be cured of idolatry, the first to have a spiritual idea of God. And this was part of their career, too. They were carriers of the God-idea."

"So now you are saying, Moreh, the Jews have two careers. They are freedom carriers and God-idea carriers."

"It's all part of the one career, Re'uven. The spiritual God is the source of freedom. There cannot be one without the other."

"How long can Jews go on carrying this idea? Isn't it about time others shared the burden?"

Moreh took the mantle and placed it on the open scroll, so that it should not remain uncovered too long. His reverence for the scroll itself was a habit of a lifetime. "Re'uven, look out at the world. Others are sharing the responsibility. As carriers, the Jews held on to the God-idea until the world grew up. Then they handed it on to a band of Christian apostles, bringing to the Roman world the God of Mount Sinai. Thus was the pagan world redeemed through Sinai. All of Europe and part of Africa and Asia now knew God. And when the tribes of Arabia began to outlive their ancient idolatry, a camel driver came who had lived with the Jews and absorbed from them their sense of career. Thus another section of mankind abandoned its idols."

"Moreh, we've wandered far from my *sidroh* and the building of a sanctuary for the Israelites."

"Not so very far. You see, there was one thing different about the temple in the desert—where it was *not* built."

I was puzzled.

"It would have been logical to build the temple at the foot of the miraculous mountain of Sinai, but the Israelites did not build it there. Instead they built a collapsible temple, a tent that could be taken down, travel with the people on their journey and be set up again when they encamped. Evidently this religion was different from others. The others had a sacred spot to which people made pilgrimage in order to be sanctified. But this tent-temple went with the people because the people were holy. This was a kind of religious democracy. The entire people was to be a kingdom of priests. This was never dreamed of before. The career of Israel thus involved not only personal liberty and the concept of a spiritual God, but it was for the first time democratic worship, where no person was superior to another. If there is any hope of this world uniting into an enduring peace, it will be through a deepened sense of human brotherhood, which cannot come except to those who have a sense of the common fatherhood of God. That is what our career as God-carriers may yet mean to the world."

Moreh picked up the mantle, placed it at the edge of the desk, and I began to read my *sidroh*. It was as though I was reciting the familiar words for the first time. A kind of magic was in the air. The magician was beside me with his wand and little box of inspiration. I ended my recitation, and the spell was over. Moreh raised the scroll high. The strength of his faith seemed to be in his arms, for it was a heavy scroll and he was not an athletic man. I rolled the staves together as he held them and bound the parchment with the cloth binder. Then I dressed the Torah in its mantle and placed the silver ornaments in position. Moreh carried his most precious possession to the Ark and set it among its companions.

He was silent, and so was I.

I was to be called to the Torah on March 5, 1927, the first of Adar I, 5687, according to the Hebrew calendar. By the beginning of February Moreh had already given me an overview of the Book of Exodus and related it to the last chapters. The *haftarah* or prophetic portion presented no difficulty since I could read it at sight. I was also to conduct the *shaharis* (morning) and *musaf* (additional) services, but these, too, were well in hand because I had often led the ritual before. One task remained, the composition of my *deroshoh*, the bar-mitzvah address.

My subject had to grow out of my Hebrew studies. Moreh would not hear of a hackneyed speech unrelated to the subjects he taught. The Old Man wanted me to speak on a Zionist theme. Since representatives from the community were expected, he was ready to help me with a rousing address in Yiddish on the Palestine *Yishuv* (Settlement) so that there would be no mistaking my sentiments and loyalties. Moreh inclined toward a Hebrew address which would gain in meaning for me what it would lose in intelligibility for my audience. I had the weird notion of wanting to say something in English because my friends and teachers from high school were invited.

During the days of pondering my dilemma, the Hebrew class read "Three Gifts" by Yitzhak Leib Peretz, a classic tale of one of the great Hebrew-Yiddish writers of the late nineteenth century. Drawing upon the rich sources of Hasidic lore and tradition, Peretz told of a soul doomed to eternal wandering and of its search for three good and beautiful gifts from earth which would ensure its entry into Paradise. It came to me that the tale would make a striking text for my speech and appeal to everyone in my collectively trilingual audience. Moreh thought it a felicitous idea. The Old Man wasn't sure, but when I pointed out that it would include a nationalist theme and demonstrate the versatility of one of his wards, he readily assented.

I can still feel the knot in my belly in the minutes before I confronted my audience. I saw the faces of the members of the Board, the matrons, Moreh, the Old Man, the Orphanage citizenry all decked out in their sabbath finery, and my friends from Machray

School to which I had transferred from Luxton on entering grade nine. Where do I get the courage to summon a nice smile, a nicely calculated deference and an unshakable faith? I am too scared to smile, too nervous for deference and shaking like a leaf inside. My hands are clammy and a cold sweat has broken out over my body. Suddenly all my words and images leave me. The Old Man has insisted that I take no notes to the dais. That is his style. He is a master of the seemingly extemporaneous address, with a memory like a camera. He hardly hesitates or gropes for a word. Isn't it monstrous to expect a similar performance from me? How can I possibly speak without a slur or a mistake? Moreh has warned me about this: "None of us knows what bread costs until we do our own shopping." Here am I trying to buy an audience and the price is terror.

I approached the railing that surrounded the altar and stood there. My face was grim and unsmiling. I opened my mouth, and another voice issued, the sonorous voice of the high priest calling the Biblical genealogies among the Israelites. Actually I was a sad little dog, all alone and baying at the moon. I picked out Moreh's face from among all the others. He nodded slowly as if to say: "I am with you and you have nothing to fear." I spoke directly to him.

I began the speech by telling Peretz's story, switching from Yiddish to Hebrew to English. I told of the finding of three good and beautiful gifts: a bit of earth from the land of Israel, the most precious possession of an old Jew, robbed and finally murdered as he tries to save it; a blood-stained pin with which a beautiful Jewish girl covered her nakedness when dragged through a city's streets on a trumped-up charge of desecration; and the *yarmulka* a whipped Jewish prisoner refused to part with. Then I launched into my interpretation of the story. Terror was no longer my companion. Ordinary fear took its place.

"A bag of earth for his grave," I declaimed in Yiddish. "The old Jew remembered the land of his fathers, the Promised Land. How long can a people be expected to remember anything—to cherish a constitution, to honour a treaty, to keep a vow, especially when it has ceased to profit them? A generation? A century? Unlikely. A millenium? Impossible. Well, this people by the waters of Babylon swore: 'If I forget thee, O Jerusalem!' That was twenty-six hundred years ago, yet it did not forget.

"Not in all history has any people remembered anything so long

a time. That Jews should have thought of Zion in times of distress
and persecution is understandable. But how shall one account for
all those who lived in quiet and comfort and security and still did
not forget?

"Just that the Jews remembered Zion and placed a little of its
earth in their graves is a miracle. Not a miracle in the traditional
sense. All that happened was that by its memory a people achieved
the impossible. Just that and nothing more!

"What were the ingredients of that miraculous memory? How
did it work?

"First, by hope. To this our forefathers clung even when it
seemed altogether hopeless. By teaching they imparted hope to
one another. Deliberately they made themselves prisoners of
hope—a hope born of love; love of land, of people and of God.
Had it been the child of hate, it could not have lasted so long, for
hate destroys not only its targets but those who practise it. Only
love endures; only love gives life.

"What is more, our people never allowed hope to remain only a
mere longing and a wishing. At every opportunity they converted
it into a will and effort. It is not true that all through the centuries
the Jews just sat and waited for the Messiah to realize their hope
for them. Nothing could be further from the truth. To be sure,
they did not use modern techniques of political negotiation and
diplomatic activity, but they never stopped trying. At the first
favourable turn, the Jews were always immigrating to Palestine.
Only their strength was slight and circumstance was always
against them, so they never achieved anything much and often it
seemed that they never would.

"But now things are changing. Circumstance, in the form of the
Balfour Declaration, is shifting. It really does not matter how ad-
verse circumstance may be; nothing can stand before the power of
the will."

The Old Man had taught me to lift my voice at the last sentence.
My Yiddish-speaking audience burst into applause. The public-
school guests looked a bit bewildered, but as good sports they
joined in.

Now came the most difficult section of the address, the Hebrew
declamation. Moreh had emphasized its importance more than the
other parts, though he knew only a handful would understand it.
The Old Man had been helpful at this point. What they don't catch
in understanding, he said, let them absorb by sound and contrast.

He had trained me to modulate my voice, really to act out my meanings. By this time fear had left me, but tension came up to bat.

"The girl in Peretz's story was beautiful," I said in Hebraic accents, "but she understood that beauty to a Jew meant 'compassion, modesty and benevolence,' as the Talmud teaches. The ancient Greeks believed in the holiness of beauty. The Jews have always believed in the beauty of holiness. What do we mean by 'a beautiful Jew'?

"Jews today show great and legitimate concern for defending the Jewish name, that it should not be dragged in the dirt. But our forefathers rose to a higher concern when they warned that bad or scandalous conduct on the part of the Jew might cause *hillul hashem*, the desecration of God's name, and weaken faith in God. More important than defending the Jewish name was offsetting the cheapening of life and restoring the notion that to be a Jew means to be held to standards of honour and truth.

"Being a Jew should mean being committed to goodness; putting a brake on the insatiable hunger for power; seeking success not in outdoing others but in outdoing oneself, in rising above one's limitations and developing one's creative talents. It is not enough for a Jew just to observe the laws of the state, with their minimum standards. He must develop a sensitive ethical conscience, must live on a standard more demanding than the legal requirement.

"Where did that beautiful girl get her standard of behaviour? From the Torah. So may we strengthen our devotion to Judaism's ideal of humanity united by ties of sympathy and understanding, in a common effort to make life worth living for every human being."

The Yiddish-speakers in my audience nodded as if I had expressed a significant thought, although most of them did not understand a word.

Finally, I retreated into English and realized what a comfort it was to be able to speak one's first language. Even the fans of Mendele the Book Peddler, for whom English was a challenge, seemed to relax. But though English came more easily, I was still timid and fearful as a bird.

"The Jew who would not part with his skull-cap, the Jew who would not give up his religious faith—what a price he paid! All of us would pay much for such a faith. Men today would like to believe that the brutalities of our world are not the forerunners of doom, but only a nightmare to be dispelled by the light of a new day. All men would welcome the belief that life is worthwhile despite suffering, that it is well to identify oneself with the good, that though the wicked seem to prosper history will produce a nobler type of man.

"Well, there is something in the spirit of the human being, some stubborn instinct of life, that cries out against letting the human drama end in a senseless farce. That instinct demands not only the survival of the human race but the survival of those values for which men have sacrificed in all ages: truth, justice and mercy.

"Consider a young man told that the golden rule in business is 'do others or they will do you.' He cannot yield to these temptations without feeling cheapened and degraded, but he may unless he can believe in a moral law which is divine and makes life worthwhile for those who abide by it.

"Consider the demand by philosophers, scientists, educators and statesmen for a rational basis for democracy, one that would arouse as much enthusiasm for the democratic way as fascism and communism seem to arouse among many people in Europe. Do we not need a faith that history has a meaning and that this meaning is a confirmation of the democratic ideal? Can economic freedom give security to everybody? Can government develop a power that will suppress anti-social behaviour yet at the same time be trusted not to suppress individual initiative and liberty? The answers to these questions must come in deeds not words, but they cannot come at all unless we believe that such answers exist. They cannot come without religious faith."

It was over. I had fought terror, fear and tension in that order. Now the richness of relief rushed through me.

The most memorable moment of my bar-mitzvah was not my speech. It came before my *deroshoh*, as I was reading from the Torah. My father, who was becoming more frail and crippled with the years, had been brought to the service. A great debate had raged between Mother and Osovsky over whether transporting a disabled man from the Home for the Aged on Manitoba Avenue to the Orphanage several miles north was feasible. Father still walked with a painful shuffle, his left arm hung helpless and his speech was becoming increasingly garbled, all as a result of his stroke. Would the bar-mitzvah ceremony be adversely affected by his presence? I wanted him, and that settled the matter.

Before the service began, I helped him on with his big woollen prayer shawl and he mumbled the blessing. I told him he would be the third person to be called to the Torah, and he looked startled. I assured him he need not worry about the blessing since I was there to help out in case he stumbled. He smiled, evidently seeing the irony of a son guiding his father to the Torah.

At the third stop in the reading of the *sidroh*, I called out in the traditional manner: "*Ya'amod*, let Meir ben Avraham Yitzhok ascend the altar." Father rose painfully. Several hands helped him to the altar steps and carried him to the table where the scroll rested. He managed the first blessing well enough and stood beside me as I read the words from Exodus, grasping my hand in a tight grip until I almost cried out. He was showing his pride and love.

After the concluding blessing the Old Man nodded to him to move aside for the next man to be called. Father would not budge. He took hold of the scroll handle with his good right hand and held it as in a vise. "Let go," said the Old Man. Father shook his head and tried to say something, but nothing was intelligible. People in the congregation began whispering: "What's going on? Why did they let that old man up there?" I heard the comments, and they upset me. Father was only fifty-eight, still young.

"*Voz iz, Tateh*? What's the trouble? Tell me." He embraced me but could not explain himself. At that moment Moreh understood. "You want to say *boruch shepetorani* [the blessing by the bar-mitzvah's father], don't you?" Father nodded vigorously. And Moreh, that loving, devoted teacher, recited with him: "Blessed be He who has freed me from being responsible for this young man's conduct." How relieved Tateh was! He was doing his duty as a Jewish father, giving his son the proper send-off. Now I was a thirteen-year-old as the great tradition intended. The tears cascaded down his cheeks, and I wept uncontrollably. His act of insistence on the continuity of tradition, though he was broken and ill, made me understand through the years why the Jewish people has survived.

Father died shortly after and made of me a real orphan.

XII

Indians

As a post-bar-mitzvah in the Orphanage, I acquired status. I monitored a table at meals, led morning services for twelve-year-olds preparing for bar-mitzvah, rehearsed the Torah portions for sabbaths and began the study of Talmud in earnest. Moreh would give David Gilman and me extra lessons after the regular daily Hebrew sessions.

For grade ten I went to St. John's Technical High School. Few of the Orphanage residents reached this educational level. By age fifteen they were expected to be independent and earning a living in the workaday world. I had just turned fourteen, having skipped several grades in elementary school, and the question of taking a job had not yet arisen. Since no one challenged me, attendance at high school seemed a natural progression.

At St. John's everyone appeared to know I was from the Orphanage and when the annual oratorical contest was announced, it was assumed I would be a contestant. "Give your bar-mitzvah speech," said Aaron Boroditsky, one of my class-mates whose father was on the Orphanage Board. I wondered about delivering that speech before an audience of Anglo-Saxon teachers and a student population of Jews, Ukrainians and Poles. A Jewish audience would expect me to talk about my origins and aspirations for my people, but a mixed audience would either turn away with boredom or hoot me off the platform. Winnipeg in the 1920s was still very British. Ethnics were tolerated but not as a normal element in the national spectrum. They were expected to conform to the standards set by English and Scottish forebears.

I decided not to enter the contest. The choice of a topic was too much of a problem. But Old Man Osovsky learned of the competition from young Boroditsky's father.

"You must enter and win," he said to me, as if the outcome was already decided. "You owe it to the Home. Think of what it would mean in terms of support for the institution that reared you."

"You can't be sure I'll win," I countered. "Suppose I lose. Other losers will be able to fade away, but the spotlight will be on me as an Orphanage kid. Losing for me will be more than disappointment. It will mean embarrassment and shame."

"You're not going to lose," said the Old Man. "All you need do is speak as you did at your bar-mitzvah, and I guarantee victory." The Old Man was a splendid salesman. He didn't convince me, but he forced me to see that I had no alternative. To refuse to enter the oratorical contest meant ingratitude to those who had laboured to make a home for the homeless.

I submitted my name to Mr. Gardiner, St. John's Latin instructor, athletic director and organizer extraordinary of extracurricular activities, but informed him that my topic was still in abeyance.

Suddenly it became a *cause célèbre* with the Orphanage Board. At a regular Sunday morning meeting, the Old Man brought the matter up after the scheduled agenda. He turned to M. J. Finkelstein, attorney-at-law, a publicist who frequently addressed non-Jewish audiences and was generally regarded as the expert on Jewish-Gentile relations. "What do you think, M. J., should be Reuben's topic?"

Finkelstein had a talent for logic and an understanding heart.

"Isn't that for Reuben to decide?"

I was called from the Hebrew class into the Old Man's office, where the Board meeting was in progress, an unheard-of departure from the rules. There I stood, small in my own eyes, made smaller by the piercing though benign eyes of the Board members, who looked imposing all in a bunch.

"Have you started to prepare your oration yet?" asked M. J.

"Not yet, Mr. Finkelstein. I have a few ideas but nothing definite."

"What ideas? Perhaps we can help you?"

"We're not supposed to get help, only advice. Those are the rules."

"Rest assured. We wouldn't presume to write your speech. But surely we can advise you on your topic. What ideas are circulating in that busy head of yours?"

"I was thinking I might speak on the subject of 'Indian Legends.' "

A heavy silence fell. The Old Man's brows knitted in anger and perplexity. Had he been alone with me, a thunderclap would have exploded from him. But this was M. J. Finkelstein's show, and he respected him too much to interfere.

"Indian legends? American Indian or East Indian?" queried M. J.

"American Indian."

"Why any kind of Indians?"

"I've always been interested in them. I have read all the volumes on the American Indians in our library—their life, customs, history and legends. They seem to me to be very similar to the Jews."

M. J. turned to the Old Man. "How did we get books on Indians into the library?"

"Somebody donated them," said the Old Man apologetically. "You know we have no funds for books in our budget. They seemed harmless enough. Reuben seems to read everything. He's impressionable and absorbs information like a sponge."

"I've been reading Indian legends since I came to the Home more than four years ago," I said, thinking to help out the Old Man. "They're very entertaining and they make me feel very Jewish."

The Board members exchanged bewildered looks.

"The Jews believed in one God," I said. "So did the Indians. They believed in the Great Spirit. The Jews were exiled from their land. So were the Indians—driven from their ancestral soil into the reservations. As Jews have mourned over their exile, so have the Indians."

The Old Man's jaw dropped, but Finkelstein was equal to the challenge. "Bravo. There are indeed close similarities. Do you propose to develop your speech on those lines?"

"I haven't started working on it yet, but Moreh Frankel likes the idea and has promised to give me some advice."

The Old Man could not contain himself any longer. "You are making a mistake. Jews and Indians do not belong together. They are as far apart as the poles. It is ludicrous to make any such parallel. You'll become a laughing-stock. It's childish and naive. I beg of you to reconsider. We have a stake in this, too. You represent us. Your words and actions reflect our entire institution. Be sensible and practical."

"Now don't go threatening the boy," M. J. interceded. "And don't handicap him with a heavy burden from the start. The whole reputation of this institution is not in his hands. Why should he carry a load the other contestants do not have?"

He turned to me. "Reuben, we want you to win. You will make us proud if you do, but if you don't you will still be our joy. The final decision as to topic belongs to you. Some of us would rather you spoke on another subject, but the power of choice is yours."

The Old Man refused to give up. "M. J.," he said, "let me try to persuade him. I have a suggestion that will put pride in him, in us and in the entire Jewish community. I propose that Reuben speak on Jewish self-respect." A few heads around the table nodded.

Encouraged, Osovsky proceeded to expatiate on his subject. "Man shares many emotions with the animals," he said. "But there is one emotion animals cannot feel. They cannot be indignant. Angry, yes; indignant, never. Indignation is the resentment aroused in us by someone's unworthy behaviour. An awareness of worth is something intellectual or moral, and man alone is capable of it.

"Judaism's most heroic figures were men of great indignation," the Old Man continued. "Consider that meek man Moses. Consider the prophets after him: Elijah, Isaiah, Amos, Nathan, Malachi. There is no social gain, from the abolition of human slavery to the establishment of parliamentary rule in our time, which has not been sparked by indignation. A human being, if he is going to live at all, let alone respect himself, cannot take insult or injury passively. The one thing a human being must have for the health of his spirit is a vigorous self-respect."

Osovsky was warming to his subject and was speaking more to the Board than to me, carried away as he was by the force of his own words.

"How should Jews react when they encounter anti-Semitism? Take fright? Hide or run away, as they did during the Kishinev pogrom? Condemn other Jews? Repudiate Judaism as though our faith and morality were at fault? No, the right reaction should be indignation, which is self-respect. We are too good for anti-Semitic treatment. All through history we have been a humane and constructive force. And that we are as a whole today. There are exceptions, of course. I am not happy over such Jews, for we cannot be content with moral mediocrity. But when I think of what our people have been and what they are now, and then when I think of the riffraff who insult us, there is only one phrase that expresses my feelings—the *hutzpah*, the brazen, unmitigated *hutzpah!*"

The Board broke into applause. The Old Man had not been speaking to me, trying to convince me to accept his topic, but to the world, the cruel world that oppressed the Jews for no good reason. He left me somewhat uneasy. What he said was doubtless true, but I could not picture myself saying such things to a mixed audience of Anglo-Saxons and children of East Europeans. They would probably be more startled than understanding, wondering why I was so vehement.

M. J. Finkelstein must have felt the same. He cleared his throat and said: "Fine sentiments, Mr. Osovsky, words we can all appreciate. But neither you, nor I, nor Reuben here at his tender age are so naive as to suppose that all we need do to solve the problem of anti-Semitism is to get indignant. Jewish self-respect is important, but it is only the first stage. Anti-Semitism, if it is to be eradicated, requires at least the following measures: a sustained campaign of education against all forms of group prejudice; the encouragement of friendships and co-operation between Jews and non-Jews as individuals and as organized groups; the preservation and enlargement of political democracy; the achievement of a greater measure of economic justice for all; the establishment of codes of fair employment and fair social practice, with agencies empowered to enforce them; the promulgation of legislation which, while protecting legitimate freedom of expression, would make it a crime to incite hatred against a group because of race, creed or colour; the development of increased unity and co-ordination among Jewish civic defence agencies."

It was obvious even to me that M. J. had worked these thoughts out long before. He sounded like a lawyer addressing the court, and the Board members showed a proper deference. Then he went on, more as a Jew than as a lawyer.

"These are the true answers to our problem. We ought to work very hard on them. But in the meantime let us be sure of one thing. Whenever anti-Semitism raises its head and we are certain it is the real thing, after every device and persuasion has been tried and has failed, then let us hit it as hard as we can. Let us, as lawyers say, throw the book at it in every way permitted by the British North America Act, the Ten Commandments and the Marquis of Queensberry. Although such tactics may not stop the anti-Semite —though I wager they will exert a salutary influence on him—it will in any case be good for Canadian democracy and very good for our self-respect."

It was an impressive meeting, but I remained unconvinced. I wasn't sure whether the best blow for the Jews was to raise the banner of war and come out fighting mad or to do it my way by associating Jews with Indians and making a plea for both.

When I reported the discussion to Moreh, he was astonished but gratified that the Board would take time to consider intellectual issues as well as budgets and fund-raising projects, but he said:

"When Jews consider the welfare of Jews and Judaism, they inevitably think in terms of fighting anti-Semitism. Too many of us Jews have no God and no Torah, no Jewish knowledge and no Jewish practices, only the penalties of being Jews. We never enjoy Judaism; we only suffer for it and even that not heroically. The Jew who is a hollow shell, a Hebraic cipher, is flooded inevitably with hostile notions about Jews. The anti-Semite convinces him. But the Jew who knows Judaism has his head and his heart too full of positive healthful values ever to be invaded by self-contempt."

Moreh looked at me closely. "It is this positive aspect you must put into your speech, Re'uven, the feeling that a knowledge and love of Judaism can make one a nobler, stronger, better human being and a more valuable citizen."

When the Old Man heard that in spite of all his and the Board's endeavours, I was still resolved to speak on "Indian Legends," his vitriol was boundless. He accused me of trying to imitate the *goyim*. "Why not be the Jew you were taught to be? Surely you're not ashamed of what you are? Stand four-square, then, and speak up for your people without fear or favour. Be true to your Jewishness without qualifications. Indians have nothing to do with the case."

I stuck to my guns, though I was aware that if I lost the contest the Old Man would blame my stiff-neckedness. Not once did he ask how I was getting on with my speech preparations. It was Moreh who encouraged me and suggested resource books for parallels between Jewish and Indian cultures. My search for affinities led me to all sorts of parallels between the sacred traditions of the Bible and Talmud and those of Indian legend.

According to the Bible, God created man out of the dust of the earth, then gave him a general anaesthetic before performing surgery, taking from him a rib out of which woman was made. The Osage Indians of the Missouri River, I found, had a similar tradition, differing in detail but with the same concept, in their legend of a snail man and a beaver woman.

The legend tells of many things contained in the first chapter of Genesis—that the Great Spirit has no form or substance and that his voice is quiet and gentle, that only one man was created in the beginning to indicate the unity of mankind, that man was given dominion over other animals and that family devotion is basic to society. I shared my discovery with Moreh who was intrigued and encouraged me to continue my research.

My quest led me to consider Jewish and Indian attitudes toward peace and war. As a fan of silent cowboy-and-Indian movies on Saturday afternoons, I had always believed that war and violence were a natural part of the North American native's society. How did one reconcile the long Jewish tradition of *shalom* with war paint, tomahawks and an accumulation of white men's scalps? But the Bible also records many battles, though the great Jewish tradition is peace. Could it be the same with the Indians? They produced many warriors but the longing over the centuries could have been for peace. One legend verified this guess. It told how Aseelkwa, the Big Chief, in patriarchal style and making concessions for peace, turned away from his enemies and sought another hunting ground, avoiding war. As Isaac received the inheritance of peace from Abraham, so Aseelkwa received it from his father Milkanops. As throughout most of their history the Jews shunned aggression and responded only to attack, so Aseelkwa fought only when his enemies fell upon him. And in the end the vision of peace is fulfilled. The tribe of Aseelkwa beats its swords into ploughshares, the valley is fruitful and the people learn war no more, just as in the prophecy of Isaiah.

What impressed me most was that the Indians suffered a great deal, as did the Jews. They suffered, according to their medicine men, so as to be cleansed of all selfish pride. Their lands were taken from them so they might be ready for the great awakening. So with the Jews, who were exiled, as they said in their prayers, "because of our sins," and believed that redemption would come when humility had run its course. Both peoples put great store in the hopeful dream. With the Jews their prophets saw visions. With the Indians their legends spoke of them.

Once there was an Indian chief who came to the end of his days. His braves brought him to the foot of a mountain where he called to him his three sons. "One of you will succeed me," he said to them, "but you must each be tested. You will climb the mountain and bring down an object from its summit. The one who brings the most desirable object will become chief in my place."

One son climbed the mountain and brought down a flower, and it was beautiful. Another climbed the mountain and brought down an attractive stone. It had been shaped by the sun, the wind and the rain, and it was beautiful. The third son climbed the mountain and came down empty-handed. "I have nothing to give you," he said to his father. "For as I stood on the mountain peak I saw a fertile valley below and thought, 'This is a good place to bring the tribe to build a better life.' I was so preoccupied with my idea that I forgot to look for something to bring you."

And the father said to his third son: "You will be the chief in my stead, for you have brought the most precious gift of all, a vision of a better world and a better future."

Jews and Indians have been dreaming dreams for centuries, dreams that have been their bread of hope. They seemed to me to be very close in belief and aspiration.

I say "they seemed to me." Actually it was Moreh's idea. He guided me so skilfully that I believed I myself had arrived at an original conclusion. It was Moreh who led me to see the Indians through Jewish eyes. It was he who had taught an ancient Jewish concept that a man's attachment to his own hearthstones should make him understand better how another man feels about his motherland. Today we Jews are losing this humanism and universalism of Judaism, all for the sake of Jewish statehood. We love Israel, and so we should, but we are so blinded by that love that we are willing to pay a prohibitive price for it. We condone acts we would declare unconscionable anywhere else in the world: nuclear weapons are wrong but necessary for Israel; apartheid is wrong, but for the sake of Israel's survival we will tolerate it; human rights are critical, but not for the Palestinians; we have a right to a state but Palestinians do not. Our racism toward Arabs would be regarded as anti-Semitism if others spoke of us in the same light. In all things we need to remember that the Jewish people and the Jewish state are but instruments, not ends in themselves; that what is good for the world is good for the Jews, not what is good for the Jews is good for the world; that the ultimate goal of the Jew, if he be truly Jewish, is to serve humanity.

Moreh assured me I had the foundation for an argument, and I proceeded to write my speech for the contest. First I set forth the common ground that bound the histories and traditions of Jews and Indians together. Then I said:

"The Indian is my brother, because we face the same dilemma

and have the same opportunity. Each of us belongs to a people with a literature and a language, a music and an art, a system of folkways, a treasury of folklore and a structure of institutions. We are, the Indian and I, heirs to two complete civilizations in addition to that of Canada. What do we do with these heritages? Reject them root and branch and content ourselves with the abundant spiritual resources of Canada, or do we wash our hands of the problem and let it go by default?

"Something binds us together, the Indian and me, with an indissoluble bond. Both of us tend to regard ourselves as not altogether wanted by the majority society of which we wish to be a part, the approval and acceptance of which we desire earnestly. My Jewishness and his Indianness expose us to a special set of insecurities.

"What is more, we have doubtless at some time or other felt that some of our frustrations—economic, social and cultural—were the result not of a personal inefficiency but of the fact that I am a Jew and he is an Indian. At times we may have been convinced by the criticisms of the Jew-hater or Indian-hater.

"The upshot of all this is that many a Canadian Jew and a Canadian Indian is in mortal peril of losing his sense of worth, his self-respect, his dignity in his own eyes. He may secretly feel ashamed or even bitter about his Jewishness or his Indianness and be tempted to conceal it altogether. He may come to feel he is somehow a human being inferior to the unlabelled Canadian.

"Now it is fundamental that a person has to approve of himself if he is to be happy and creative. He must be realistic, sharply critical of himself. But he must in the end respect what he is. No meaning in life is possible without this precondition. And this health requirement is what the Canadian Jew and the Canadian Indian are in danger of losing.

"What can we do? We can be indifferent and refuse to think about the whole business. We can hope like Micawber that it will all somehow come out right in the end—even though it will not come out right by itself.

"Or we can try to liquidate ourselves, deliberately try to lose ourselves in the majority and dedicate all our creative energies to the enhancement of Canadian life, undistracted by the demands of another tradition. Such a goal is impossible of achievement. An occasional Jew or Indian may lose himself in the unlabelled Canadian world, but most Jews and Indians are going to have to remain Jews and Indians, no matter how they may struggle against that fate. Most of all, we must reject liquidation or assimilation because it means wanton waste, the deliberate throwing away of valuable cultural traditions capable of enriching both the individual and the broader society. It is no more a solution of Jewish and Indian problems than suicide is a solution of individual problems.

"What is the alternative? For me, deliberately to adhere to my Jewishness and for my Indian brother to adhere to his Indianness. What do we get out of our respective heritages? A world outlook in light of which the individual is clothed with dignity and the career of humanity with meaning and hope; a morality, humane and elevated and sensibly realistic; a system of rituals which penetrates our daily routine and invests them with poetry and intimations of God. Because my Jewishness and my brother's Indianness are positive, the haters will loom less large in our lives than in those of many of our fellows. We will be less susceptible than escapist Jews and Indians to infection by self-contempt. We will not be tempted to flee, nor will we be bitter.

"Canada should approve, or to put it more modestly, should have no quarrel with my Indian brother's or my enterprise. Is it not the essence of our political theory that the state exists so that the individual may find fulfilment where his conscience directs? Canada will be immeasurably benefitted if its Jews and Indians respect themselves, if they are mentally adjusted rather than disaffected and if they are richer rather than poorer in spirit.

"There is great promise in cultural pluralism, and we Jews and Indians can show the way. It is out of differences meeting in mutual understanding that cultures bloom most luxuriantly. That is what happened in the age of Pericles, the Renaissance, the eras of Chaucer and Shakespeare. We ought to preserve the common ground of government, language and culture we all share, and also our second diversities, and then as a matter of planned policy arrange for their mutual meeting. Out of such husbandry of the spirit may well emerge a life richer than history has known before. That is the opportunity for me the Jew and for my brother the Indian."

There were some twenty contestants in the oratorical contest. For two weeks preliminaries were held in the school auditorium at noon hour, when students from grades ten and eleven were free to attend. They had a fine time, cheering their favourites and assessing the speeches afterwards. On the Monday following the final series of speeches, the judges, members of the faculty, posted the names of the semi-finalists. My name was not among them.

I turned away from the bulletin board with a heavy heart. How was I to face the Old Man and members of the Orphanage Board? They were right. I was a stubborn kid with delusions about my superior judgment. I should have listened to the voice of experience, M. J. Finkelstein. He said he didn't hold me responsible for the Orphanage's reputation, but he must surely be thinking the opposite. As for Osovsky, my goose was cooked. Henceforth he would treat me as a pariah, an outcast, a heretic who dared challenge the established wisdom of an entire Board of Directors. I felt like the solitary goat in the Passover hymn which was eaten by the cat, which was bitten by the dog, which was beaten by the stick, etc. A whole chain of humiliating consequences would result from my failure. I would no more be one of the "favourites," and would have to perform menial chores. I would lose my status as a senior inmate.

All these base thoughts welled up inside me as I descended the high school's entrance steps on my way home, when a shout stopped me short. It was Mr. Gardiner, director of extra-curricular programs. "Reuben, wait up . . . very important." What further calamity could befall me now? "Forgive me," said Gardiner, the bearer of good news, "a clerical error . . . your name was omitted from the list of semi-finalists. How disappointed you must have been. Don't let it discourage you. There are still the semi-finals and the finals. And I hope you go all the way. Congratulations!" A new list, including my name, was posted the next day.

I was chosen as one of the six finalists. The competition was stiff. One of the six, Stephen Maitland, spoke on "The Indian Way," a topic related to mine though different in concept. Maitland, who must have spent time on an Indian reservation, described Indian styles and custom. He explained the costumes of the men, women and children and illustrated their songs and dances. His war whoops were entertaining, and the audience was enchanted.

Even more impressive was Irving Brotman who spoke on "The Power of Will," how some people stand up against the blows of ill fortune that land on them and the cruel billows of circumstance that roll over them, people like Epictetus, a slave and crippled, and William Wilberforce, "the shrimp" who fought the slave trade.

"Nobody ever *finds* life worth living," he said. "One always has to *make* it worth living." He spoke simply and with suppressed intensity and received an ovation.

The finals were held in St. John's United Church which was filled with students, friends and assorted relatives. As a finalist, I was alloted several reserved seats, and I invited the Old Man. He was preparing for his annual fund-raising trip to the west and could not make it. But he was gracious and said something encouraging. Moreh came but would not accept a reserved place. He sat in the back row. The only member of the Board who showed was David Spivak, the cattle dealer, who loved the orphans as if they were his children and was a *mechuton* (celebrant) at all the events of their life cycle. It was Spivak's groan I heard when the judge announced the winner, Irving Brotman. Then the adjudicator held up his hand for silence. "This year," he said, "the judges were impelled to name another winner because of the lesson in his address, the lesson that love for one's own people can teach love for mankind. Our second winner does credit to those who reared him." When my name was announced, Spivak let out a great Indian war whoop. I was rather less elated. The whole ordeal, from the confrontation with the Board to the finals in the church, had taken all my strength and energy.

The Israelite Press commented in an editorial: "All power to the Jewish Orphanage, our pride and joy." I was again called out of Hebrew class to appear before the Board meeting, where I gave thanks to the Old Man, the members of the Board and to Moreh, who was hardly noticed but whose name should have been on the medal I received.

It was Moreh who put the incident into perspective. "So now you have two speeches under your belt," he said, "the bar-mitzvah *deroshoh* and the one that brought you a medal. I shared the agony of their preparation and sensed the fear in you as you were giving them. It will probably always be that way." Moreh then smiled, a sidelong, crooked smile. "But don't be smug, Re'uven. Don't think that because you have given a speech you have done something. A speech is just a thought preliminary to action. If no deed follows, the speech isn't worth too much. It's simply an exercise for you, and a misery or enjoyment for your audience, depending on whether you bore or interest them."

Moreh was brutally simple. He made sense, though I did not acknowledge it then: "As for the contest and your tussle with the

Board, chalk it up to profit and loss. You lost something: the sense of urgency, the desperation that drove you into the conflict is always ephemeral, a kind of firefly thing. But you also gained something, I hope: an insight that the rhythm of the days is more satisfying and productive than short frenetic bursts of energy. Trust the rhythm, Re'uven, rather than the highs and the lows."

XIII

Spinoza

One day, in my fourteenth year, I was reading in the Orphanage library, where I spent much of my time, when the Old Man came in and sat opposite me. "What are you going to do with your life?" he asked. No preliminaries, just a flat-out question.

"Do you mean it's time for me to be making my own living?"

"Partly yes," he replied. "But I am thinking you might want a career rather than a job."

"What's the difference?"

"If you opt for a job, you go to work in a factory or a store as soon as you finish grade ten. If you want a career, you will need more schooling."

"I've been thinking of university."

"But have you thought who would support you as a university student?"

It was a question that had not escaped my interest.

"I can arrange for you to continue your education."

The Old Man smiled at my surprise. The Home had been in existence for more than a decade. At no time had any inmate been financed for post-high-school education.

"You mean I can start planning to attend the University of Manitoba?"

"Oh, I didn't say that."

"But you said. . ."

"I said I could enable you to gain more formal education—but not at the local university. If you want to study, you can do so at the Chicago *yeshivah*."

That wasn't a new idea. He had broached it several times before. The Hebrew Theological College in what was then America's second city accepted students without tuition from all over the continent. But was it for me? A *yeshivah* student spent most of his time studying traditional subjects, mainly Talmud. Would I be able to get a general education at the same time? I put the question to the Old Man.

"I have made all inquiries, and the answer is that *yeshivah* students attend secular institutions of learning in conjunction with their courses in Jewish subjects. Rabbis today need academic degrees as well as *smichah* (ordination)."

"Are you saying you want me to become a rabbi?"

The Old Man wasn't pushing hard. "You could do worse."

"How much time do I have to make up my mind?"

"I'd like to know in a week or so."

Old Man Osovsky had prepared the ground before he approached me. He had turned to the scholarship fund established by the Bronfman brothers, successful Winnipeg liquor distillers, and was assured that funds were available for two Orphanage inmates to travel to Chicago, there to be provided board and room for several years of study. The offer was made to David Gilman and me. David had no interest in the rabbinate whatsoever, but he was attracted by the opportunity to acquire knowledge. The decision to become a rabbi could be made later. I wasn't entirely repelled by the prospect of a *yeshivah*, but my plans had inclined toward law rather than rabbinics. However, neither David nor I had a choice. It was the *yeshivah* or pants-pressing.

Mother was delighted with the offer. She was traditional enough to recall how Jewish mothers in the East European *stetl* dreamed of their sons studying Torah. To have the dream come true for her was a special blessing. She urged me to accept with dispatch. Moreh was more contemplative.

"Do you know what it means to be a *yeshivah* student?"

I quoted the Talmud to him: "A student has no more than a crust of bread with salt, a measure of water and he sleeps on the ground."

"It's harder even than that," said Moreh. "Your whole life-attitude must now change. We call ourselves orthodox, but it's only a label. You have to have a certain type of mind to be orthodox. Orthodox Jews may possess brilliant intellects and be gifted with fine sensibilities, but they crave fixity, order, permanence, and they will achieve it at all costs, at the price of the most audacious intellectual somersaults. Sometimes you have to defy reality to be orthodox. Can you?"

"I don't know what you mean."

"Well, you know the difference between what is natural and

what is supernatural: the natural is the life in nature, the supernatural is the breaking of natural law. Joshua ordered the sun to stand still in Gibeon, a supernatural feat. According to orthodoxy, the Torah is *min hashomayim* or supernaturally revealed. It was given to Moses on Mount Sinai. That was a suspension of natural law. Can you accept that?"

"You mean Moses was just a pen in God's hand? God dictated and he simply wrote?"

"Yes. The orthodox Jew believes that God can do anything. All things act according to the will of God. He causes the sun to rise and set or He can stop it in its tracks. In such a universe of thought there can be no distinction between the natural and supernatural. Only God is the reality. You have to accept him without question."

"No questions? But you have always said that you can't learn without questions."

"True enough. But orthodox Jews insist that questioning has limits. When it comes to God, all challenge stops. You have to accept him on faith. Can you?"

"I'm not sure. It will take getting used to. You never said I couldn't question."

"Well, now you have a taste of what it means to be orthodox. Let me give you another test. An orthodox Jew believes that every ceremonial and every ritual is a *mitzvoh*, God's direct command to the individual Jew. That includes daily prayer, *kashrus* and the sabbath. The great majority of Winnipeg Jews, as well as those elsewhere on this continent, have cast aside these institutions. Our observance of them in the Orphanage falls below the standards of orthodoxy. Our rituals are not part of the immutable divine law given to Israel at Mount Sinai. You're going to have to change your ways. Can you?"

Moreh presented an enormous challenge, and I decided to confront the Old Man with it. If he wanted me to attend an orthodox *yeshivah*, he would have to cite some good reasons to justify orthodoxy.

"Do you agree," I asked him, "that I must accept unquestioned faith in God and observe rituals we violate here? I'm not sure that I want to go to a place where I can't ask questions. You have always encouraged them. And I'm not used to a sabbath with all kinds of ritual restrictions. You're asking me to take on ways you yourself don't seem to believe in."

"I want you to be a rabbi because I want you to help save the Jewish future. In every generation many Jews have rejected God's law. We are the sinners, the masses of us. But if the sinners do not turn penitent there will still be *she'or yoshuv*, a saving remnant. Who says that Jews must be numbered in the millions? God can accomplish his ends and fulfil the destiny of the Jewish people through a loyal remnant. I want you to be part of that remnant."

He was telling me that I had to be an exception to the rule, better than all the rest, and it was hard to receive. I shook my head.

"Reuben, what have I taught you in the five years you have spent here? That Jewish life is a unique way of experience and needs no further justification. The various interpretations of Jewish doctrine and practice, the meaning of God, the abstract values and concepts are but the after-thoughts of what Jews felt and suffered. The recital of *shema Yisro'el* ("Hear, O Israel, the Lord is our God, the Lord alone") was traditionally one of the most dramatically meaningful practices, not because of the abstract meaning of Judaism which it expresses, but simply because it provided an occasion for experiencing the thrill of being a Jew. The religious observances, too, claimed our loyalty primarily because they were a unique way of self-expression. Orthodoxy for me means the most authentic way of being identified with the Jewish people."

I objected. "What's the good of all our observances in the Home if we don't do them the orthodox way, as Moreh says we don't?"

"That's why we need you as a rabbi, to help keep up the standard. And meanwhile, even with our errant ways we help the Jewish people to survive. When we keep *kashrus*, for example, faulty as it may be, we are made to think of our religious and communal allegiance on the occasion of every meal."

"But since we don't observe the rituals the orthodox way, why should I go to an orthodox school? Let me study with Moreh and attend university here, and then apply to Schechter's seminary in New York or the Reform College in Cincinnati. Reform and Conservative Jews have observances and rituals, too. They can maintain the same feelings of Jewishness in us."

The Old Man began to sputter, a sign of his anger. "Schechter's and Cincinnati are assimilationist. They will be the death of Jews and Judaism, because they do not feel the Jewish momentum, which over twenty centuries has given rise to institutions, undertakings, commitments and languages."

"But aren't Schechter's and the Reform seminaries institutions and therefore part of what you call the momentum?"

"They are marginal, away from the mainstream. They fail to understand Jewish attachment to Hebrew and Yiddish, and callously introduce English into the synagogue. Imagine, English prayers! As if the synagogue were a church!"

The Old Man himself sometimes delivered addresses in English in the synagogue in order to communicate with the orphans, but he considered it an intrusion when it came to prayers. Once Rabbi Samuel, the incumbent at Shaarey Zedek synagogue, delivered an English prayer for the royal family at an Orphanage service, and a row ensued. English for the Old Man was an instrument for measuring the degree of alienation from the core of Judaism. So I took my life in my hands with my next question:

"Why are you so opposed to English?"

"I'm not against the English language. I am for Yiddish and Hebrew. A language enables the individuals of a nation to enter into communication with one another, and at the same time develops in each one an awareness of his people as different from other peoples."

"Can't I be as good a Jew in English as in Yiddish?"

"No," said the Old Man explosively. "Each language has not only its idioms but also its specific overtones. The most sacred and intimate experiences of the Jewish people cannot be faithfully reproduced in a foreign tongue. A language helps to keep alive the collective consciousness of a people. Israel Zangwill said it for all of us: 'A people that speaks is not dead; a people that is not dead speaks.' "

"But why Yiddish?" I remonstrated. "Not all Jews speak it, and it came very late in our history. Can't we do with English what we did with Yiddish?"

"Reuben, you are forgetting the most important things taught you in this institution. Yiddish is bound up with our suffering and our ability to endure. When it comes right down to basics, Yiddish is mostly Hebrew in its everyday expression, its connection with the prayers and holidays, its relation to the way we behave, its devotion to the values of the Torah. Should Yiddish ever fall into disuse, we will be alienated from the true spirit of Judaism."

The Old Man was able to make such an all-encompassing generalization because he could back it up with the realities of the Winnipeg Jews of the late 1920s. Most of them spoke Yiddish, attended the Yiddish theatre, read local and imported newspapers in that language and supported a thriving educational system founded on the vernacular of East European Jews. One reason

why the Reform and Conservative movements made no headway
among Winnipeg Jews of that period was the disinclination of the
new denominations to use Yiddish as a vehicle in communication.
It took only a decade and a half for conditions to change. Osovsky
lived to witness the disappearance of Yiddish as the language of
the sermon in the city's most influential synagogues and their use
of English in prayers and homilies.

But in 1928 he was unalterably opposed to any seminary which
had abandoned the Yiddish language. It was the Chicago *yeshivah*
or nothing.

Moreh, though *mameh-loshen* was dear to him, did not give it
the same significance. He believed that of the two languages Hebrew was by far the more indispensable. His favourite example
was the community of more than a million Jews who lived in
Egypt in the first century. In spite of persecution, massacre and
forced conversion to Christianity and later to Islam, a remnant
would probably have survived had these Jews not dispensed with
Hebrew altogether, contenting themselves with translations of
their literary heritage. They were enthusiastic Jews, their zeal at-
tested by their efforts to convert the heathen population around
them and the numerous writings they left behind. Yet they disappeared from history because they lacked one of the fundamental
elements of Jewish survival, the Hebrew language. For Moreh Hebrew was the instrument by which the most vital interests of the
people found expression.

Moreh's preference, therefore, was for the Jewish Theological
Seminary in New York, popularly known as Schechter's after its
founder, rather than the Hebrew Union College in Cincinnati
which in those days did not have as rigorous a Hebraic emphasis
as today. However, he advised me to accept the Chicago *yeshivah*
offer. "You need an academic degree to enter Schechter's. Meanwhile in the next four or five years, you can be getting a grounding
in Talmud at the *yeshivah* and working for your degree at one of
Chicago's universities which are subsidized by the municipality
and charge only modest fees."

"But I am not an orthodox Jew, Moreh. You yourself have
shown me how far I am from orthodox requirements of belief and
observances."

Moreh was ready for this question. He reached into his briefcase
and read me a passage from "The Nineteen Letters of Ben Uzziel,"
by Samson Raphael Hirsch, an orthodox scholar who reckoned
with the challenge of modern thought and life:

"Whoever in his time, with his equipment of powers and means in his condition, fulfills the will of God to the creatures that enter into his circle, who injures none and assists everyone according to his power to reach the goal marked out for him by God—he is a man! He practises righteousness and love. . . . His whole life, his whole being, his thoughts and feelings, his speech and action, even his business transactions and enjoyments—all of these are service to God."

Moreh looked deep into my eyes. "Now have I taught you anything different from this stirring passage? Hirsch says it is study of the Torah that teaches us the nature of what is good, true and beautiful. He condemns in the strongest terms the identification of religion with mechanical observance. Judaism, he says, must be lived and handed down not as a habit. Only through the spirit can it properly be transmitted. Now Re'uven, have I taught you any differently?"

Moreh was making points. If this was orthodoxy, why need I be suspicious of it? According to Hirsch, said Moreh, "the Jewish people is a vessel or instrument for the fulfilment of a certain purpose. It is a kind of living parchment. When it calls itself a holy nation, it does not lay claim to being holier than any other nation. All that it states is that it is consecrated to the task of proving by its mode of life the possibilities of holiness that inhere in the human being."

Said Moreh as he tried to help me make up my mind:

"Israel's mission consists in the faithful discharge of the task it chose through the centuries—to serve the good of mankind. Mankind would probably in the course of time have benefitted by its own experiences, and after a great deal of tragic blundering might have learned to become aware of its own true destiny. But the Jews have helped save mankind age-long effort. Israel, by pursuing peace not power, has served as an example, a guide and an inspiration to the rest of the world. It can continue to do so. Orthodoxy can help you understand that. At least Hirsch's orthodoxy can. He can be your standard and guide at the *yeshivah*."

"But suppose the Chicago *yeshivah* does not follow Hirsch. It seems that there are several orthodoxies: yours, Mr. Osovsky's— then there's Rabbi Kahanovitch and others like him who frown on girls singing in the choir."

"Not to worry," said Moreh. "Suppose they ask you at the *yeshivah*, 'What is the purpose of being a Jew?' And suppose you reply, 'My purpose is to learn a true sense of values and that

wealth and power are ephemeral.' Wouldn't that constitute an orthodox answer? The true purpose of the Jew is to study and practise the Torah which teaches us to withstand persecution and blan-
dishments and serves as a training school in the exercise of true
heroism. Can you say that?"

"It's probably something I can eventually learn to say. I have no
quarrel with it."

"Well, then, why are you afraid of being orthodox?"

I succumbed to Moreh's arguments and left for the *yeshivah*
with David Gilman. We were driven there by the Old Man and his
daughter Susie, who took turns at the wheel of a brand new Whip-
pet automobile. The trip was a disaster. The car broke down several times, and we had to be towed to garages in small towns
where the necessary replacement parts were not always available.
In addition to the physical discomfort and delay, David and I experienced spiritual shock. One morning we came down to breakfast at a guest house—there were few motels in those days—and
found the Old Man and his daughter enjoying—our eyes simply
could not take in the sight—bacon and eggs! Here we were on our
way to an orthodox *yeshivah*, being given an unforgettable demonstration in the violation of orthodoxy's sacred dietary laws. It
was to serve as the first of a series of disillusionments.

Moreh was incorrect in his assessment of orthodoxy at the *yeshivah*. No one was interested in my approach to Judaism à la Samson Raphael Hirsch. Only the dean of students Rabbi Greenberg
had ever heard of him. The philosophy of Judaism was neither in
the curriculum nor in the minds of my teachers and fellow
students.

Their heavy concern embraced study, with which I had no quarrel, and ritual observance, which was a severe trial for me. By
nature I am not a literalist, and I found it ponderous and boring to
have to be fastidious about every detail of the sabbath and dietary
laws. I learned not to ride on the sabbath, to walk briskly to the
synagogue and slowly away from it, even to tie two handkerchiefs
together and bind them around my waist so that I would not be
carrying even this bit of impedimenta in a public place on the day
of rest.

But I never ceased having trouble with the kosher diet. I eventually discovered that not all signs saying kosher were validly so.
Some were just kosher style, others did not carry the imprimatur
of a pious enough authority. I refrained from eating ice cream on

the suspicion that it might contain animal gelatin, although some authorities permitted it because the quantity of gelatin was only one-sixtieth or less of the other ingredients and was not intended as food but simply as a binder.

I learned the difference between ultra-orthodox, neo-orthodox and modern orthodox, but the distinctions left me cold. I respected the orthodox emphasis on knowledge and tried to emulate the scholar, but when rank at the *yeshivah* depended on the number of pages of Talmud a student stored in his memory rather than understanding of Talmudic concepts and the ancient attitudes that generated them, I lost some of my enthusiasm for studentship. Bible study, Jewish history and modern Hebrew literature were secondary subjects at the *yeshivah*, though they were of primary interest to me, and undue preoccupation with them earned a reprimand for inadequate attention to the main course, Talmud.

On the one hand, anxiety about ritual observance gave me stomach ulcers; on the other, exacting curricular demands taught me the meaning of self-discipline and regular study habits. As a result, I found my courses at the university easier. The combination of academic and *yeshivah* training kept me in classes of one type or another from eight in the morning until eight in the evening, when I had my dinner and then set about working on university assignments. It was a heavy load, but I relished the independence and responsibility.

Daily I was exposed to the drumming that orthodoxy is superior to other approaches in Judaism, that utter conformity to the minutiae of ritual makes for greater honesty and deeper understanding of human obligations. I tried with all my might to believe this claim but found no basis for it, as I have since found no basis for the claim that religious Jews of whatever persuasion possess higher integrity than secular Jews.

I was puzzled by orthodoxy's arbitrariness regarding Jewish law. Jewish religious law is codified in the *Shulhan Aruch,* the *sanctum sanctorum* of super-orthodox Jews. This classical code by Joseph Karo is divided into four books and the rules and conventions in all these sections are equally binding on all orthodox Jews. The first book comprises the laws of the annual cycle of holidays; the second deals with dietary laws; the third with personal status, marriage, divorce and inheritance; and the fourth with civil law, torts, evidence and procedure, and criminal law including theft, robbery and what-is-mine-and-what-is-thine.

My experience, however, was that while orthodox Jews adhered to every jot and tittle of the first three sections and regarded anyone who deviated from them as a heretic, an entirely different attitude prevailed with regard to the demands of the fourth section. They belonged to a sphere other than religious law and could be ignored or broken without calling into question a man's status as an observant Jew. A man is orthodox and accepted as such if he observes the rituals and family law, even if he is a thief, but let him violate the ritual requirements and he places himself outside the pale. This rigour struck me with great force as a *yeshivah* student.

Still I hung on, even when David Gilman left to devote himself exclusively to secular studies. I envied his courage and was tempted to follow. The Old Man, back in Winnipeg, was delighted at my resoluteness. I wrote him long Yiddish letters and Hebrew ones to Moreh. They answered in kind. I explained my problems to both. Osovsky ignored my intellectual and emotional turmoil and expatiated on the glories of learning and the rewards of academic success. Frankel commiserated with me but reminded me also that toil and sacrifice are the price every student, whoever he is, must pay. He urged me to focus on the goal at the end of five years, when I would be the possessor of a university degree and able to apply for admission to the Jewish Theological Seminary in New York, where I could live under less exacting ritualistic clamouring.

Two years passed, and the Old Man commanded my presence at the Orphanage synagogue for Rosh Hashanah and Yom Kippur. It was time to show how I had progressed in my studies and whether they had enriched my insights. I was to be the preacher at all services. A news story, adorned with a photograph, appeared in the Israelite Press announcing my visit and the titles of my sermons. The Old Man had composed the titles without consulting me, a rather high-handed action, I thought. The first day of Rosh Hashanah I was to deliver an English sermon on "The Prayer Book and What its Pages Tell"; the second day a Yiddish address on "The Voice of the *Shofar* (ram's horn)"; at Kol Nidre on the eve of Yom Kippur another Yiddish oration on "The Marranos of All Ages"; and on Yom Kippur morning a final Yiddish dissertation, "*Yizkor* and *Kaddish* (memorial prayers)—Testimony to Jewish Pain." The topics reflected the views and philosophy of the Old Man, and I pondered the wisdom of following him so slavishly. After all, if my visit was to be an accounting for two years of study under the Home's auspices, it should demonstrate my acquisition and my development, not what the Old Man sought to represent as me. I determined to speak my own heart. It was a fateful decision.

Rosh Hashanah went well. I spoke Yiddish both days. My facility with the language had improved at the *yeshivah* because I used it every day in the exposition of the Talmud. In my speeches I used Talmudic phrases liberally, a sign for my hearers that I had made an acceptable adjustment to my environment. The second Rosh Hashanah address in particular was a smash hit. It developed the Biblical story of Abraham and Isaac "walking together" to Mount Moriah. Abraham, the patriarch, I said, typified the fathers, the supporters of the Home, and I was emblematic of Isaac, one of the sons of the institution. We walked together in the early years and we would walk together in the years to come, I assured them, to our common destination, Moriah, the Temple mount, the symbol of a life of meaning and purpose.

The Old Man and Moreh were elated, but the joy did not last. At Kol Nidre, the most solemn moment of the Hebrew calendar, when young and old crowded into the Orphanage *shul* to hear the plaintive traditional melody, I chose to deliver an English sermon, so that all would understand, and proclaim my declaration of independence.

I began softly, as the Old Man always did, reminding my audience of the poignant music of Kol Nidre, reflecting in its minor key the persecution and dispersion of the Jews over the centuries. In those lands where Jews, under duress, made vows to accept another faith, the recital of Kol Nidre, a legal formula for the invalidation of vows, often brought relief to their tormented consciences.

I reviewed the history of Jewish dispersion. Before and after the fall of the Temple in the first century the Jews spread abroad into every corner of the Mediterranean—to Athens, Alexandria and Carthage, to Rome, Marseilles and to "the end of the world," Spain. Eventually Jewish wandering followed two streams, one along the Danube and the Rhine and from there into Poland and Russia, the other into Spain and Portugal with the conquering Muslims. Wherever the Jews went they created and contributed, in central Europe as financiers and merchants, and in the Iberian peninsula in the schools of Cordoba, Barcelona and Seville, absorbing the mathematical, medical and philosophical lore of the Arabs, transmitting ancient and oriental culture to western Europe.

"Who does not thrill," I asked, "to the ring of the famous names—Judah Halevi, Abraham and Moses Ibn Ezra, Solomon Ibn Gabirol and the greatest of them all, the many-sided genius Moses Maimonides?" I paused and looked at the Old Man who was smiling.

I changed the mood. The Moors were expelled from Spain, the Christians supplanting them, and with Christianity came persecution. The dreaded Inquisition in 1492 gave the Jews a choice, baptism or exile. The great majority chose the hard road, exile. Some took ship for Genoa and other Italian ports, were refused and sailed in misery and disease to the coast of Africa where they were murdered for the jewels they were believed to have swallowed. Venice accepted a few, knowing how valuable Jews were to its maritime development. Others financed the voyage of Columbus, hoping that through him, perhaps a Jew himself, a place of refuge would be found. A number sailed up the Atlantic between the hostile coasts of England and France to Holland, the only country to extend a hand of welcome to Jews.

I paused again. Out of the corner of my eye I caught the Old Man, arms folded, hugely enjoying this review of history of which he heartily approved. I continued: "The Jews were happy among the Dutch, building their first synagogue in Amsterdam in 1598. Then controversy erupted. Uriel da Costa, under the influence of the challenging spirit of the Renaissance, wrote a treatise attacking belief in life after death. This was not necessarily against Jewish doctrine, for even in the Talmud a difference of opinion occurs among the scholars concerning 'the world to come,' but it was contrary to the essence of Protestantism, the faith held by the hospitable Dutch. Rather than incur their disfavour, the Jews compelled da Costa to retract. They made him lie down across the threshold of the synagogue while members of the congregation stepped on his reclining figure. Degraded beyond endurance, da Costa went home, wrote a fierce denunciation of his persecutors and took his own life."

I paused once more. The Old Man looked somewhat bewildered. What was I getting at? "I come now to the hero of my story," I went on. "Baruch Spinoza grew up in Amsterdam, aware of how his people were driven out of one country because of their beliefs, were welcomed into another, then turned around and kicked out one of their own number because of his beliefs. Spinoza was a brilliant youth who, unlike his merchant father, preferred to spend his time poring over books, the Bible, the Talmud, the commentaries of Maimonides, Ibn Ezra, Ibn Gabirol and even the Cabbalistic mysteries of Moses of Cordoba. He found more questions than answers in Maimonides' 'Guide to the Perplexed,' and more doubts than assurances in Ibn Ezra's explanations. He turned to Christian thinkers to discover what they had written on the great questions of God and human destiny. He mastered Latin and explored the treasures of the ancient and medieval philosophers. It was Descartes, a man of his own seventeenth century, who influenced him most and taught him three Latin words which embraced a whole universe, '*Cogito ergo sum*', 'I think, therefore I am.' "

I pronounced the phrase with flair and avoided looking in the Old Man's direction lest he discourage me from proceeding. "Like Uriel da Costa, Spinoza at twenty-four, filled with the knowledge and doubts of Jewish and Christian masters, was summoned before the elders of the Jewish community on the charge of heresy. Was it true, they asked him, that he did not accept the ancient God of Abraham, Isaac and Jacob, that he spoke of angels as simply chimeras and that he told friends the Hebrew Bible does not contain the idea of immortality? True or not, he was offered an annuity of $500 if he would consent to keep his unconventional ideas to himself and maintain an external affiliation with the synagogue. To his eternal credit, Spinoza refused and was thereupon placed in *herem*, excommunicated with all the doleful ritual prescribed by tradition: the *shofar* sounding; long black candles extinguished one by one, signifying the extinction of the spirit of the excommunicated one; and the reading of the curse."

I intoned the curse with sonority: "None shall hold converse with him by word of mouth. None shall have communication with him by writing. No one shall do him any service or abide under the same roof with him or approach within four cubits of him. Nor shall anyone read any document dictated or written by him."

A breathless stillness hovered over the congregation. Most of them became aware of the scenario I was painting for the first time and were fascinated to learn that such an event had ever happened among the Jews. I kept my eyes away from the Old Man and plunged on:

"Was this the end of Spinoza? No, our loss was the world's gain. He was alone, isolated from his people, rejected by his father, cheated out of a small inheritance by his sister, shunned by his friends. But his intellect grew, and his ideas, powerful as they were, spread. Spinoza speaks to our time. He said that the Bible contains nothing contrary to reason, but men interpret it literally and thereby fill it with errors, contradictions and obvious impossibilities, as that the Jews were favourites of God and the Red Sea was split by his omnipotent hand. But the great thinkers, said Spinoza, penetrate the mist of allegory and poetry and make intelligible its truths. The people will always demand a religion clothed in imagery and encased in the supernatural. The scholar, however, knows that God and nature are one being, acting by invariable law. It is this majestic law the understanding man will obey. Spinoza was the first modern. How tragic that he was disowned by his own people."

I turned and looked full into the face of the Old Man whose eyes were now flashing, and put to him and the congregation a rhetorical question: "Were the Jewish leaders right in excommunicating Spinoza? One can understand their plight. Protestantism was not then the liberal philosophy it later became. The war between Luther and the Pope left their followers entrenched in their respective creeds. What would the Dutch authorities say to a community of Jews that repaid Christian tolerance by turning out in one generation a da Costa and in the next a Spinoza? Gratitude to their hosts seemed to demand the excommunication of a man who struck at Christian roots as vitally as at Judaism.

"Nevertheless," I hammered away, "the Jews should have run the risk and kept Spinoza within the fold. The Jew is the eternal dissident. All through the ages Jews died to defend their right of conscience. Abraham challenged even God on its behalf. Rabbi Akiba, Rabbi Haninah ben Teradyon and all the martyred sages of the centuries chose death rather than surrender their convictions. The Jewish people was hounded and humiliated, tortured and burned at the stake for the sake of Torah, the ultimate document of dissent."

Years later I might not have been so brash in my judgment. The Jews of Amsterdam, under friendly rule, considered themselves the only protected community in Europe, on whom the survival of the rest of the Jews of the world depended. Had they their own state, their own establishments of power to compel internal cohesion, they might have been more tolerant. But their religion was their patriotism as well as their faith, their social and political life as well as their ritual and worship. Under these circumstances they must have thought tolerance suicide.

But in 1930 I was speaking out of the misery of the intellectual tyranny that obtained at the *yeshivah*. I was being strangled by conformity and yearned for relief. Moreh understood. He embraced me after the service, assuring me that I spoke in the spirit of Hillel who differed from Shammai, Abaya who disagreed with Rava, Rabbi Johanan who clashed with Rabbi Ishmael. But the Old Man never forgave me. Thunder rolled out of him as he confronted me in his office.

"You burst in here like an angel of the Lord," he said, "and deliver your little judgment on matters you know nothing about, except by hearsay." How did I dare revise history? What *hutzpah* to question the miracles of the Bible, the chosenness of the Jewish people, the wisdom of the leaders of a Jewish community. It was this last bit of agnosticism that most rankled in him. The majority had to rule; therefore it was right. It never occurred to him that on matters of the spirit the majority is usually wrong, that political democracy is essential but moral democracy ruinous, that humanity stands or falls by the courage of the spiritually élite.

My mother, who had long since left the Home and was working as cook in private residences and in a local kosher restaurant, was at the service to hear me preach. I caught sight of her upturned face as I was spinning out my cocky judgment of history from the pulpit. But she was not interested in history, only in her son. After the service, she pushed her way through the crowd excitedly discussing "the brazen young man who was impatient to change the fate of the Jews," embraced me and asked: "*Vos far a vort iz Spinoza?* What kind of a word is Spinoza?" I laughed uproariously. She broke the tension for me. She was right in her innocence. What was I to Spinoza or Spinoza to me? I had things to do, promises to keep, a thousand books to read and worlds to conquer.

I returned to Chicago and the *yeshivah* after the holidays. The Old Man never wrote to me again. After a few months the cheques also stopped. But I managed to survive. The *yeshivah* opened a dining-room in order to control the kosher diet of its students; out-of-towners were served without charge. Though the economic depression descended upon the land, I discovered parents who were willing to pay for the training of bar-mitzvah boys, an activity I performed on weekends. On the High Holidays I was engaged by Canadian synagogues—in Fort Rouge, a suburb of Winnipeg, and Melville, Saskatchewan—to conduct services, sound the *shofar*,

read the Torah and preach the sermons, all for what congrega-
tional executives considered one bargain price but for me was a
bonanza. It was a hard and uncertain life financially, living on less
than $300 a year, but I finally made it out of the university, bade
farewell to the *yeshivah* authorities, who shook their heads over
my departure, and headed for New York and the Seminary and an
environment I hoped would allow me to air my doubts and put my
questions.

In later years, when I became the incumbent at McCaul Street
Synagogue in Toronto, I kept meeting the Old Man at Zionist
meetings. He had moved from Winnipeg to become the director of
the local home for the aged. We were always at opposite poles of a
public debate. At one meeting, celebrating the establishment of the
state of Israel in 1948, I addressed the Toronto Zionist Council as
its president and expressed the hope that in our joy over the emergence of the Jewish state we might be moved to remember the
plight of the Palestine Arab refugees and help to rehabilitate them.
When Osovsky asked for the floor, I recognized him as "my mentor and a formidable Zionist." He condemned my feelings for the
Arab refugees and concluded: "I guess I am a better Zionist than a
mentor." I did not see him or hear from him again. He died later
that year.

Moreh Frankel did not stop writing to me until his death in 1963
at the age of seventy-seven. I made a point of visiting him every
time I stopped in Winnipeg. His last words ring down the years: "I
am an old man with the clocks set against me. You have youth and
a new horizon, something I can't buy. The secret of keeping your
youth is to speak your mind and heart. Outspokenness will bring
you loneliness, but don't be afraid of being lonely. Everybody is.
There are no pills to cure that, no formulas to charm it away. If
you retreat from it, you end in a darker hell: yourself. But if you
face it, you will remember there are millions like you who want to
speak out and, for one reason or another, cannot, and in the end
you will be lonely no longer." He was always Moreh, teacher, and
will doubtless be to the end of my days, a teacher who understood, perhaps more than anyone I ever knew, that the essence of
life is compassion, a pity for the living.

Epilogue

I visited the Orphanage but seldom in the years following my declaration of independence in 1930, once to celebrate the twenty-fifth anniversary of its founding and twice on private inspection. On my private visits I envied the inmates. I wanted to be like them again. When you have been aboard awhile, the ship becomes a womb. You are warm, you are fed, and once you are used to the motions you are so comfortable you never want to leave it. With the departure of my contemporaries, I became an outsider. I no longer felt as possessive about the institution as when Osovsky ruled it as a benevolent tyrant.

H. E. Wilder had taken over, but our relationship was mutually deferential since he did not know me as a child. He was a splendid man with progressive ideas which inevitably led to the dissolution of the Home. In 1939 he succeeded in forcing a change of name, from the Jewish Orphanage and Children's Aid of Western Canada to the Jewish Children's Aid Society, arguing for the elimination of the word orphanage because the Home was not merely a temporary shelter for children but an educational institution where they prepared themselves for future life, as it had always been. Osovsky's management was old-style, formal but shrewd; Wilder's modern, open, hewing to the latest sociological trends.

The name change was a signal that the Home would have to succumb to the foster-home plan, where children would be distributed among private households and their upkeep paid for by a communal agency. Efforts to forestall the demise of the institution were tempestuous. Those who looked back nostalgically on the struggles to keep it going through the years—men like David Spivak and Aaron Osovsky—fought mightily.

The Old Man urged that the building be turned into a school for Jewish children, where they could learn general subjects and at the same time absorb the positive values of Jewish tradition. As such it would have been the forerunner of the Jewish day school which became popular in Canada and the U.S. in the 1960s and 1970s. But his was now "a still, small voice," and no one paid attention.

Had the building become a day school it would still have fallen short of the Home's standards of Jewish identity. In the Home children were totally immersed in preparations for later responsibilities; the Hebrew school and the life situation were governed by the same authority. But the day school, though its Jewish focus is strongly positive, cannot follow the child home to guarantee that standards be sustained. The Orphanage faced no such contradiction. It was an exceptional institution with an extraordinary opportunity to transmit Jewish values. When it was dismantled, something unique went out of the life of Jewry in Western Canada and perhaps in the entire country.

Spivak visited me in Toronto in 1947, pleading that I intervene to save the Orphanage. He pointedly used the old name to enforce his appeal. I wrote a passionate letter to the Jewish Child and Family Service of Winnipeg—though my heart was not in it because I knew the end was unpreventable—and received a respectful but sophisticated reply. The community had to decide for itself, I was told. It did in 1948. The building was razed in 1952.

But the Home did not die. Almost thirty years later about 150 alumni converged on Winnipeg from points east and west in Canada and from California, Israel and points between—musicians, merchants, dentists, accountants, clerks, businessmen, lawyers, a cantor and a rabbi. I have recorded their names in the preface of this book. Many I did not know; they were from the generations after mine. Some I had not seen in over half a century. But I saw in them and they in me the inchoate youngsters we were. There was so much enthusiasm it bubbled like spring water.

For four days we talked, far into the nights, sang the old songs and chanted the familiar prayers: "O, come, my beloved, to meet the sabbath bride" and *"Hallelu es hashem*. Praise the Lord, all ye nations." Ours was a continuity of experience, a common past, a common faith. No matter how scattered we were by geography, how stringently bound by the monotony of our daily round, we had a tribal dream to make us one, a dream that was funnelled to a whole people. We talked about that dream—the stories, the legends, the attitudes. They all linked together, joining past and present.

We remembered the violence, the beatings, the cruelty and the tyranny, but we were mostly aware of the grace, the beauty and the generosity. We recalled, in one united chorus, the obscure people who served us, who knew life's most important message, that compassion is the one thing that grows as you spend it.

We celebrated our cherished Orphanage: its practical success—the fact that of the 838 children who had been trained in the building on Matheson Avenue only one turned out to be a delinquent—and its power as a spiritual centre.

We looked at the Home and found it good. Good in itself, good in the people who had made it, who had pity, fear and love. Man does not live by spirit alone, but neither can he live without it. Those devoted communal servants—Frankel, Osovsky, Wilder, Spivak, Rafalsky, Finkelstein and all the others—knew better than most that, to be human, neither the flesh nor the spirit could function except in and through the other. Earth and grass and tree and animal were of the same creative act that produced a man or a woman. They were good in themselves and in the laws that governed their growth and decay. Only misuse could debase them to instruments of evil. To plant a tree, to make barren earth flourish was to share in the act of creation. To teach children, especially parentless children, was to make them, too, participate in a divine plan.

It is easy to talk roundly of faith, hope and charity as if they were a fetishist's incantation. But for the men and women who built the Home faith was an inspired act of will, their answer to the terrible mystery of where we came from and where we are going. For them hope was a child's trust in the hand that led it out of the terrors of the dark. For them charity, which in Hebrew is the same word as justice, meant hands dabbling in sickroom messes, wiping running noses and erasing infection from body sores. At meetings and conclaves they spoke not in the jargon of the sociologist and economist but in the simple language of the grocer, the baker and the shoemaker.

I look back now at the 1920s and see myself in a frail cockleshell, alone, unshackled, thrust up from the deeps. In the Home I began to know without knowing, to see without seeing what had drawn my people out, millenia ago, from their east Mediterranean haven into immensity. I understand now something else, too: that for a small people, fragmented by migration and enormous distance, bound to a monotony of simple, concrete rituals, the fountain of dreaming and creating was always in the ones who remembered and in the knowing. No matter that they were oppressed, humbled. Their spirit made them proud and privileged, set at the centre of events. It was in the Home I learned that this spirit, the spirit of an eternal people, is a treasure for humanity and a man's greatest comfort.

Index

Grand to be an Orphan
Reuben Slonim

This vivid and fascinating memoir combines a description of an extraordinary Canadian institution, the Jewish Orphanage and Children's Aid Society of Canada, with an account of its formative influence on Canada's most controversial rabbi. Reuben Slonim lived as an orphan in the building on Matheson Avenue in Winnipeg between 1923 and 1928. At this time, and indeed until the dissolution of the Orphanage in the 1940s, the Jewish community poured out its compassion, pride and joy over the orphans, who were drawn from the whole of the Canadian West, and over their scholastic, cultural and oratorical achievements. All work and all play were devoted to fostering reverence for the centuries-old traditions of the Jewish people.

As Rabbi Slonim brings to life his two main teachers — Superintendent Osovsky, the vociferous promoter of Jewish self-respect, the stern and unbending political Zionist; and Shimon Frankel, the Hebrew teacher and gentle custodian of the spiritual values of Judaism — it becomes clear that his concern is also with vital contemporary issues. He reveres both men, but worries that too much Jewish opinion today resembles the strident, anti-dissident voice of one teacher rather than the conciliatory and compassionate voice of the other. His intent is to show that Jewish values are a treasure for humanity as a whole.

This is a poignant, and pointed, evocation of a remarkable institution. Its focus is on a group of immigrant Jews who produced an institution of charity, but it is no less an aspect of Canadian social history and ultimately speaks to the human spirit.